THE ROAD TO
AUM

SECOND EDITION

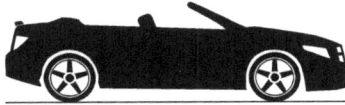

Driving Assets Under Management
through Effective Marketing and Sales

SANDRA POWERS MURPHY

THE ROAD TO AUM
Driving Assets Under Management through Effective Marketing and Sales
By Sandra Powers Murphy

Published by Noble Ark Ventures LLC
www.noblearkventures.com

Amazon Author Central Page:
http://www.amazon.com/author/sandrapowersmurphy

Acknowledgements

Where to begin? There are so many people to thank.

To the institutional research professionals who took the time to speak with me at length about their experiences with managers of all shapes and sizes, thank you. Your insight is invaluable. For those of you overseas and in different time zones, who made your calendars work to accommodate this project, my heartfelt thanks. In the day-to-day hustle to accomplish our own agendas, it is often difficult to take time out to support someone else's. You have made an immeasurable difference for thousands of organizations, past, present and future, who elect to heed your words of wisdom. The market is better for your participation. I can not thank you enough for entrusting me with your candid feedback.

To the managers who keep trying. Like Forrest Gump, you keep running. You inspire us all with your passion. The road to growth is long and challenging, but it is worth it. Thank you for all the stories you have shared, the inquiries you have made, the fits and starts you have had and for the opportunity to make the road a little bit smoother through this exercise.

To my team, Keith Garte, Franz Loeber, Jeannette DiBiase, Lisa Welch, Karen Gendron and Christine Donahue. Your ideas, support and patience with what has been a true labor of love has been unrelenting. You inspire me every day in countless ways. Thank you.

To my colleagues, particularly on the board of the Third Party Marketers Association, you are incredibly thoughtful, candid and passionate about investment management, marketing, and sales. Thank you on behalf of the managers and research professionals you have served over the years. It is a daunting task and you do it with grace and humility. Special thanks to Steve Rubenstein, Donna DiMaria, Scott Nance and Brian Fitzgibbon for your support in completing this project. Your insights and feedback were invaluable and will help many, many managers. Additionally, to Lisa Roth, who provided a steadying hand in working through the specifics of this project. Thank you.

To the ladies of WPO, our Women Presidents' Organization chapter in Boston, you rock. I am incredibly inspired by all that you do to support your respective industries. A better group of women has never been assembled. Special thanks to Coventry Edwards-Pitt and Kim Emberg who provided much needed support and the inside scoop on the world of publishing. You were a godsend. Thank you.

To my dear husband, Kelley, who has been steadfast in a way that brings tears to my eyes. You inspire me every day. Your support has been unwavering.

To my six beautiful children, Dylan, Henry, Jack, Isabelle, Ryan and Scarlett. You are my inspiration. May this book give you confidence that you can do anything you set your mind too. Thank you for your endearing love and patience. Special thanks to Henry, for assisting with modern technology on this project, and to Isabelle, for her artistic vision for how the book is presented.

To the other four fabulous S's, Susan, Stephen, Stephanie and Sheryl Powers. This project took away from everything for a little while. I am eternally grateful for your support and patience.

To Bruce Jones at Bruce Jones Design who walked me through the design, publication and distribution of this project. Your efficiency is astounding. Thank you.

To Kelley Riley at Kelley Riley Photography, for your incredible vision for the cover. You are correct, there is value in simplicity.

To the editor, Sheryl Mayette, who was incredible in keeping the process moving. You provided structure, patience, support and ideas that added tremendous value to the book from beginning to end. You put other projects aside to support the timeline of this endeavor. You taught me how to write better. Thank you.

To Brian Johnson at BKJ Productions who provides incredibly valuable web support and other ideas far beyond a simple screen. You are kind, engaged and committed to your clients and colleagues. Thank you for all your suggestions and support.

To marketing and sales professionals everywhere, you have a tough job. You believe in what you do, have passion for the clients you represent, and bring a degree of structure and order to the process that is desperately needed. Market conditions will ebb and flow; keep flowing with them. Ideally this book will help firms understand the process better and in so doing, make your jobs a little easier.

Introduction

"Much good work is lost for the lack of a little more."
— Edward H. Harriman

The road to asset growth is simultaneously exhilarating and tedious. It can deliver the thrill of a cliff hanging drive through a mountain pass. Conversely, it can provide the agony of detours, speed bumps, stop signs and construction along the way. *The Road to AUM* offers investment managers and business owners, as well as marketing and sales professionals an efficient roadmap to institutional asset growth based on the direct feedback of asset allocators. It was written for firms seeking to understand what matters to institutions. Whether a firm is new to the market, or has been pursuing the next level of asset growth for a decade or longer, a better understanding of institutional investors' perspectives and priorities is paramount.

Going for Gold

I wrote this book because I like to win. I believe in going for the gold. I come by this perspective honestly. Growing up as a competitive swimmer competing in long-distance events, I trained incredibly hard. Numerous hours were spent outdoors at the crack of dawn, still dark, diving into frigid water while everyone else was cozy in bed. I would go to sleep every night praying that my father's alarm would not go off; that we could sleep in just one time. That never happened. He knew what I was capable of, better than I did. Our training was brutal; twice a day, more days than not. We ran the bleachers at Harvard Stadium at night, up and down, up and down again until it was too dark to see the next step. We ran around the Charles River in Cambridge, MA. Did I mention that we were swimmers? Our coach was obsessive about training and preparing. This, coupled with sufficient talent and a large dose of perseverance, made us great champions. It put us in contention to win.

The first goal was to get in the top heat, so you would be a contender. Everyone in the top heat earned a ribbon. There are many different colors of ribbons beyond the first three finishers; whether you naturally think of blue, red and white or gold, silver and bronze. But, who ever wanted the lime green ribbon? Not me. I wanted to win. It was not about being in the race, it was about racing for the gold, for the blue, for first place.

In the realm of institutional investment management marketing and sales there are lots of 'ribbons' that could be given out for effective marketing and good sales efforts. These ribbons do not pay the bills. What managers want, and what business owners need, is to win the gold; to get the blue ribbon often enough to be a viable entity in the market. This book is not solely about being in the hunt. It is about understanding what will take a firm from an outside lane to center stage, from medal contention to a top candidate. It is about launching an investment management organization into the race and giving it the best chance to win.

The Gold Standard

This book is designed to point out the roadblocks that business owners and investment managers face, often self-imposed, in the marathon race that is institutional asset raising. As a result, the ideas presented may seem nitpicky and vexing at times. For those who believe that performance is the only factor that matters, it may be frustrating. After all, stepping back, making meaningful changes, and focusing on the smallest details as well as the overarching factors impacting growth is a notable commitment. Keep the gold in mind.

The golden ticket of institutional asset management is rare indeed. Anecdotal evidence indicates that 75% of managers will not fully reach their stated AUM capacity goals no matter how much they spend, how hard they push, and how many different avenues they try. This statistic is generous. Failure rates can be as high as 90% in certain market segments, product structures and strategies when basing this rate on who "makes it" in the institutional market place, beyond friends and family and a short list of known connections.

Competition reigns supreme in the institutional investment management arena. At the time of print, the market recognizes more than 13,500 registered investment advisers who are registered because they advise or manage assets professionally. These numbers do not paint a complete picture; an additional cohort of managers exist that are either domiciled outside of the U.S., or are too small to require SEC registration. Additionally, there is a cohort of this data set that is not serving in the capacity of investment manager; they are solely investment advisers. Regardless of these population adjustments, the competition among investment managers for institutional assets is humbling.

A further review of the breadth of investment managers across specific asset classes and product structures can be had by tapping into any number of databases such as eVestment Alliance, Investment Metrics and PSN Informa particularly for traditional long only separate account managers, Albourne and HFR for hedge fund managers, Preqin for private equity and real estate managers, FIN Searches for search activity in the institutional market (at least that which gets publicly announced), and Morningstar for mutual funds, among others. The depth of competition is inspiring; the large majority of managers have a compelling growth of $10,000 chart and can tell a good story. Only a select few will be hired by enough institutions to fully reach their asset raising goals.

Investment management marketing and sales professionals alike have a passion for managers; we want to see more managers succeed. There is an emphatic belief that the industry benefits immensely from competition and diversity—diversity of thought, process, strategy, culture and team. Yet, with so much competition for time, attention and dollars, how can a manager break through the noise and become institutionally recognized? How can the firm know that it is meeting institutional standards sufficiently to win business?

Questions Answered

The Road to AUM is designed to openly acknowledge the pitfalls that stop managers in their tracks, and outline the opportunities that managers regularly miss throughout the asset gathering process. It profiles the institutional investment management research professional's direct feedback. It asks the questions, from the mundane to the paramount, and provides the unscripted responses so that firms can manage their time and resources in light of what matters to institutions.

Managers are in the weeds, focused on performance, and guided by a passion for the way they elect to manage money. Institutions have a different perspective; they have the advantage of seeing the forest through the trees. This book seeks to give managers the institutional view and a roadmap to methodically define their offering, positioning, and marketing. Managers deserve a direct response to the questions that should be asked and answered before embarking on a costly, multi-year institutional investment management bid including:

- Is this an institutional offering?
- What is the best target market for this specific strategy and structure?
- Is the firm and offering ready for prime time?
- Is the time right?
- Where are the opportunities?
- Why hasn't this manager been hired already?
- What should be done differently?
- Who can help?

A Familiar Tale

A conversation with a manager who had been through three distinct marketing partnerships over the past few years tells a familiar tale. The manager intelligently wondered if they were barking up the wrong tree, and how could they find the right resources to help them grow their assets under management. One look at their product offering clarified the confusion. They were attempting to sell a retail oriented product in an institutional structure, targeted at institutional investors. It is no surprise that institutions were not interested, and the retail market was unlikely to touch the product as offered. The problem was not the marketing effort per se (although marketers bear some responsibility in not raising the red flag sooner), nor was it the performance. There was a broader structural issue that required resolving before spending resources on marketing would make economic sense.

This manager, and thousands like it, want to grow their asset base. They come to market with exciting stories and compelling track records, but they have no context in which to structure their organizations, product offerings and marketing efforts to drive results. Additionally, they lack the knowledge and understanding of the market in terms of buyer behavior and priorities. What makes the difference in institutional asset raising? Why isn't performance enough? How can managers build and market a firm that meets investor objectives efficiently? The inquiry that led to this book sought to ask these questions and many others directly of institutional investors so that managers can make informed decisions about resource allocations, and better manage their own expectations.

One important distinction is that of marketing v. selling. Marketing and sales are not the same. Marketing can be accomplished, and revenue can be earned when a manager is not ideal—not ideally prepared, presentable, or sellable. Marketing does not necessitate specific near-term results to be a viable business. Marketing gives a manager the sense that "something" is happening. Indeed, good marketing *must* happen and in most cases for a long time measured in years—not in weeks or months—to lay the groundwork for effective institutional sales.

Selling, being on the hook for commission-based sales, particularly to experienced institutional investors, requires a deeper look in the mirror. Selling is what investment managers ultimately need in order to grow assets.

The Beneficiaries

Research on the subject of marketing identified a variety of books that provide strong motivation, yet they all lacked context to the task at hand. These books are not written by professionals whose livelihood depends on the ability to grow institutional investment market share, nor do they provide the voice of the institutional buyer. Institutional investment management marketing and sales professionals spend their days trying to see the forest through the trees on behalf of their clients. Where are the opportunities? What are the competitors doing? What is sellable? What do institutional investors want to see and hear from managers? Their livelihood depends on an ability to get on the right path efficiently. Investment managers must get there as well. Four constituents will benefit most from this book—those new to market, emerging, stuck in neutral, or undiscovered:

1. *New to Market:* Firms, or individuals, who are new to the market all together, whether as a student of the market seeking to understand investment management business development, a spin out from a much larger firm, or as a home-grown talent inside a family office.

2. *Emerging:* Managers who are considered "emerging", defined as any manager who is sub $5B and more often sub $1B at the time of institutional market engagement. *[Definitions range widely as to what constitutes an emerging manager. The numbers can go as high as $10B. Regardless of size, managers will need to be employee owned (not an affiliate of a larger entity) to qualify, and may need to meet certain diversity standards in some cases.]*

3. ***Stuck in Neutral:*** Firms who have plateaued, stuck at the same assets under management level they have been at for years, and who wish to grow past this asset hurdle.

4. ***Undiscovered:*** Managers of significant size, but with an 'orphaned' or 'underserved' strategy, or an unrecognized brand; those who are rolling out to a new channel or with a new product targeted to the institutional market for the first time.

Curious what type of manager you are and how this book can help you most? Use this QR code to take a preliminary assessment. It will take you all of 10 minutes and will highlight areas for special attention as you get on the road to AUM.

Road Trip to Gold

This book is about getting to the finish line efficiently. It is about managing expectations and understanding what must be done—and done better. It suggests areas in which firms can save resources, and defines how firms can put their best foot forward based on the direct feedback of institutional investors. It will not solve poor performance or the wrong structure. It will provide the motivation to fish or cut bait where needed. It can put a manager on the map, and into the fast lane on the road to AUM.

What's Changed in this Second Edition

While we consider the game plan provided by *The Road to AUM* evergreen in its 12-element construct, a few market changes of significance have occurred that necessitated this update. Here are the highlights:

1. ***Digital Marketing Has Taken Off:*** The biggest shift for *The Road to AUM* was the expansion of Chapter 10 on Digital Marketing. While institutional entities continue to focus their analysis on data found in third party and/or their own proprietary databases, managers can no longer avoid the need to engage digitally. A movement that had been underfoot for the past few years, the global pandemic launched a digital imperative virtually overnight. Traditional marketing professionals struggled to respond, as did sales professionals, often referred to as road warriors, who typically prefer getting out and shaking hands. Ultimately, the opportunity to embrace a digital age, to build interactive content and connectivity for future generations, and the ever-expanding globalization of communications with no limits to potential reach created a transformation in traditional business development that warranted this second edition.

Importantly, the conversations around best practices in face-to-face business development were left in as we fully anticipate a return to in person activities. After all, human nature drives our collective need for connection. The new normal will certainly be a hybrid. What is more, organizations realized that they could be perhaps more productive in certain aspects of their business, and simultaneously spend less on superfluous travel through this experience. Now, several years later, rather than a short-term blip, we acknowledge a permanent change in behavior. We see cultural shifts that reinforce the value of virtual communications in all aspects of business engagement, including marketing. Whether investment firms are seeking distribution in intermediary or institutional channels, the need to implement, monitor and maintain an active digital presence is unquestionable.

This new age of communication provides a broader array of mediums in which to reach investors, often at lower costs and with greater efficiency. For those seeking to engage the next generation, the rationale for going digital is multiplied. We are encouraged by the permanence of the shift and believe organizations, both large and small, are embracing this new norm on the road to growth.

To help reinforce the value of interactive engagement with the book's content, a QR code was provided in the introduction that permits organizations to assess where they are right now, before diving in, to make the most of their time and focus on the key areas most urgent to address. A second QR code is provided at the end of the book, so that organizations can easily pull the content they wish to engage including resources, self-assessments, team workbooks and interactive tools. The future is digital, and the future is here.

2. ***Diversity Matters:*** Of course, it always did. But the market was not making active decisions to improve diversity, until now. A newfound focus on diversity, equity, and inclusion (DEI) permeates our culture in a way never before experienced. While discussions of expanding diversity, and supporting women and diversity-led organizations have occurred for some time given the abysmal numbers, these important factors have all benefited from a substantive expansion of the conversations happening in our homes, in our communities, in our schools and in the workplace. As a woman owned business ourselves, we have first-hand experience in understanding the need for this conversation and the intense energy that surrounds these important topics.

Upon review of the first edition before we went to print several colleagues asked me if I would, if I could, include a chapter on my experience as a woman in business. I elected not to do that. Like many women and diversity professionals, I wanted the focus to be on the work, not on my personal experiences. As might be anticipated, I have had amazing experiences and offensive ones. Where would I even begin on this topic? Having recently sat on a panel for DEI in NYC, a panel composed of all women representing many cultural backgrounds, I realized how empowering the experience was. In our industry, it is incredibly rare to have another female at the table in an externally facing and/or C suite role. In reflecting on this experience I realized that I had never been on a panel of all women before. Not once in 30+ years. To me this represents a sea change. Despite the difficult times we live in today as a nation and as a world, I am excited for the future. I am excited for my daughters. I am confident in my sons who are growing up with a vastly different sense of equality in every aspect of life (if you read the forward, you know I have six amazing children now 11-22 who have grown up on 'the road' journey). For me, sharing my war stories is not as important as acknowledging how much things have changed, and how pleased I am to finally see it.

We've always represented and consulted with women & diversity led firms. I am sure that is because we connect with them, we share some of their experiences. And most importantly we know how incredibly difficult it has been, as witnessed throughout my work history of more than 30 years, for this industry to create, support and invest in equality. I hope this is the beginning of a new chapter in our society.

3. *We Are All Rethinking Our Impact:* ESG, Impact, Sustainability, investing in companies with solid ESG and in those making an active and positive difference for our planet are broad and varied topics. From an environmental and sustainability perspective, we continue to see the challenges of performance comparison and competing priorities in portfolios when it comes to making 'good' ESG decisions. This is most easily witnessed when discussing energy policy and investing. More broadly, addressing ESG has become a requirement for all managers (even if the response is 'we don't') as the regulators have required it. The trickledown effect means that database providers have added some 40+ questions to their profiles asking for data on the topics of both DEI and ESG. To the dismay of many managers, this has not been focused exclusively on what they are investing in, but also on their own organizational profile — the team that is doing the investing.

We expect to see a continued push to general improvements in ESG among all companies, investment managers and the companies they invest in. After all, doesn't it improve risk management to have good ESG anyways? We expect this will become the norm and that the changes are more than just marketing hyperbole now. When it comes to Impact—which we would differentiate as strategies and services that are actively seeking to make an impact as part or all of their mandate, not just to prove their holdings have good ESG—it is still a long game. The regulatory changes, global implications, current world events and realities of supply chain, goods, and services costs, etc. will all affect how quickly the impact investment space can grow, simply because it will impact the outcome of those investments.

In the early days of impact investing, there was significant push back about the performance of impact solutions— the notion that you were 'giving up' return to make a difference was and still is prevalent. Overtime, however, with a global focus on sustainable practices and impact across industries these companies have more support and are doing better, creating more opportunities for growth as citizens individually seek to make better decisions about their own impact and the impact of goods and services on themselves and their families. For these reasons we think this market will continue to grow, albeit slowly. What came in like a fire storm, however, and is here to stay in a more tangible way across all investing is the focus on good ESG as a general 'good business' set of standards.

PART I

Out of the Weeds: A View of the Forest from Institutional Investors

Investment managers and their resources are in the weeds. They work tirelessly to get in the hunt, to get recognized and to get hired. Rarely do they take the time to step back, look at the forest through the trees, and seek to understand what obstacles are in their way. These obstacles are seldom about performance. Yes, performance is required, but numbers alone will not get a manager hired by institutions. It is the human condition, and certainly part of the entrepreneurial spirit which this cohort has in spades, to push forward seemingly apathetic to these obstacles. It is natural to want to avoid looking squarely in the mirror; to rely on the numbers alone. Particularly when it seems that so much work has already been done.

Managers of all types will spend millions on inconsistent and ineffective efforts to grow long term assets under management again this year. Efforts that have no hope of succeeding based on the firm's current profile, level of commitment and approach. Stop wasting time and resources. Stop marketing the unsellable. Start building a complete and durable value proposition the firm can grow meaningful assets with.

The goal is to help investment management firms, their portfolio managers, marketers and sales professionals gain institutional market share. The catalyst for this growth is a better understanding of the institutional investment research process, including defining what needs to be done, and what cannot be done, in institutional product development, marketing and sales. By understanding the process, and what matters most to institutions, investment managers can focus their resources on the establishment, management, marketing and selling of a more successful investment firm.

The Road to AUM provides the market with the direct feedback of senior level institutional investment research professionals worldwide (the large majority in the US), supported by the anecdotal experience among a series of institutional marketing and sales professionals over the past decade. It is about helping managers understand how to put their best foot forward in asset raising. As the research carried on, it also became about something bigger. Managers must do more pre-planning. As the adage goes—measure twice, cut once. The book serves as a roadmap to assist managers in the process of firm development, or more likely with re-evaluation. For organizations already in the market, this book will ask firms to revisit their offering, their commitment and participation in the process, as well as their marketing approach. It is about making meaningful changes now that will greatly increase the odds of success down the road, and then stepping in completely—committing to a long-term game plan to grow assets.

The institutional market is challenging in many ways, but it will always be a great panacea, with larger asset pools to manage, more knowledgeable and experienced investors to discuss markets with, and fewer client relationships to worry about. Despite the challenges, including fickle boards, transient staffing and priorities, competitive fees, extensive due diligence and high hurdles, institutional assets are generally "stickier" and require less staff to maintain than their more retail counterparts. This allows managers to manage and institutions to grow.

CHAPTER 1

Methodology

Years of experience do not compensate for asking the direct questions. This book was created to provide managers with the voice of the institutional market.

The Format

The book was conceived around the notion of a deep dive interview with a sufficient sampling of senior level institutional research professionals. The goal was to ask precise questions about what matters. What is value-added and what might toss a manager into the penalty box? What accelerates the process and what terminates it?

The interviews were conducted over a 12-month period in a combination of in person meetings and extended conference calls. One hundred percent of the interviews were conducted with senior level institutional research professionals. The large majority to whom I had been marketing and selling, in most cases for the better part of a decade. I spoke with more than 50 institutional research professionals in all about these topics to gain their wisdom and perspectives, 32 of which were formal interviews.

The interview covered 10 major topic areas represented by a roster of more than 60 questions. In each formal interview, all topics were covered with ample time to ensure full review of the key question set, although not all questions may have been asked. To ensure maximum value for readers, respondents provided anonymous feedback that has been merged together by topic to define a consensus, in most cases. The hope was that respondents would be more forthcoming with their feedback without concern for identification.

The Respondents

The respondents represent global asset pools that exceed one trillion in assets under advisement; their focus is on institutional investment management research for a variety of product types including traditional long only and alternative offerings in a variety of structures, both liquid and illiquid, direct and pooled. These individuals sit within industry leading organizations. Respondents represent global consultants, large multifamily offices, single family offices, endowments and foundations, corner office ultra-high net worth intermediary teams, insurance companies, bank trusts and independent wealth advisory firms of size. These are not retail advisers; they are not interested in rounds of golf or steak dinners (at least not as a means of selecting managers). These are senior level institutional investment research professionals and often investment committee members. This is not meant to slight the value of good relationships and the importance of taking the time to build them (nor is it a slight on the retail business which fuels our market in many ways), but to differentiate these respondents as buyers.

The institutional investment management research professional is driven by the data and by their client's needs. They are pursuing managers that can handle somewhere between $10M – $500M in assets in a single client account or pool of client assets, if not more. They are not paid on commission. They are interested in identifying the "best" managers for their institutional investors as they define it. As a cohort they are consistently averse to unnecessary risk. They are making the decisions on who to hire and who to fire. Every single one of them has the potential ability to change the endgame for an investment management firm.

"Potential" is used deliberately here, given that we all understand these professionals are part of a much bigger ecosystem. Often, managers have the negative perception that research professionals can't move the needle at all. Yet enough of them can and do.

The Interview Topics

The interview topics around which the questions were posed are defined below. There are several key aspects of a successful firm that are not explicitly identified as a topic below because they are not subjects which naturally lend themselves to a direct question to respondents. A firm's offering and branding are excellent examples. These components are not only insidious to the ultimate result and covered in Part II *Stepping Back*, but will surface among the feedback of respondents regularly. For example, the establishment of a firm's brand is integrated into all aspects of its marketing effort, and is reflected through the understanding and experience of the institutional buyer without a direct question on the same. ***Getting the offering and branding correct, as well as affirming the firm's commitment to the process and its understanding of prospects and timing, are initial hurdles that require undivided attention before any successful launch into the institutional market.***

The interview topics start where most managers dive in, at the initial point of contact with institutions. The interviews were designed to capture the institutional investment management research professional's experience, which begins the moment they receive an inbound inquiry for review and often ends years, if not a full decade, later. Key interview topic areas included:

1. The Competition
2. Tools of the Trade: External Data Points Used in the Evaluation
3. The Story and Its Content
4. Initial Outreach and the Successful Introduction
5. The Live Meeting
6. Technology in Meetings

Each component of the process has a series of questions designed to gain market feedback on efficient and effective interactions that move the needle. Every interaction a firm has can be pivotal; it can propel a manager to the top or to the bottom of the list, in spite of the numbers. The reality of institutional marketing and sales is that it takes lots of time and resources. Time and resources are limited. The questions are precisely those that impact where a firm spends their time and money so that they can prioritize what matters most.

The Resource Prioritization Matrix (RPM)

Based on the interview feedback, each key element of a marketing and sales effort is given an overall rating in terms of relative importance in the process to these respondents. Ultimately, all elements of a successful campaign are critical; prioritizing them will get a firm on the right path sooner and for less time and money.

To keep the diagnostic simple, the *RPM* evaluates the primary elements of the institutional investment management marketing and sales process, and rates the importance of the quality of each element on a four-point scale. The rating seeks to highlight the relative importance of these limited touchpoints, so that firms can apply resources where it is most appreciated and noticed by institutions.

A disclaimer is required here; all aspects of a firm's story, marketing and sales are important, or they would not have made it into the book. Any red flag raised at any point in the process no matter how subtle is sufficient to exclude a firm from consideration, now and in the future.

The institutional investor is not always forthcoming with direct feedback to help guide this resource spend. Unfortunately, red flags, particularly less obvious ones, are rarely well articulated back to the manager or to its sales and marketing representatives. In other words, *"there is something wrong here, but we just can't put our finger on it."* This is not the response firms need to maximize their efficiency, to minimize their budgets and to grow assets. The book is designed to lay out many of these red flags, some large, waiving, and overwhelming signs of distress, others so small they might not be noticed. It is best to leave no stone unturned in the competitive world of institutional investment management. The *Resource Prioritization Matrix (RPM)* is designed to provide a structure around how a firm might think about investing in its sales and marketing effort: what simple changes can and should be made, and what is better left to a "future enhancements" bucket list because it doesn't appear to move the needle in a meaningful way.

RPM Rating

Rating	Description
De Minimis	This aspect of marketing and sales was not important to respondents at this time—no respondents highlighted this as a necessary element to success; minimal time and resources should be spent perfecting this item.
Core	This aspect of marketing and sales was considered a core element and was important to respondents at this time—the majority of respondents identified it as necessary, but that it was more "expected" than value-added; a sufficient amount of time and resources should be spent perfecting this component up front and consistently delivering on it over time.
Priority	This aspect of marketing and sales was considered a priority element and was extremely important to respondents at this time—respondents were excited to talk about this element and could identify specific scenarios in which it made a difference; a significant amount of time and resources should be spent assuring accuracy, efficiency and best positioning.
Game Changer	This aspect of marketing and sales was considered critical and could be justification for immediate and permanent exclusion from consideration if not done well. Respondents clearly identified this topic as a hot button, something that made a material difference; extreme thought and preparation should go into the exact wording, timing, content and delivery of this component of the marketing and sales process.

Given the scarcity of resources, it is imperative to understand market expectations and needs, and to spend those resources in line with a "highest and best use" protocol. The *Resource Prioritization Matrix* is designed to prioritize firm activities in this way, spending time where it is most noticed and appreciated by institutions. Of course, readers will often disagree with the rating. These priorities are subject to change and will vary from professional to professional; the rating is provided based on the consensus of respondents.

Key Takeaways

Each element of the marketing and sales process reviewed with respondents has an overall *RPM* rating, proceeded by a deeper dive into the subject matter. Respondent feedback is summarized into a set of comments and best practices for readers to digest, followed by a section which incorporates the questions asked to respondents and the consensus answer. *Words to Drive By* follows. This section provides a sampling of direct quotes from respondents on a variety of aspects of each subject. The goal is to provide firms with actionable and efficient market feedback, and to give respondents a voice in the process, a voice that might be more meaningful to readers than the suggestions and consensus response alone. Concluding each chapter is a *Summary* of key takeaways.

Let's Get the Show on the Road

Having screened hundreds of managers over the past 25 years, and having invested great time and care in corralling the feedback and voices of institutional investors for this project, one universal truth stands out. Managers consistently have good intent without the necessary understanding, skills, process or perseverance to get to the finish line. This book was written to provide managers with a view from the inside. It is a unique opportunity to hear from the experts themselves, whether firms believe institutional research professionals are experts or not, in how they perceive what comes to them and what is going to move the needle.

Firms and their representatives will find out where to spend their time and where to stop wasting it based on the realities of the market and the processes and procedures generally consistent among this institutional buying group. This book is full of practical guidance to provide managers with the reminders that marketing and sales professionals often need themselves, or have a hard time delivering to their manager clients because managers can be infamously insular in their view of themselves and the market's response to them. This insular view has its benefits; it is what fuels a manager's passion and dedication to their philosophy and process. The joint work is in finding the best way to structure a sustainable and competitive investment offering, and effectively implementing a meaningful sales and marketing plan to engage the market in order to grow assets.

Institutional buyers are different. The factors that drive a decision are deeper than performance or a handshake; the factors will be outlined in detail. Managers can exit these pages with a game plan to get them where they want to go. Take the time to look a bit deeper in the mirror. Figure out what is working and what is not. Executing the critical changes required to succeed is up to the firm; every member of the team must be on board, knowledgeable about the process and committed to the firm's success. The book provides a series of process steps from pre-launch (and in the case of most who have already gone to market in some way, stepping back) through full scale implementation. Complete the whole process prescribed: step back, then step in and step out into the world of institutional investment management marketing and sales. Do this whether you are on day one, Fund III or year ten. Ideally, if done thoroughly and completely, the firm will only have to travel the road to AUM once. These are the rules for the road. This is the view of the forest through the trees.

CHAPTER 2

The Institutional Lens

There are a few guiding principles that are important to clarify out of the gate. They are profiled here so that firms are aware of the institutional lens through which they are viewed.

Our World Has Changed

Technology and the globalization of our economy have together proven to be great equalizers in the field of marketing, creating efficiency and access that has largely leveled the playing field worldwide. This has created its own equal and opposite chaos in the realm of data overload and cyber risk, further complicated by the very fact that this is the money business. Organizations, both institutional and intermediary driven, have tighter processes for screening, selection and ongoing monitoring than ever before. Business is no longer done on a handshake. Regulation is increasing. Technology's capacity to track, screen and monitor massive amounts of data, both current and historical, is on the rise. Global competition is up. Meanwhile, budgets and time are down.

Firms and Managers Are One

Managers and firms are one in the same for the purposes of this book. Firms can be quite small, but must be legal and formal entities to be considered for institutional mandates. The terms 'manager', 'managers', 'firm' and 'firms' are used interchangeably throughout.

Institutional Investors Are Different

The wealth of generations is in the hands of institutional investors. Investment management is important business. Is an institution going to risk their reputation and perhaps even their livelihood on a particular manager? Should they risk it? Institutions are naturally risk averse; they possess the knowledge, the resources and the mandate to look far beyond the numbers. Anecdotal evidence shows that the components of the process managers want to dismiss as unnecessary or "not a priority" are exactly those that separate the long-term winners from the rest of the pack. Performance is not one of them. Performance is a given. A manager will get nowhere without good performance. Truly good performance is not the kind where the firm has re-engineered a new way to look at alpha, selected a weak benchmark against which they look stunning, or decided which time periods are relevant to the market and which are not. Institutions understand these games managers play with regard to performance. They are adept at understanding data and they prefer to avoid unnecessary risk. Despite the short-term mentality of the world today, institutional investors are generally seeking long-term solutions as well. For a good understanding of how long-term their thinking is, visit www.fcltglobal.org and review a variety of pieces on the subject, including FCLTGlobal's *Institutional Investment Mandates: Anchors for Long-term Performance*.

Outperformance Is Not a Panacea

Institutions will give up a fair amount of exceptional outperformance to work with a "comfortable" choice; a stable and well branded manager with a lengthy track record and deep asset pool—a good "CYA" manager.

It has been said often, *"You never get fired for hiring Blackrock"*. While this may be true, institutions want and need to find other managers. Institutions are naturally drawn to undiscovered gems with more capacity and a different story. It is also preferable to hire investment managers and not asset gatherers, leading institutions to seek managers with sufficient capacity remaining. Institutions want to know their investment managers well and prefer to be more than just a number on a client roster. Institutional investment research professionals also want to keep their jobs interesting. They want to outperform where and when they can, provided they perceive the risk/reward trade-off to be manageable.

Institutional Investors Defined

Institutions and institutional investors, for the purposes of this book, are defined as organizations with a structured research protocol and dedicated research resources. They include both global and regional organizations that provide product selection and oversight for a wide variety of institutional investors. Institutional investors include public pensions, private pensions, endowments, foundations, family offices, multifamily offices, consultants, insurance companies, sovereign wealth funds, sub-advisory entities, bank trusts, affinity groups, high-end wealth advisory firms and intermediary platforms among others. Products that may be relevant to institutional investors include separately managed accounts, private placements, limited partnerships, mutual funds, exchange traded funds and co-investment structures among others. Where product specificity is necessary, it is clarified throughout.

Assets at Work

The assets of institutions are generally invested, except for a small percentage required for liquidity purposes. While a certain amount of asset ebbs and flows are normal over the course of a multi-year period, and there are periods when cash allocations run high as market cycles move, it is rare to see an institution with an entirely available asset pool to invest. As such, the majority of allocations come from replacement searches. The firm will most often be competing against an incumbent, one whom the very institutional researcher they are marketing too may have participated in selecting. In most cases replacement searches occur because the manager is underperforming, or the investment life cycle is complete. Replacement searches can also occur because the institution changed its mandate parameters or asset allocation, leading to a necessary change. In any case, managers are most often contending for an existing slot; the assets are already at work. Firms may presume this does not apply to them in certain cases. For example, if they are offering private equity, venture, limited partnerships, co-investments or liquid structures, they may believe timelines are shorter as they once were in certain channels. Times have changed. With few exceptions, the notion of a long road, deeper due diligence, higher hurdles and full platforms are the norm.

The Fine Balance of Marketing and Sales

While marketing and sales are not the same thing, like the two side rails of a ladder, climbing the rungs successfully requires both to be level, balanced, steadfast and sturdy. Marketing and sales need to work seamlessly together. They generate one set of feedback from the market.

Combine the need for integration with the extremely tight budgets and resources of most growing investment management firms, and marketing and sales tend to become more intertwined. *"We all wear multiple hats"* is the normal response of most growing investment managers when asked who is doing what. This response is accurate. However, a distinction should be made when it comes to marketing v. sales activities and the skills required to achieve success. A good example is when a portfolio manager (PM) attempts to serve as a sales professional. The PM is critical to the process, but is rarely a phenomenal presenter. The things that make a person good at being a PM can hurt in the sales process. An active marketing and content development role for the PM? Yes. A critical voice in live meetings and conference calls specifically displaying their passion for their investment management philosophy and process? Absolutely. Leading the sales effort while trying to run the money? No. Even if a portfolio manager's sales skills are unusually fantastic, this is not where their time should be spent. These distinctions are critical for firms to understand and to fully vet in regard to resource management. Formal definitions of each function are listed below:

Marketing

According to the American Marketing Association Board of Directors, "Marketing is the activity, set of institutions, and process for creating, communicating, delivering, and exchanging offerings that have value for customers, clients, partners, and society at large."

Selling

According to Dictionary.com, the verb "selling" is defined as "1. To engage in selling something. 2. To be on sale. 3. To offer something for sale. 4. To be employed to persuade or induce others to buy, as a salesperson or a clerk in a store. 5. To have a specific price; be offered for sale at the price indicated. 6. To be in demand by buyers. 7. To win acceptance, approval, or adoption."

Marketing refers to the process of creating and communicating a brand, the firm's story and its offering(s). Sales refers to the physical presence of a firm in front of, visually or vocally, the target audience, with a focus on closing business. When firms separate marketing and sales, the resources may be deeper as they are by design more dedicated, but often they don't work well together. This book incorporates a broader discussion of marketing and sales respectively, and provides specific recommendations in considering these two critical side rails on the firm's climb to the top. The most important consideration being an acknowledgement that marketing and sales are different.

Buying v. Hiring

Investment management is not a product that is bought. Managers are asking to be hired for investment management services that will be provided in the future. A wise manager once said, "the past is not prologue" in looking at the companies they are choosing to invest in.

Selecting investment managers only differs from a product sale by its complexity and the exponentially greater difficulty in unwinding a hiring decision. "Past performance is no guarantee of future results." This disclaimer is plastered on all marketing materials and sales literature for good reason. Firms will benefit from keeping this simple distinction, buying v. hiring, in mind in everything they do. Whether preparing for a marketing campaign or a sales call, the firm is being interviewed, an offering of services under certain terms is being made, and the firm is seeking to be hired. Do not confuse this endeavor with a simple product sale. A manager's fantastic performance is always in the rear-view mirror in asset management.

Internal v. External Resources

This book is not about whether to build internally or to engage external resources to help support a growing investment management firm. Ultimately, that series of decisions is dependent on multiple variables. Often a combination of internal and external resources is required, and even more often the needs of an organization will change over time. However, institutional investment management research professionals were asked about their experiences and views on internal v. external resources regarding marketing and sales, and in relation to vendor selection and prioritization. Where views on internal or external value propositions are relevant (and there are certainly clear value propositions to both) they are included for context. Resources will be addressed in *Chapter 17: Resource Management*.

Entrepreneurialism Rules

Take a pause before you dive in and remind yourself how amazing you already are. You have either created your own company or you are thinking about it. You have stepped out from a much larger firm to run your own strategy, or signed up to market and/or sell on behalf of a growing investment management organization. You are living off the fruits of your own labor. Who does that? That is amazing. Entrepreneurs are amazing. You have the courage, the fortitude, the stamina and the commitment to do all the things that make a company viable in the first place. Whether you have already been in the market or are new to it, you have already accomplished something truly exceptional that most people only dream of. This book was written to celebrate what you have done and where you can take yourself from here. However, the path is long, and the firm probably isn't at full capacity nor fully prepared just yet. This book will help the firm figure out what it needs to do, or do differently, to get there.

Product Structure Timelines Have Converged

There is an assumption in the market that certain product structures are more expedient to sell than others. Readers are cautioned to consider how these timelines have converged over the past several years. Changes in regulation, globalization and the simple time in market of many product structures have driven this convergence. For readers who believe the timeframes outlined in this book do not apply to them, keep in mind that these timelines are based on getting a manager to full capacity, not to first allocations. Certain product structures do lend themselves to quicker allocations in specific channels such as a small broker-dealer or registered investment adviser who onboards a liquid mutual fund early in its lifecycle, or a family office who jumps into a private equity Fund I solution or a sub $10M limited partnership. Typically, senior level marketing professionals will not get involved with a manager until they have reached certain thresholds. For example, the coveted $100M in AUM, or completion of the challenging Fund I and II raises. At this point, part of the timeline has already been baked in. Managers should expect a three-year timeline at a minimum, regardless of product structure, if they are new to the institutional market or in the early stages of business and product development.

Thanks Bernie

We live in the Post–Madoff era. Managers miss the significance. Google "Post–Madoff" and you will be greeted with "Post–Madoff Reforms" at www.investor.gov authored by the Securities and Exchange

Commission. The degree of difficulty is exponentially higher thanks to Bernie. His $18 billion fraud perpetrated on investors and the industry at large was the largest Ponzi scheme in history. Significant due diligence, right down to the minutia of individual trades from years past, is the new norm. Managers are consistently thrown by the degree of due diligence implemented not only by institutions of all shapes and sizes, but by potential vendors, marketers and sales agents. The regulatory environment took on a life of its own coming out of the Post–Madoff period. These regulations are here to stay. Firms who can create more automated ways to demonstrate compliance and to provide due diligence materials will fare well in the decades ahead. Firms must embrace the call for full transparency to be viable candidates in the institutional market.

PART II

Stepping Back:
Getting in Position to Win

Managers are excited to get the show on the road; to bring their numbers and story to institutions far and wide. Managers want to hear what these institutions think. More assets under management are needed to thrive, perhaps even to survive, and firms want their fair share. They believe they are ready.

Market experience, reinforced by the institutional investment management professionals interviewed, indicates most managers are not fully prepared. Lack of preparation makes the task tougher. For 75% of managers or more, regardless of strategy or structure, the road will not lead to a viable institutional investment management business. The carnage is all around us in the form of fledgling firms that never fully took off.

It is worth noting that investment managers can run a very efficient and prosperous business without ever tapping into institutional assets. In fact, many of them should; their profitability might well be higher and their stress, lower. ***However, if a manager believes they are a good fit for institutional asset management, and they want to expand beyond high net worth, digging deeper and looking past performance to achieve success is necessary.***

Success is based as much on what is done before a firm launches its institutional marketing effort, as it is on the marketing plan itself. Remember, firms have one chance to make a first impression. In this instance, "first impression" is not referring to a manager's opening monologue or their presence when they walk in the room. It defines the overall package—what the firm is offering. The competition for attention is fierce. Firms may be unaware that they are one of 100 inbound manager inquiries received in an average week by institutional investment management research professionals. That is a big pond.

Whether a firm is contemplating its first outreach, or it is knee deep in a broad distribution list and multi-year sales effort, a pause is likely in order. What is the rush? Yes, patience is painful. Managers will say, "but we've got it—we are performing better than X, we are 'within the fee range', and we have a longer and better track record than 'Y' big box firm." These comparisons may or may not be accurate. They may not even matter much to institutions. There are many variables at play. Part II is dedicated to defining these variables, so that what the firm brings to the table, and who they bring it to, is the best match it can possibly be.

CHAPTER 3

The Institutional Asset Gathering Marathon

This book is about understanding what works and what does not in institutional investment management asset raising. Firms want to know how to create an effective and compelling offering, where managers stumble and what elements must be in place to achieve results. The research delivers this direct feedback through the eyes of the institutional investment professional on the other side of the table, from the very first outreach to ongoing communication. The book provides rules for the road, and a series of reflections that managers can take back to their own organizations to ensure they are doing what it takes to succeed. Not only on day one, but throughout the grueling marathon that is institutional asset gathering. Appreciating that this is a marathon and not a sprint is rule one.

Managers want to catch the elusive lightening in a bottle. Firms that appear to have caught lightening have a lengthy back story, or they do not last. Rome was not built in a day and investment management firms won't be either, no matter how good their numbers are. There have been some spectacular rises and falls in the investment management arena, particularly in the hedge fund space. The world watched them leapfrog to the top virtually overnight, and then crash and burn just as quickly. They are the anomaly of the investment management world and they are hired on a combination of big brand, connection and outsized performance. Managers are unlikely to see their star burn so brightly, nor crash so brilliantly. Shame on the industry for continuing to let these examples exist at all. The tape has been played too many times. Like the Bill Gates example of skipping college, it is an anomaly that is unlikely to pay dividends for the other 99.9%. Institutional investment management research professionals want managers to come prepared, and to understand the process in order to maximize efficiency for the manager and the institution. One comment from a respondent sums up institutional perspectives on the process quite well; *"What do you bring to the table, who is it a fit for, where does it fit? There is a normal course of asset raising: friends and family, college contacts, board/network/ colleagues, small wealth advisers, seed firms, smaller institutions seeking to differentiate who are more flexible, and finally, the big boys and girls. KNOW YOUR AUDIENCE! Who the prospect is, what do they want, what are they willing to invest in?"*

Stepping Back to Get Ahead

What does stepping back mean? It means taking a step back from the drive to market and sell an investment management capability for long enough to ensure that the offering is the best it can be. It is asking the tough questions and confirming their answers before a full scale institutional marketing and sales commitment is made. What needs to happen, beyond performance, before engaging the market? What needs to be in place for the firm to be successful? Does this team have what it takes? What will the market require of the firm beyond the numbers they have posted? Where are the red flags? What does the firm know about its prospects and competition? ***Managers consistently skip the tedious work of asking and fully answering these questions, preferring to plow full steam ahead into an unknown market. In the end, this makes the process longer, not shorter.***

Find a Devil's Advocate

Firms must resist the temptation to dive into institutional outreach without first laying the appropriate ground work. Managers can undoubtedly find marketing and sales resources who love their story enough to plow full steam ahead right along with them. These resources, whether internal or external, may encourage managers to jump in, feet first, with the assurance that this is possible, in less time and with less resources than imagined. Why? These resources want to believe it is possible too; they don't want to focus on the risks because they are focused on the promise of institutional assets, the excellent story the manager has told and performance they have posted in the past. What these resources do know, however, presuming they are well established and experienced, is that the process of building a business, bringing an offering to market and gaining institutional market share is hard. Managers must be highly confident they have vetted all aspects of the business and value proposition; that they have all of their ducks in a row.

This moment belongs to the managers. It is their opportunity to take a pause; to think through their business, offering, commitment and desired client base. The market can and will wait. Experienced marketing and sales professionals will support this pause fully. In fact, they will insist on it. Firms will benefit from identifying a devil's advocate, whether a potential advisory board member, an interested colleague, or an outsourced marketing and sales partner, who can provide a series of likely market objections and other considerations regarding the firm's offering and commitment. This will ensure that firms are more prepared for what institutions might push back on, perhaps providing the opportunity to correct course before engaging the market.

The Numbers Are So Good—Why Not Step In?

Firms tend to want to dive in; to outreach before they are ready, to skip the self-reflection and competitive analysis, and to avoid the realities of the market environment. They believe performance trumps everything. Sometimes managers move too slowly but more common are those who move too quickly, without fully vetting the opportunity set and what they bring to the table. Firms may have sat on the side lines for years building their track records, waiting for what they perceive to be the right time. They presume this track record alone means they are ready. They jump in, casting a wide net without context and proceed to tread water as they impatiently wait for the market to respond. This inevitably results in multiple iterations as the firm attempts various approaches, swapping out resources and repositioning a team and strategy already introduced to the market, all to compel the market to respond. Institutional investment research professionals know this, and they do not like it. Managers get one chance to make that first impression. As one institutional investment research professional quipped, *"We are not guinea pigs; we don't give our clients' assets to managers who haven't cut their teeth yet. It is not just about the ability to manage the assets well in terms of performance, it is also about being able to trade outside your firm, being able to present to a board, investing at higher volumes. It's about experience."*

Outreach Is Evergreen

Stepping back and shoring up the foundation is not only good business to avoid wasting lots of time and money on the wrong effort, but it is also good business because what is put out in the market is permanent. Materials and introductions sent out are forever saved in institutional databases. It is extremely difficult to back paddle. Firms need to ensure that they have the right team in place, the best offering they can provide and the most differentiated story they can tell so that they resonate with the institutional market on day one. Ideally the firm is not just ready for primetime, but is presented in a highly professional way that will stand the test of time.

Platform Rationalization and Replacement Searches

The world has changed, and the investment management landscape has changed along with it. While the 2000s were spent building out extensive and diversified platforms of investment options, the 2010s were spent unwinding them. Easiest to unwind is liquid and separately managed account structures, but private equity, venture and limited partnership investments have not been immune to these trends. Whether institutions run their own platform, or outsource to an entity that focuses on investment manager selection and monitoring in the form of consulting or a dedicated platform, manager rosters are robust. Over the past several years, platforms have gone through an ongoing rationalization process of shaving down their inventory of offerings. With an increase in regulation and strong momentum behind the major indices, platforms have sought to reduce their offerings in order to maintain a more efficient solution set. By reducing the quantity of managers, institutions save costs. Platforms can be managed with far fewer resources.

The market cycle has only supported this trend. With passive management largely outperforming active across asset classes, institutions and their investors have further rationalized that passive provides the best cost/benefit equation in certain asset classes. The result is a reduction in active management opportunities and far fewer new allocations. Managers are largely reliant on replacement searches, opportunities in which institutions determine they must replace a manager due to size (it has grown too large or too small), performance or other investment management or firm changes the institution is not comfortable with. Platform realizations and a focus on replacements as the primary search rationale has changed the landscape for investment managers seeking to grow institutional market share. Even in the case of liquid products, and those at the other end of the spectrum with long-term holding periods such as private equity, venture and some limited partnerships, manager rosters are on the decline. Institutions of all shapes and sizes are simplifying and downsizing their manager rosters. Re-upping on subsequent offerings from the same manager is down and investing in early stage funds is on the decline. While these trends will surely shift, the days of readily available capital and limited due diligence are unlikely to return. As you read this book today, where are we in the cycle?

Stepping Back: Firm First, Market Second

In Part II *Stepping Back*, the focus is first on the firm itself; the market and marketing must wait. The importance of the firm's story—its team, offerings, brand identity and capital commitment to the process are the firm's top priority. Confirming that a manager has something sellable, that any red flags have been internally vetted and that the firm is ready to make the capital commitment required to engage the institutional market is paramount.

Once the firm has been fully vetted, it is time to focus on the institutional market. First, institutions will be discussed as prospects— how to understand and approach them. Then the competition will be discussed. These variables: (1) the firm; (2) the institutional prospects; and (3) the competition, require careful consideration before we dive into the institutional investment management research interviews conducted. Otherwise, the book would only be about the process of active marketing and selling of a pre-defined solution, when the solution itself might be the very reason a manager has not and will not succeed.

This "miss" is a primary thesis of the book: not only can the marketing and sales approach of the firm fail, poor pre-planning and offering definition upfront can result in failure too. The marketing and selling is ancillary; these activities only matter if the hard work of firm infrastructure, product viability and capital commitment is squarely in place. Firms are otherwise assured of wasting money and time that they don't have on the wrong efforts, and destroying the viability of institutional prospects along the way. The *Resource Prioritization Matrix* rating was introduced in *Chapter 2: Methodology*. If we were to apply an *RPM* rating to the element of stepping back, it would be an unequivocal *game changer*.

Summary on the Marathon of Institutional Asset Raising

It's a long road—be prepared.

Find a Devil's Advocate
Look Beyond Performance
Proceed Only When Prepared

CHAPTER 4

Firm First: A Pre-Launch Puzzle

Managers who are passionate and articulate can tell a great story. Too often, passion wins over process; the firm and its resources are willing to go to market with something that is not quite right. The story has "red flags" or "fleas" or whatever label one would like to ascribe to it. Perhaps the performance is stellar, but the terms are wrong. Perhaps the manager is exceptional, but the team is wrong. Or worse, there is no team. Maybe there is one teeny, tiny, red flag—a regulatory blip or a performance blooper that happened "years ago". Managers talk about transparency, but then can't seem to get the data "ready." There are thousands of permutations of what can be problematic, and it only takes one red flag to derail the process. The pre-launch puzzle is about putting the firm first, ensuring the firm has the right framework in place before getting on the road. It starts with an acknowledgement that performance is not the only criteria to win institutional mandates, and that managers have histories and stories; they are not perfect.

Experience Is Never Perfect

When things look too good to be true, they typically are. Firms often want to hide their flaws: investments that didn't work, changes to process that went undocumented, blips in the track record, regulatory events, organizational changes, and so on. Burying details is ill-advised. Institutional investment management research professionals want to work with investment managers who "get it"; managers who are comfortable enough to be honest and forthcoming about their history. Perhaps these professionals believe there is a correlation to being forthcoming in the future? Due diligence requires that institutional investment management research professionals fully vet all aspects of a firm and its offering. It does not, however, require perfection. Managers have stories and histories—this is their strength. An investor looking at a private equity offering whose materials showed no signs of stress despite 21 unique investments, wrapped up in a pretty bow and with the manager touting "excellent market conditions" once begrudged, *"we know you are going to have some dogs; everyone has a few dogs"*.

What is expected is an honest reflection and the ability to articulate these lessons learned. Experience tells us that every firm has a few molehills to climb, and that molehills become tall mountains in the highly competitive world of institutional investment management, precisely at the time firms need them not to be. How many molehills can be identified? How many obstacles can be removed before the firm steps in? Nothing changes the color of the face of a sales professional quicker than an investment manager who uses a hard-won meeting as true confession time. The team has gone over and over the investment process, firm history and story. The team has it down. The materials and the numbers look great. Then the manager drops a bomb. A big, awkward, game changing confession in the form of a process "update", portfolio "tweak" or team "transition" that should have been factored in long ago.

Now is the time to factor that in. Right now. All of it. Before the firm spends countless hours and dollars in a market that has a long memory and too many options. We are going for the gold. It will take hard work and honest reflection, but the outcome is well worth it.

Vetting the Firm: A Four Corner Framework

How do you start a puzzle? Do you lay all the pieces out and turn them right side up? Getting those first pieces in place is critical because they provide a structure; they give us a frame in which to create. We tend to start with corner pieces and then the flat edges because they serve as guideposts. Similarly, there are four preliminary corner pieces of the puzzle that should be laid out before firms do anything else. Each one is a game changer. These are the four corners:

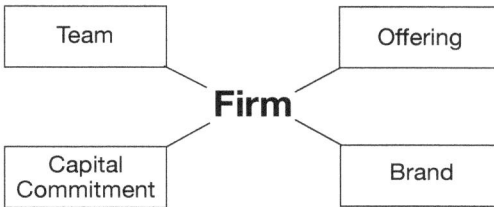

Puzzle Piece #1: Team

The firm's offering begins with the team offering it. The firm is seeking to get hired. Here is the first lesson in institutional priorities. Institutions don't like press, particularly negative press. They don't want or need to worry about the longevity of a manager with whom they have entrusted a percentage of their client's assets. They like their jobs and they want to keep them. The team is a critical element of the evaluation, and more important than firms want to believe. There is a primary portfolio manager who has some support structure. Getting under the hood and understanding how broad or limited that "team" is serves as a cornerstone of institutional investment management due diligence. Here are some risks worthy of consideration: (1) insufficient resources; (2) inconsistent resources; (3) risky resources. It does not mean that firms can or should change up their team to meet an institutional prototype, but it does require extensive forethought. How is the team positioned and resourced? How does the firm intend to manage various adverse scenarios with the constraints inherent in its team structure? What is the firm's three to five year game plan in regards to addressing resource limitations?

Here are a variety of the potential limitations that institutional investment management research professionals are factoring in regarding the team, and for which firms should be well prepared with an explanation:

Team Hurdles

1. Key man/woman, or married couples' business ownership and/or portfolio management
2. Family business ownership
3. Partnership/Ownership structure
4. Private equity ownership
5. Organizational sustainability/Burn rate
6. Competing interests/Other businesses (*i.e. wealth management*)
7. Seed capital controls
8. Lack of pedigree
9. Insufficient team
10. Unaligned incentives/Lack of an incentive structure
11. Turnover
12. Regulatory history (*firm or individuals*)
13. Legal history (*firm or individuals*)
14. Firm three to five-year game plan

A recent manager inquiry presented a spousal team. The team was just that; two married individuals seeking institutional assets to manage. The strategy presented was quite complex and there were no analysts or additional support professionals. The presentation provided placed their two photos, first and matching last names, on page one. No additional resources nor resource discussion followed. What institution could bypass the elephant in the room? Is everyone aware of the divorce rate? Could you work with your spouse? The game plan must clearly define the team and organizational path. Firms should outline their succession plan, incentive compensation structure and internal and external resource commitments. Newly established capabilities may not have these pieces in place, and institutions of course can simply terminate if a major change occurs (this is a new manager's typical retort when asked about succession planning). However, institutions don't want to take that risk and they don't need to. Planning is required and expected, particularly when organizations are familial or have roots in a single family. Firms must take special care to acknowledge and plan for unforeseen changes. The market has seen the tape reel play too many times. Immunity is created by infrastructure, good planning, appropriate incentives and team diversification. Success and sustainability is never assured but the odds are greatly improved with meaningful planning in place. Firm infrastructure, available resources, and how to build and manage a growing organization in this context is the subject of its own book. For now, understand that the firm itself, or lack thereof, is a game changing element in the institutional investment management research due diligence process. Performance will not overcome a risky infrastructure. More will be discussed on this topic in *Chapter 17: Resource Management*.

Puzzle Piece #2: Offering

When moving into the content of the interviews, it will become clear that a notable frustration among the institutional investment management research community is manager (and marketer) lack of context. This comes into play in the next puzzle piece, the firm's offering. Institutional investment research professionals expect that firms have done their homework, that they know what is relevant and what is not. Keep in mind that investment researchers have context that firms don't, and they expect firms to come in knowing more than they typically do about how they "stack up" in relation to an undefined peer group. How can managers put their best foot forward? Start by getting the structure right.

The Offering in Context

Firms are not selling their services in a vacuum and institutional investors are not buying based on performance alone. Firms are competing against many factors, the most obvious being other managers and their respective offering profiles. What may be less obvious is how critical comparing apples to apples is in the world of investment management offerings. Two managers can have identical track records, while offering an entirely different value proposition to investors. Varied vehicle choices (separately managed account, limited partnership, private placement, mutual fund, exchange traded fund, etc.) and their related terms can make a monumental difference in the market interest in, investor experience with and results of an investment. Firms must stretch their review beyond performance of the most likely peer group to understand how their offering stacks up.

When marketing a registered product, such as a mutual fund or exchange traded fund, gathering competitive information is easy. Firms can pull up Morningstar or any one of several other resources and quickly ascertain who the competition is and how the manager stacks up well beyond performance. For hedge funds, searching the universe can be done, although true competitors can be more difficult to identify given broader product flexibility by design, and broader based indices. Hedge fund product descriptions can be vague and naming conventions, as they relate to a specific strategy, are rarely clear. For separately managed account strategies, private placements and direct investment opportunities, understanding the competitive landscape is even more difficult. It requires market intelligence and access to datasets that are not readily available without expensive database subscriptions, if at all.

Competitive analysis, regardless of how it is compiled, should be completed immediately; not later in the process, after the firm has invested significant time and resources, and has been out in the market trying to figure out why their awesome numbers are not doing the trick. To this end, a lot more than a rudimentary performance comparison is required. Detail will be provided in *Chapter 6: Redefining the Competition*. For now, as part of the pre-launch puzzle framework, for the piece dedicated to the firm's offering, be sure that the team has extensive competitive data on hand from which to evaluate its offering.

Don't Offer Too Much

A multiple product offering can be quite problematic. Understand that if the investment team is small, and the firm is going to attempt to market and sell multiple products at once, the effort has a greater likelihood of failure. Institutions instinctually know what is possible for a small team to handle. It is also a distraction to be asked to weed through multiple products when there is generally just one that would be an institutional fit and timely given current market trends. Rethink the firm's primary offering in this light. Less is more. This does not mean that managers cannot or should not incubate products, and that multiple products cannot coexist.

On the contrary, particularly given the oft style box nature of institutional investors, seeking great specificity in their mandates, having stand-alone strategies can be compelling. There are also natural derivatives of strategies that lend themselves to an additional offering, such as the small-cap manager that believes they can offer a compelling SMID (small and mid-cap) offering or believes their 'early' ideas would make a compelling micro-cap offering, or the manager who runs a quantitative screening process on U.S. equities and believes they can apply this to international equities. Managers are encouraged, however, to focus on their most compelling offering when it comes to initial outreach. Large, well branded and established managers can and do provide a product matrix, on a single page for institutions to consider their offerings in snapshot format. Smaller firms with a single investment team should remain laser focused on their lead product for now.

Offering Structural Considerations

Managers can have their strategies in the wrong structure, and this can make all the difference. Strategies that should be in a separately managed account (SMA) vehicle, but are instead in a limited partnership (LP), are in an LP and instead should be in a mutual fund, or are in a mutual fund but could be in an exchange traded fund structure (ETF). The strategies can exist in these multiple forms, but the competitive landscape often dictates where it will sell. Understanding vehicle norms and related terms for a specific strategy is critical. Institutional research professionals are incredibly adept at quickly ascertaining whether the structure is "right". They possess an extensive list of competitors that are offering the structure in the "correct" format at the "correct" fees, competitors they typically have known and monitored for years.

Institutional investment management research professionals may talk harshly about the "games managers play" and "creative structuring" when discussing managers who can have a perfectly good strategy and highly competitive numbers, but its offering is all wrong. How are firms going to argue against that? But, they do. They want to justify a structure or a term or a set of terms, a fee schedule that is too high and a net return profile that is too low.

Marketers too often legitimize this behavior by accepting manager imposed offering constraints believing that perhaps the "story" is *that* different, the opportunity is *that* good, or the fee is not *that* much higher. Marketers believe that if they tell the story just right, if they access a new market segment with it, etc., they can overcome a structural abnormality. What institutional research professionals know better than anyone is that a structural abnormality, such as higher fees or restricted terms, can seem ok and "worth it'" at the time of sale, but often these abnormalities hurt down the road when it can least be afforded. When a manager under performs and the fees are higher than the norm, this underperformance is inflated; when a manager under performs and the vehicle provides no liquidity, the client is trapped.

Put some pen to paper on this one. Often looking visually at a matrix of competitors, vehicle structures, fees, vintage, assets under management, return profiles and terms goes a long way towards helping managers and their organizations realistically assess the inherent challenges they have created through their structure (a matrix template is provided in *Chapter 6: Redefining the Competition)*. The best laid sales and marketing game plan will not generally overcome a poorly executed offering. The market simply has too many options. Here are a few structural considerations to review prior to going to market:

The Vehicle

Take the time to evaluate what competitors are running a similar strategy in the same vehicle structure. Also consider competitors who are running a similar strategy in other structure(s). Each vehicle structure brings with it an inherent set of typical terms and fees. Is the structure consistent with that of most competitors? What terms differ and by how much? For example, are minimums higher? Hold periods longer? Are redemption fees higher? Is the investment process more complicated regarding paperwork, tax treatment, etc.? Is the offering attempting to move the market into unchartered waters with its vehicle structure? Bringing something new to the table, when the firm itself is new, is a tall order. A small tweak here or there that stands out as value-added is one thing, but redefining how the market sees a strategy structurally is either a labor of love or a recipe for disaster, and either way it will not help get to the goal of institutional AUM efficiently.

The Fees

Fees are one term in a long list of product structure considerations, but such a significant one that they require special discussion. Managers will often look at competitors, but will not look at fees closely enough, and certainly not in relation to AUM, length of track record and performance. Managers may cite a wide variety of fee points ident-ifying themselves as "in the ball park", only to find that there are a few (sometimes all it takes is one) significantly lower priced offerings with great reach and market acceptance who are already in the que. This is problematic not only because many firms will draw a line in the sand as to the maximum fee they will pay for a specific strategy and vehicle structure (quite common), but they will also consider the risk of fee impact in a performance downturn. For example, if the fee is 50bp above a strong competitor, in a down market the higher priced product is going to look significantly worse with the double hit of underperformance and a higher fee. Fee variances are exacerbated in extended periods of underperformance, to which no manager is immune. Getting the fees correct cannot be overstated.

Emerging managers count on these fees to support a growing busi-ness with a smaller than average base of assets. Regardless, managers will have a hard time catching any fire if they are not extremely competitive on pricing. The one exception to this rule, more powerful than exceptional and long-term outperformance, is when the incum-bents have capacity constraints and they are no longer viable candidates.

There is consistent market coverage on excessive fees and the regulators have come down hard on them. As a result, platforms have set thresholds and most firms in the institutional market, even those who paid a traditional 2% management fee and 20% performance fee (2 and 20) in the past, are extremely fee driven. Investors might look the other way on higher fees if it is a strategy that they believe they need exposure to and there are no other viable candidates currently in the market. However, this is rare and should not be relied upon to justify excessive fees. If raising assets is a top priority, assessing fees that are not only within the range but highly competitive is a necessity. Yes, firms need to cover their costs in order to build a sustainable business, and institutions understand this, but that is a far cry from 2 and 20.

In the separately managed account space where emerging managers often have a high net worth fee structure, for example, fees can be more than 1%. This is not a viable fee in the institutional investment management arena for separately managed accounts, not even micro-cap, and the promotion of such a schedule is highly indicative of a wealth advisory focused organization. We will discuss the wealth adviser becoming an institutional investment manager conundrum in later chapters. Define a workable fee scale that is in line with industry norms and provided openly to institutions that is south of 100bp in most cases where account size exceeds $10M. Managers may want to consider further highlighting that the fee is "negotiable pending mandate specifics" or some similar wording indicating that they are interested in working with institutional investors and willing to compromise on fees within reason. Understand that while asset pools are larger, institutional fees are generally lower due to economies of scale. Firms can and probably still should charge their low balance accounts in the 1% range to cover the costs of servicing them; just be cautious about how this is presented to institutions. Other fee thresholds will apply to different vehicle structures.

Other Terms

Once the vehicle structure has been defined, a series of terms flow from it. Clearly, if managers select a more detailed vehicle structure such as a limited partnership v. a separately managed account, they are inherently creating additional terms that will impact the sale. These terms include less liquidity and longer required hold periods, higher (or lower) minimums than desired, fee variances as discussed above and the option to charge performance fees. It is rarely if ever advisable for a long only equity manager to be in a limited partnership format and attempting to market with a typical management and incentive fee structure. The vehicle will also dictate variances in terms of the amount and depth of paperwork associated with the investment. The structure can even impact the strategy itself, with certain vehicles maintaining requirements for liquidity and generally resulting in more transient investors than other structures by design, for example mutual funds.

Every aspect of the investment structure should be mapped out v. competitors who are managing a similar strategy in the same vehicle structure and in other vehicle structures to paint a complete picture. Institutions might well prefer less liquidity and higher minimums; these terms are not raised to suggest otherwise. In fact, they typically do prefer these terms for a variety of reasons. Carefully vetting all aspects of the firm's offering is paramount, not just the numbers.

Timing Is Something

Vintage plays a role in the offering. Perhaps, a first-to-market solution can get away with something (a higher fee, a shorter track record) that later entrants cannot? However, attempting to be first in a new vehicle when everyone else is managing under a different set of structural terms might be the "right" thing to do, but it is not an easy road. The manager becomes the educator without a peer group. Ideally, the story takes hold and they become the industry leader, but this is exacerbated if the firm is trying to introduce something new as a relatively small, unknown capability; now they have got two things to introduce—themselves and the strategy. Keep the launch timing and firm's market reach in mind when considering structure and structural norms. The market needs pioneers and fresh ideas, but it is a risky proposition for lesser-known managers who are under timing, resource and budget constraints.

Here is an example. A manager who had been in the market as a registered investment adviser, offering separately managed account strategies, determined that its investment management approach would be the perfect fit for an ETF series. The manager was virtually unknown in the institutional community. The competition for the type of strategies offered by the manager were within a mutual fund structure, not an ETF structure. The strategy was more efficient and cheaper for investors to invest in within the ETF structure v. its mutual fund counterparts, but it looked quite expensive in relation to the ETF market in which it existed. This was a noble move; offering a strategy in the right structure that is more economical and efficient for investors. However, it was ill-timed because the manager did not have the market cachet to be 'first', at least not until it had built a multi-year track record proving out the thesis that the strategy was indeed more efficient in an ETF wrapper v. a traditional mutual fund.

Puzzle Piece #3: Brand

Who is this firm? What are they known for? Are they known at all? What does the firm stand for? Does it have a brand? What does brand application even mean? Many managers will start to get uneasy at this point. They don't really think brand matters all that much. Managers want to focus on the numbers. They fail to acknowledge that the numbers are past tense. Keep in mind that firms are marketing so that they can be hired for what they do in the future, not what they did in the past. Brand defines who the firm is, and likely what the institutional buyer is getting if they hire them. How professional is the firm? How committed are they? How clear and organized is the firm's messaging? *A firm's brand, like it or not, intuitively tells the market how serious the firm is, and how seriously to take them.*

Brand Defined

According to *BusinessDictionary.com*, brand is a "Unique design, sign, symbol, words or a combination of these, employed in creating an image that identifies a product and differentiates it from its competitors. Over time, this image becomes associated with a level of credibility, quality, and satisfaction in the consumer's mind . . . Thus brands help harried consumers in crowded and complex marketplace[s], by standing for certain benefits and value."

A firm has a philosophy about who they are and what they do. There are key words they prefer to use and perspectives that they believe best express who they are. Brand is a representation of this in an experiential sense. It is what the market sees, hears and experiences when interacting with the firm or a representative of it, in any format. Brand is an opportunity to state who the firm is and what is important to it in a consistent and meaningful way so that the market comes to know the firm as an entity with purpose. When done well, brand will combine the best of what a manager does and who they are into a single set of messaging. Brand will be the manager's presence in the market and it will overlay everything a firm does in marketing and sales. A good brand is a living and breathing identity—it should permit the firm to grow and improve while always retaining the best of what the firm set out to create. What is the firm's brand today? Would someone be able to easily identify it in a crowd of materials, logos and identities? What would institutional investment management research professionals say that the firm stands for if they have been receiving the firm's communications or speaking with the firm's representatives for the past year or longer?

Brand Is Not Purely Visual

Defining a brand comes first and it includes having a professional logo, clear tagline and/or mission statement that is consistently applied across all media. A good brand demonstrates consistency and continues to tell the firm's story in the use of key words, images, colors, fonts and 'personality' in everything produced and distributed on behalf of the firm. Consistently applying a quality brand is the hard work of good marketing, and of the entire organization. The most junior analyst must understand the firm's brand and represent it well. Be dogmatic about protecting, supporting and enforcing brand. The brand can and often will define whether a firm is perceived as 'retail' or 'institutional'; use of various colors, sizing of fonts and word use are all indicators.

Target Audience Influence on Brand

Firms often struggle with brand particularly when they are trying to succeed with two very different constituents, for example with high net worth investors in a wealth management framework and with institutional investors in an investment management framework. Branding can be expensive and time consuming; where should the resources be applied first? Step back and consider the primary recipient's frame of reference and likely comparative universe. Who is the firm up against? We all want efficiency, but sometimes it can muddy the waters too much. Seek clarity in branding by defining the target audience. Determine if the brand campaign must factor in different audiences, and how this will be achieved in a cost-efficient manner. Differing audiences may necessitate multiple versions of branded materials, with slightly different messaging, but the same overall brand identity. Firms can adjust their brand positioning to meet the target market's expectations through more efficient layering of content, and use of various versions of materials, including websites, to specifically address audience needs.

Good Branding Is Consistent

How consistently has the brand been applied? Managers are eager to get into the market. The desire to share their story is often implemented too soon and inconsistently. Here is a good test project. Produce a hard copy of everything with the firm's name on it that the firm has created and disseminated to anyone over the past four weeks (longer if this has not been an active marketing period). Include team members' business card(s), firm letterhead, any commentary, fact sheets and presentations, one-off pieces, RFI/RFPs, team members' email signatures, the firm website, video recordings, client reporting, and firm brochures or mailings, for example. Virtually anything that has been used to communicate with anyone about the organization should be produced in color. Lay all pieces out on a large flat surface. Walk past each one and complete the following checklist:

Brand Checklist

- ❏ Is the brand identity clearly displayed?
- ❏ Is the brand consistently applied; do these pieces go together?
- ❏ Does it represent the firm well?
- ❏ Is everything consistent in look and feel? What is not?
- ❏ Are the materials professional?
- ❏ Do they provide enough context to be meaningful?
- ❏ Are they engaging?
- ❏ Are colors/fonts/logos consistently applied?
- ❏ Are the pieces consistently highlighting the firm's strengths?
- ❏ Do they demonstrate the firm's value proposition?
- ❏ Are there any outliers that do not belong/do not make sense?
- ❏ Which is the strongest? What is most representative of the firm?
- ❏ Do the materials provide clarity of purpose?
- ❏ Are pieces streamline, efficient representations of the Firm's work?

Brand Is Not Just Design

Firms might logically think of the visual aspects of brand: logos and colors, business cards, website and firm written communications. Brand is deeper than this. Brand is about who the manager is and how they communicate. Some managers will get the visual branding right, but the content they provide will not support the brand. We will discuss content marketing in greater detail in *Chapter 7: The Firm's Oeuvre—Creating the Content Library*. Brand is much more than design. It is not only what the messaging looks and feels like, but what it says about the firm it represents.

Clarity Is King

Research professionals are highly unlikely to review verbose, multiple paragraph dissertations on a strategy unless requested to do so by a close connection, and even then, they are not happy about it nor likely to hire the manager. Respondents indicated they were quick to dismiss based on countless potential and seemingly minuscule red flags, from the email address (Gmail is too personal), to the subject line, to the very first sentence. Proper use of grammar and avoidance of typos, not to mention the content itself, are all opportunities for dismissal. Be clear and concise in firm communications.

One interesting insight from the research indicated that managers are avoiding the most rookie of mistakes—the non-business email address, typos, sole dependence on third party articles to support their thesis with no articles or materials of their own. Research professionals lamented having to *"dig deeper"* to figure out if a manager was *"legit"* in terms of sufficient depth to be considered as the materials are generally *"solid."* This is good news for the market overall. For our purposes regarding brand, understand that everything and anything can impact a firm's brand, and can be the red flag that eliminates a manager from consideration. ***The manager's job is to stay in the game by raising no red flags, defining who they are and then demonstrating it through thoughtful, consistent and robust communications.*** A brand lens must be applied to everything the firm does to ensure consistency; every opportunity should be taken to advance the firm's brand presence in the market. This book will lay out many red flags that impact a firm's brand along the way. Review it in its entirety, take notes, and most importantly go back and compare it to what the firm has delivered to date.

Performance Is Not a Brand Strategy

Managers want their numbers to be their brand. Performance is a given to access the institutional investment management market; performance is not a strategy and it is not a brand. A brand is about what the firm stands for well beyond its past performance. All firms believe they have great numbers and if they do not, they will not be hired anyway. The philosophy a firm has about money management, and how the firm works or intends to work with its clients is what differentiates it from the competition.

Brand Types

Managers fall into four categories in relation to brand. Firms should evaluate their brand history and seek to ensure that it is on target as outlined below:

1. ***No Brand:*** No notable or strong identity; the firm is trying to throw enough against the wall, often performance related, to see what sticks. The firm uses third party articles and academic research to support its performance claims but without a baseline firm branded collateral system to back them up. There is a lack of structure regarding outreach.

2. ***Inconsistent Brand:*** No professional logo, color and context consistency. The firm speaks from many different voices and angles; nothing is consistently applied. There is a lack of correlation across mediums (web v. business cards v. presentation v. fact sheet v. commentary). Inconsistent branders have some decent components but no inherent system or clear brand identity.

3. ***Overboard Brand:*** Firm has gone overboard and branded everything, so much so that it appears they are massively overspending (and they are) and perhaps insular in their views. Brand is overbearing and overly structured, creating too much formality and the sense that materials are created for branding sake, rather than to share valuable content. Brand is overly gimmicky, too punchy, and potentially controversial. The firm has branded everything in their office except for the sidewalk leading up to it.

4. ***On Target Brand:*** Firm has an identifiable brand and consistently applies it across media. The firm works to reinforce its brand through creative content development, well timed marketing, and active ongoing communications.

Brand and the Budget

There are many books available on establishing and building a brand. For the purposes of institutional investment management marketing, it is most important that a firm demonstrate consistent, accurate and error free communications to build its reputation and the case for an allocation of size. Firms do not need to overspend on brand nor throw excessive dollar amounts at regurgitating their content. Firms, particularly those seeking institutional investors, do not need to overly engage the market with the most modern of technological advancements. It is unnecessary to spend a year's salary on an agency designed pitchbook at this stage. Managers need a consistent, clear and error free voice that the market can come to recognize as its own. Once established, managers must actively exercise that voice.

Puzzle Piece #4: Capital Commitment

Managers most often fail for no reason related to their investment management capabilities and results, but rather due to the challenges of owning and operating an investment management business. They tend to be inadequately funded and inconsistent in their pursuit which leads to failure. Institutional investors know this. A sound marketing and sales strategy takes time to create and even more time to implement, and it requires the right offering at the right time to be a win. Managers need to balance their investment management activities, with their business management activities, and the firm's need to market itself all at the same time. Having a well-defined game plan, including how long the firm will give a specific effort and how many resources will be applied to it, is paramount.

Capital commitment is not referring solely to a manager's individual investment into its own offerings. While this is an important aspect of capital commitment, the total investment made by the firm into their business development is what matters most. Resources, invested capital, long-term business planning, and funding are all aspects of a firm's capital commitment.

Managers are rarely committed for a sufficiently long window to get the results they seek. Perhaps the mentality of investing factors in here. Managers are constantly vetting, screening, buying and selling in the market. Why not do the same with their marketing and sales plan? Being consistent for the long term is challenging and it is outside of the comfort zone and likely the intended commitment of a manager no matter how many professionals have attempted to provide this guidance along the way. Their story and numbers are different after all, right?

The commitment risk is exacerbated when managers have gone to market prematurely, without fully vetting their firm resources, offering and positioning. It is understood that stepping back takes time and resources in and of itself. However, consider the consequences of skipping the pre-launch. Managers rush to market and then realize, as it so often happens, that they need to regroup, reposition, and restart. They have now added a significant chunk of time and notable cost to their game plan that was not anticipated. They have also put content into the market that will be in the institutional files of those whom they marketed to forever, long after they have moved on from it themselves.

Firms will benefit immensely from completing the pre-launch work such that the game plan never requires putting their vehicle in reverse. If reversing course is required at this time, as it too often is, just do it. Don't try to dance around what isn't working, whether as a business owner, portfolio manager or marketing resource. Step up to the plate, take the hit, and get moving in the right direction. A famous quote often attributed to Einstein comes to mind. *"The definition of insanity is doing the same thing over and over again and expecting a different result."* Stop the insanity.

Committing Resources

An effective game plan will outline the firm's capital commitment, the offering priorities and the types of resources to be applied. It will also define in writing for how long the firm is committed to the plan. A careful review of market channel opportunities is necessary to determine the most efficient path to success. Managers are wise to think through likely outcomes; how would they respond in the face of changing market environments, requests for negotiated fees, discussions of capacity and concentration, periods of poor performance and lack of sales results?

A decision regarding the type of resources to be utilized is crucial. What is the firm's culture? How much does the firm outsource in general and how well does that strategy work? Are there internal resources willing and able to play a role in the firm's efforts and what are the specific skill sets? How quickly is the firm seeking to grow? How committed are they to a certain type of client profile and how long will that take to attract? The answer to these questions will depend on the channel(s) a firm wishes to pursue and in what order they do so. A solid three years of capital to cover the desired game plan must be earmarked for most efforts. If this type of capital is not available, firms can consider a variety of possible adjustments, including cutting back on proposed channels, delaying full scale marketing until the track record is further developed, taking in seed capital or other JV type opportunities, or repurposing existing firm resources where feasible.

Managers consistently underestimate the cost and time associated with institutional asset raising. There is a "if we build it, they will come" mentality among many firms. Remember, firms are seeking to get hired for future results. This requires a deeper level of trust and commitment; trust that is built through a lengthy marketing and sales process. Put the economics down on paper and ensure broad based support for the game plan before putting the show on the road.

Have Some Skin in the Game

Managers speak eloquently about their compelling investment solutions. They encourage investors to consider them above all else for their capital allocations. A key question from institutions is always "How much of the manager's own capital is invested in this strategy?" It is logical to presume that managers will invest in their own strategies, and that they will do so with a significant percentage of their personal capital. This investment puts the manager in the client's shoes literally. They are now 'playing' with their own money at risk too.

A manager well known in the industry for his deep pockets rolled out a highly compelling offering and the market watched an incredible three year track record develop. But institutions were not diving in despite the strategy's strong profile and the manager's reputation in the market. Why? The manager had not put a single dollar of his own capital into the strategy. The market perceived this as a notable issue and dismissed the offering. They were not willing to take on a risk that the manager did not deem worthy of his own portfolio.

It is feasible for managers to limit their exposure to a strategy if they can provide a compelling explanation for this decision. For example, a highly volatile investment profile might deserve a minimal allocation of no more than 5% of an investor's capital, despite its potential upside. However, managers who make this argument should not expect investors to invest beyond this stated threshold. What is good for the goose is good for the gander. Managers must invest their own capital if they expect investors to follow suit.

On the Road to AUM:
The Natural Progression of Institutional Sales

As firms think about the capital and time commitment they are willing to make, the offering they have and how they want to position the firm, understanding the natural progression of asset raising is helpful. There are a series of channel norms which largely dictate where marketing might be most effective in a phase one, phase two, phase three and so on framework. Certain audiences will be more receptive at different stages in a firm's development. A natural progression for managers follows, keeping in mind that the offering specifics will dictate the viability of certain channels. Anything is possible in terms of gaining traction in one or more of these subsets earlier or later in the process based on any number of criteria. This is a sample blueprint of how most investment management firms grow.

The Typical Path to AUM

1. Friends and Family
2. College Contacts/Past Colleagues
3. Boards/Network/Current Peer Group
4. Past Employers
5. Existing Relationship Driven Wealth Advisory Firms and Family Offices
6. Seed Firms/Emerging Manager Programs/Public Funds with Emerging Manager Programs
7. Large Wealth Advisory Firms/Single and Multifamily Offices
8. Sub-Advisory Opportunities/Insurance Companies
9. Regional BDs/Platforms/Bank Trusts/Affinity Groups
10. National Platforms
11. Mid-Tier and Regional Consultants/Small Endowments and Foundations
12. Global Consultants/ Large Direct Plans, Endowments and Foundations

As one might expect, different channels and vehicle structures have different lead times and requirements. A firm's time in market will also have a notable impact. For example, a Fund I v. Fund III offering, a new launch v. a five-year track record. The lack of an offshore vehicle when certain channels require it. While these examples may be intuitive, managers often will engage a multi-channel game plan and have consistent expectations as to the timing and allocations of these various audiences.

Firms should consider a multi-channel game plan, but with different deliverables, time expectations and commitments to each. Getting the firm's name in the market is important; it takes years to build a solid reputation. Yet, firms need assets short term. This conundrum is faced by all managers and it explains why most pursue a multi-channel game plan out of the gate. However, should this effort be full steam ahead across a wide variety of channels, each with their own needs and expenses and all at once? No. The game plan must clearly delineate expectations and commitments, including the length of time the effort is expected to take and what the firm is committed to implementing, by channel. Factor in the herd mentality that often accompanies the asset gathering process. A channel that looks perfectly suitable on paper might see its constituents piling onto a competing offering that was simply quicker to market or had a slight nuance that this offering did not. Alternatively, the channel might simply not be interested in this asset class at this time. These subtle variables can make or break the timing and perceived value of a channel. Patience, market intelligence and efficiency must be applied to ensure the longevity of the effort.

The firm's commitment defines the final puzzle piece of the pre-launch. At this point, ideally the firm has carefully vetted itself across four critical measures: its team, offering, brand and capital commitment. It is now time to see what is out there; to take a good look at the forest through the trees. It is time to move beyond the firm and get to know the prospects and competition.

Summary on Pre-Launch

Take the time to fully vet your firm before
an institutional marketing push.

Take a Step Back to Avoid Costly Mistakes

Complete the Pre-Launch Puzzle Analysis:
Team, Brand, Offering and Capital Commitment

Understand the Typical Growth Path

CHAPTER 5

Understanding Prospects

Managers who have established their own investment management organization, having built a track record, team, and process around a strategy they feel passionate about, are eager to dive into marketing and selling. This is understandable; it is an exciting time for the organization and the costs of running that team and strategy are piling up. Performance looks great based on the manager's self-assessment, and perhaps the market has even taken notice, resulting in some inbound inquiries and assets. Now more assets, and bigger assets under management are needed to complete the picture. But which assets? Managers are myopic in their views at this stage. *Chapter 4* discussed the need to step back and complete a full review of the organization—team, offering, brand, and capital commitment. Managers feel confident they are ready for prime time whether they have completed the *Chapter 4* exercises or not. Yet, the stepping back process is not complete.

There are two additional factors at play, significant ones, which must be carefully vetted before diving into a multi-year institutional marketing and sales game plan. The first factor is understanding the prospects.

Start Where the Client Is

How much does the manager really know about their prospect organizations and whether they are prospects at all? Intuitively we know that not everyone will be a good fit. It is the quintessential square peg in a round hole conundrum. Perhaps if a wide enough net is cast—surmises the manager and its marketing and sales resources—something will get hooked. Does understanding where the prospect is coming from really matter? The fine art of "starting where the client is" means understanding the prospects and what is important to them. In so doing, managers can determine where they will be a "good fit" and thus where an allocation is most likely. Which prospects are predisposed to coming around to the manager's way of thinking in the time allotted? How many institutions on the prospect list does the firm really know? How many questions below can the manager or its representatives answer about these prospects? Who is a legitimate prospect in the first place? If an institution is not, then what? What needs to change for the institution to become a viable candidate?

Consultants, Priorities, and Criteria

Three key pieces of information from the research team of the prospective institution will improve efficiency and reduce the risk of pushing too hard on a poor fit: (1) whether the prospect utilizes a consultant; (2) the prospect's current research priorities; and (3) the prospect's investment criteria. The latter is certainly the most critical piece of information as it is less likely to change nor to be swayed by a great story and numbers, particularly among the institutional investor population where mandate guidelines are strictly applied. Research priorities are very important, but they are subject to change. The more information that can be captured, the better. At a minimum, ask these questions of prospects upfront:

1. *Can you share with me your research priorities at present?*
   What areas are you considering right now?
   (For first time inquiries: How often might these priorities change?)

2. *Can you review with me your firm's criteria for investments? Specifically, do you have minimum standards in terms of:*

   ❏ Firm AUM
   ❏ Strategy AUM
   ❏ Length of Track Record
   ❏ Size of Team
   ❏ Firm Ownership
   ❏ Structural Requirements and Terms
   ❏ Fee Requirements
   ❏ Asset Class Restrictions
   ❏ Restrictions on Characteristics *(i.e. leverage, concentration, capacity)*
   ❏ Manager Concentration/Percentage of AUM

3. *Does your firm work with a consultant? Who would you suggest we speak to in order to have our firm considered?*

The consultant question is asked last; however, this will typically be the immediate response of an institution if they are covered by a consultant when they pick up the phone. If this occurs, managers are encouraged to request the best contact at the consulting firm to follow up with. If not, it is helpful to save this question for last so that more information on research priorities and criteria can be gained, which might not be readily offered by the consultant.

Gaining this information achieves two equally important object-ives. It creates a dialogue and helps the manager to understand the institution's priorities and at what point the firm's offering might be a potential candidate for consideration. The realities of timing and fit are good reasons to retain an outside marketing firm that represents more than one product. All strategies are unlikely to be a fit all the time and for everyone. Outside sales resources have the benefit of offering more than one solution, providing a rationale to keep the dialogue going even during periods when a firm's strategy is not in favor, meeting requirements, or in need. There are certainly reasons to have full time dedicated staff representing the firm as well. This is one of many trade-offs to consider. *Chapter 17: Resource Management* will address this consideration in greater detail.

Ask First

Despite multiple respondents indicating they wish managers would take the time to ask these questions, to learn this information and to be thoughtful in presenting solutions that fall far outside of the institution's area of interest and criteria, it is not always easy to get this level of detail from a research team. Additionally, investment priorities can change quickly as markets, firm and client demands dictate. There can be exceptions made to stated investment criteria as well. Managers will ask "well, how did XYZ firm get into the portfolio? We are better than them; better performance, better pricing, bigger, etc."

Institutional investors and their investment consultants can muddy the waters with misinformation. Senior level institutional representatives will often speak out in the market indicating the institution is interested in pursuing certain types of investment strategies and managers, or that they are making certain types of changes in specific windows of time. The research teams from these institutions are not always singing the same song. Regardless, it is smart selling to be curious, to ask questions and to engage the audience. A good sales organization in the outsourced marketing space is having this dialogue regarding areas of interest and criteria regularly with its network. Managers with internal marketing representatives should too. Pursue this basic information at regular intervals. Ask first; sell second. Curiosity is a great attribute when marketing to institutions.

The Prospect's Own Garden

In addition to understanding where the prospect is coming from at present—what their research priorities and investment criteria are—seek to gain an understanding of how the prospect's process works and who their clients are. What is the institution seeking to accomplish? What do the weeds look like in their own garden? Potential questions to ask include the following:

1. What types of clients do you have? What is a good prospect for your organization?
2. What is your organization's investment thesis? *(Questions can be tailored to the manager's expertise and/or key offering attributes as appropriate to ascertain fit i.e. Are you focused on low cost solutions? Are you seeking diversity in your offerings? Are you allocating to certain asset classes and product structures? Do you prefer major brands or emerging managers? What percentage of your portfolio management is passive? Is there a preference for growth or value managers? For fundamental or quantitative investment management? How do you incorporate alternative investments?)*
3. Who are your competitors?
4. What is your prospect asking for?
5. What are your clients' generally willing to invest in?
6. What are your firm's investment platform goals? Do you anticipate any significant changes to your core criteria and offerings?
7. Is platform approval required? *(When pursuing a registered investment advisor, broker-dealer or other institution which provides investment management solutions to more than one advisor/advisor group/client base.)*
8. Should we go through research or straight to the advisors/field?

Managers should not expect that a full set of questions will be permitted nor answered. The objective is to engage the audience. Engaging in a dialogue that is not all about the manager is valuable in establishing a relationship. Is that not true in any relationship?

Prospects Move

There has been massive turnover among the institutional investment research population over the years. Not only have individuals moved from big firms to small ones and vice versa, but organizations have changed how they meet their institutional investment management research needs. Keep in mind that the goal is to build a relationship with the individual—not just to sell to the institution. The institutional investor representative is likely to be in the industry for quite some time. In fact, this individual may elect to move to a new organization overnight for which that manager is a much better fit. Keeping this in mind changes the tone of the dialogue. Get to know the institutional investment management research professional as a source of market intelligence; expect to work with them and to follow them wherever they go. Institutional investment management researchers are insightful, engaged, passionate investment professionals; they have quite a bit in common with investment managers. When managers treat introductions as opportunities to establish a collegial dialogue about what they do v. simply selling something, the relationship takes on its own meaning. Do not consider institutional investment management marketing a binary event; the relationship is worth much more than whether a manager gets hired today or not. Taking time and interest in understanding prospects will pay dividends.

Track Talent

Managers, or their marketing and sales professionals, should maintain a contact relationship management (CRM) system to track professionals in the industry. Prospects and clients are most readily maintained in a classic CRM database. Salesforce is an example, with many other firms providing applications that can be utilized on desktops, on mobile devices and in the cloud. Firms are encouraged to establish a client relationship management tool day one, to train their staff completely on its use and application, and to track their marketing and sales efforts through this tool. Integrate email into the system where possible, tracking materials provided and the timing of outreach. The data set created can assist firms in understanding what channels are the best fit, what areas of the country or world are most responsive to their inquiries, and what size and profile of organizations are the most likely responders to their marketing efforts. Understanding prospects is a key factor in successful marketing. An institutional marketing and sales effort is a long road; collecting, maintaining and maximizing data on prospects is particularly important in ensuring efficiency.

Creating Your Avatars

Ideal client profiles are often referred to as avatars. What does your avatar look like? Do you have more than one? To learn more about defining your prospects through efficient avatar profiles, take advantage of the tools accessible here:

Summary on Prospects

Understand your prospects and build a data set around them.

Start Where the Client Is
Ask Good Questions
Use a CRM; Track Talent

CHAPTER 6

Redefining the Competition

RPM Rating on Competition

DE MINIMIS	CORE	PRIORITY	GAME CHANGER

*R*edefining the Competition is the first chapter that formally launches the specific interview topics covered by the book's research. Accordingly, it is the first to incorporate the *Resource Prioritization Matrix (RPM)* rating. A complete review of the methodology, including the core topics covered with respondents and a description of the *RPM* rating, is provided in *Chapter 2: Methodology*.

Competition takes many different forms in the investment management space; it is a *game changer* according to the *Resource Prioritization Matrix*. The game change is not in the mere existence of competition, but in the manager's understanding and reflection on that competition before diving into an extensive marketing effort. Often, a manager's competitive lens is focused solely on the performance of a minimally sized peer group within their immediate vehicle structure cohort. This limited lens gives managers not only the green light to proceed into unchartered waters of institutional investment management marketing and sales prematurely, it also reinforces managers' perceptions—and misconceptions—of their value.

Institutional research professionals look at competition differently. Institutional decision makers utilize a lens of risk management and opportunity cost in evaluating managers. As one respondent noted, *"We have so many factors to consider in making these investment management decisions. They are not made in a vacuum. We have a board to consider and the existing manager roster we have already committed to. We also have what the market is serving up."* Managers are wise who focus on the same by broadening their view of the competition. To broaden the lens, competition is best considered across the following measures, many of which were outlined in *Chapter 4: The Pre-Launch Puzzle.*

Competing Product Considerations

1. ***Demand***
   Does demand exist for this offering today? Is the market currently interested in this space? What trends are drawing investors to or against this asset class/strategy/vehicle type? Here is an example: an institutional investment management research professional, in discussing demand and the importance of timing, wondered aloud who could possibly have considered launching an active U.S. large cap equity strategy post 2010? A surprising number did. None have succeeded in any notable way. The trend was and clearly has been away from active U.S. large cap equities.

2. ***Vehicle Structure***
   What vehicle structures are trending up and down? Are hedge fund structures on the sidelines save for a few globally recognized capabilities? Is the structure of current interest in relation to the specific strategy and asset class? If yes, to whom? Are more mutual funds than exchange traded funds being launched at present? Why?

3. ***Terms***
   The importance of terms, specifically fees, cannot be overstated. Is the offering competitively priced and structured? Managers

can have great numbers, but if they are too expensive—which is the most common issue—they have priced themselves out of the market and the offering will not sell.

Let's stay focused on the high fee conundrum for now. Institutional investors know that when a manager is under-performing, which they will, and their investor is still paying the same high fees, the investment quickly ceases to make sense no matter how good the net outperformance was at the time of engagement. This example is magnified the longer the underperformance occurs, creating a larger and larger gap between the investment and its peer group, and particularly when shown against the relevant "fee-free" index. Managers can remind investors that the index is not investable, but there surely are passive investment solutions available, and other competitive offerings that are holding their own just fine when compared to their higher fee, active counterparts. Firms should do enough research to be certain that the offering is cost effective and priced no higher than the middle of the competitive pack; not simply below the highest priced competitor that can be identified. A part of something is better than a whole lot of nothing. Fees are more prominently displayed, discussed, and utilized as a screening mechanism in registered products and limited partnership offerings, yet they are relevant for separately managed account solutions as well.

Other challenges related to terms are driven by the wrong vehicle choice which can lead to unnecessary restrictions and requirements for investors v. competitive offerings in the industry standard vehicle choice for that strategy. For example, traditional long only investment managers will find their natural competition in separately managed account and mutual fund structures, not in limited partnerships. Term differences based on structure that can make a meaningful difference in investor interest include liquidity, paperwork, tax consequences, minimums, performance fees and a wide variety of additional ancillary fees related to investments (typically in the case of private placements) and redemptions, among others. Managers must do their homework or have sufficient guidance from industry experts. They should know when competitors are offering similar strategies at lower fees or through a more accessible vehicle structure, regardless of performance.

4. ***Direct Competitor Comps***
   For competitors managing the same structures at similar terms, what is their respective profile beyond performance including: assets under management as a firm and in the offering, offering vintage, brand recognition, platform availability, capacity and target raise, for example.

5. ***Performance***
   Managers will always compare performance, but often through a strategically defined lens. Perhaps rolling periods are more compelling than calendar years? Is downside capture more compelling than upside capture? Is performance shown gross of fees in a high fee product, for which excess performance is quickly washed away on a net basis? Even when comparing apples to apples on standard performance measures, managers tend to discount the complexity of a larger size asset pool and a longer history in comparing performance; institutions do not.

   For example, a manager may have a stellar three-year track record, yet they were not in the market prior to this period. Their peer group managed through a market cycle that was quite challenging for the space approximately four to five years ago. This manager missed out on it all together. Alternatively, a competing manager has a much larger asset pool to put to work, forcing the firm to "dig deeper" into their "best ideas" list to meet the allocation demands of investors. Institutions understand that more assets = increased complexity and money to put to work. This typically leads to increasingly muted returns over time and institutions accept this as a trade-off for stability. Institutions anticipate smaller managers will have the same challenges over time. As a result, they may discount the value of some of a manager's outperformance while managing a significantly smaller pool of assets, certainly regarding expectations for future returns. Managers can and should highlight if they are managing "to capacity". In other words, are they holding themselves to the same restrictions they would be under if they had a full asset pool to invest. If not, their performance is representative of their capacity to "cherry pick" holdings in a way that is not apples to apples. ***Be certain to screen a sufficient universe in the asset class, regardless of vehicle structure, to get a complete picture of who the firm is competing against and what attributes the firm has in relation to competitors other than performance.***

The Index Is a Competitor

How does the manager compare relative to the index? The use of "the" index is intentional. There is generally one most appropriate index for each strategy in the traditional long only and hedge fund space; private equity and venture strategies have significantly less conformity to benchmarks. Research professionals are adept at knowing what the "best fit" is. Managers know this too. When managers seek to show their performance against a different index because it "shows better" for any number of reasons, it will raise an immediate red flag. Take a step back before finalizing the offering to a broader and institutional audience. Matrix the offering out against a series of competitors big and small, in the same vehicle structure and in other vehicle structures, and against the most appropriate benchmark. Ensure that the offering is not just "in the range", but comfortably within the ranges across terms and compared to the most appropriate benchmark. The benchmark should be consistent with that of the peer group.

Display Competitive Advantages Wisely

Scrap the growth of $10,000 chart v. any benchmark unless it tells a highly differentiated story. When we step back far enough, most growth of $10,000 charts look rather similar and they don't provide enough specifics to be a good use of real estate in a firm's limited marketing materials. Managers surely have better statistics and visuals to demonstrate how they are different from the rest of the pack. Generic, broad based metrics like the growth of $10,000 chart do not belong in institutional investment management marketing, at least not as the largest visual offered to potential investors. The newer the manager, the more likely they are to plaster an oversized line graph across their prime material real estate. As managers mature, they realize they have better data points. At a minimum, they generally reduce the space they dedicate to broad based visuals that provide little in the form of details. Find effective ways to show what is different about the offering and how it fits in a diversified portfolio. Make a list of the top ten ways the firm can show value-added visually, whether through charts, graphs or tables. Where does the growth of $10,000 chart stack up in this list?

Complete a Formal Competitive Analysis

Complete a full matrix of all offering attributes, not just performance, and include a set of competitors that range in size and length of track record. Be sure to map this out on paper and include ALL fees (particularly relevant for venture, private equity and private placement strategies) and other known variables. Managers are encouraged to map out their offerings at a minimum within the framework on page 75, with no less than ten competitors, to determine viability and hurdles to overcome. In the case of private placements, be sure to pull out the fees in the Private Placement Memorandum (PPM), not just the obvious ones, to ensure an accurate comparison.

The Competition Is More than the Manager Next Door

Beyond the peer group and benchmarks, and beyond how an offering will fit within an existing portfolio, are market realities. Market realities are a significant source of competition for the time and attention of institutional investment management research professionals and their investors. Managers miss this entirely. As one respondent noted,

Competitive Analysis Worksheets

Strategy	Benchmark	Vehicle	Mgmt. Fee(s)	Incentive Fee(s)	Other Fee(s)	Total Fees	Firm AUM	Offering AUM
Offering								
Comp 1								
Comp 2								
Comp 3								
Comp 4								
Comp 5								
Comp 6								
Comp 7								
Comp 8								
Comp 9								
Comp 10								
Benchmark								

Strategy	Performance Calendar YR Since Inception	Performance By Quarter or Month; YTD; ITD Since Inception	Performance Rolling Periods (1 3, 5 YR)	Portfolio Concentration	Track Record (YR or Vintage)	Turnover	Platform Availability
Offering							
Comp 1							
Comp 2							
Comp 3							
Comp 4							
Comp 5							
Comp 6							
Comp 7							
Comp 8							
Comp 9							
Comp 10							
Benchmark							

"they believe, because they have showed up, wrapped up their offering in a lovely package and spent the time and effort to introduce it, the market should pay attention." Managers are appropriately laser focused on their firm and strategy, and they generally do understand that they have a competitive landscape to be aware of which they attempt to market themselves against. What they miss is that the biggest competition is often not another manager, but the market overall.

Defining the Market Itself as a Competitor

What market realities are impacting managers' advancement in the asset gathering process? Examples include: (1) consolidation among firms; (2) outsourcing; (3) political shifts; (4) regulations; (5) asset class trends; and (6) product trends such as fee compression, platform simplification, reduction of alternatives, etc. In addition, institutional demand and capacity change rapidly and are not always related to the strategy or asset class itself, but to the institution's existing portfolio. In many cases, "search" may not even mean there is an active search; it can mean reallocation or moving money among pools of capital. Institutional investment management research professionals have clients themselves, sometimes they have significant control over what these clients invest in and sometimes they do not. They also get fired, replaced by other providers, or simply squeezed so much on fees and account size that the opportunity set is simply not there. Seeing the institutional research team as a conduit, and not as the decision maker, is important in managing expectations. Researchers can fall in love with lots of managers and offerings, but market realities can keep them from investing nonetheless.

Good Competitive Analysis Means Asking Questions

Once in the market, realizing the competitive landscape is constantly changing, an active component of the dialogue can and should be asking direct questions to potential investors including:

- What is the best manager that you've seen in our space? Who do you like?

- Is this a space you've seen a lot of other managers in? Any other teams come to mind?

- Do you expect to see more, or less opportunity in our space moving ahead?

- Are there any trends we should be aware of in relation to terms or structuring with this type of strategy?

Managers will benefit from not only creating a competitive matrix as provided above, but by amending the competitive list as new names are surfaced and as other managers close, underperform, etc. The matrix should be produced regularly to provide a constant view of the competitive landscape, to see what is changing among the competitors and how the offering stacks up at the time of launch and ongoing. A robust competitive matrix requires a deeper look in the mirror; the entire organization should be aware of this competitive lens.

Liquid managers are encouraged to run the competitive matrix, or at least a subset of it, as often as daily (the data can be fed directly from a mutual fund or ETF database source). The competitive matrix can serve as a constant reminder to the marketing, sales and investment teams regarding the strategy profile and how it stacks up, where it is trending in terms of performance, who is coming into the market, who is struggling and who is succeeding. This does not mean changes should be made based on daily results. Rather that the regular drumbeat of this data set is an important reminder to stay the course and understand what the firm is up against. Managers in illiquid strategies and those running separately managed account solutions will not benefit from this frequent of a review. The data gathering would make it rather impossible as well. A quarterly check in on the competition, or at least a semiannual assessment, is suggested.

The Institutional View on Competition

The competition is the first component that taps directly into the formal interview process. Questions related to the competition focused primarily on the sheer volume and source of requests received. Respondents reported receiving 10-30 new requests for manager review per week on average, with the majority in the 20-30 range. Another 50-100 updates on average were received per week with the majority in the 50-75 range. When asked what percentage of inquiries came from a referral/someone you know, research professionals ranged widely, but the majority indicated that the requests *"that they were looking at"* came from someone they knew 50-75% of the time.

Institutional Investment Management Research
Weekly Volume of Requests for Review/Updates

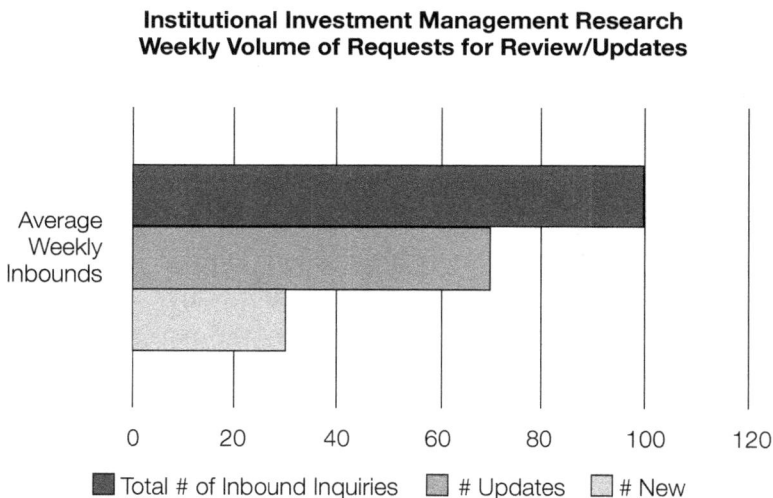

Average Weekly Inbounds

0   20   40   60   80   100   120

■ Total # of Inbound Inquiries   ■ # Updates   □ # New

When asked what percentage of inquiries came from managers directly v. through a third party marketing resource, the respondents indicated that *"on average"* the breakdown was about 50/50. This was surprising; the results speak to the sheer volume of growth in the outsourcing model. Institutional investment management research professionals seemed to consider any non-manager call to be a "third party marketing" entity, without differentiating among prime brokers, marketing firms and outsourced full-scale marketing and sales organizations. Respondents did, however, differentiate third party marketing from robocalling, mass mailing efforts, and other forms of general solicitation.

Redefining the Competition in Practice

The competition is not solely a benchmark, nor simply a short list of other managers. It is the competition for attention in a rapidly changing and highly regulated market. Patience is crucial. Managers get easily frustrated, believe their marketing efforts are failing and demonstrate their disappointment in words and actions that do not help their candidacy. Patience with the process often runs out when managers need most to stay the course, and to instead demonstrate steadfast passion and commitment. Timing is everything, but having good timing is rarely random.

Another source of the competition is the firm itself. Other priorities and interests among team members, short term success with one channel or product offering, and general fatigue from the overall effort—these are all forms of competition.

Being in the Hunt

A key component of perceived "good timing" is being in the hunt when the right time comes. Managers cannot simply show up and expect immediate consideration against a cohort of competitors that have been actively reaching out, informing the audience and engaging in dialogue over the course of several years. Having a wider competitive lens will help managers see the bigger picture. Managing resources for the long haul and having realistic expectations will help smooth the ride. It may also help to inform the types of marketing and sales activities that are value-added in differentiating a manager from the competition in its many forms. To be in the hunt fully, devise a game plan that the firm can both afford and commit to implementing month in and month out, quarter in and quarter out, year in and year out until the opportunities come.

Questions Asked

Respondents were asked the following questions in bold face text specifically in relation to this chapter. The consensus answers are in italics and immediately follow the question asked.

Approximately how many manager inquiries are you getting a week? A year?
10-30 new and 50-100 updates per week on average.

What percentage of inquiries come from a referral/someone you know?
50-75%

What percentage of inquiries come from managers directly?
30-50%

What percentage of inquiries come from marketers?
50-70%

Do you respond differently based on the source?
We try not to, but yes. We tend to respond to those we know most readily.

Words to Drive By

The following quotes provide a broader sampling of the respondents' direct feedback in relation to the above questions. Firms are encouraged to drive their marketing and sales activities with these rules for the road in mind.

On Source

60-70% is through a referral or someone I've met, or a colleague has met; 30-40% cold; a referral increases the likelihood of a look.

Some clients/advisors [are] more highly thought of so when they come up with something, we focus on it.

Coming in with a referral is much more advantageous than just coming in cold—[our] preferred [process] is to start with the research group and show the respect to let us determine from a high level what is needed and what is appropriate.

[We are] seeing a larger number of scheduling services; [I] hit ignore. It used to be a lot of internal wholesalers but now schedulers; a lot of times they send a short fact sheet after the email and say, "let us know if you are interested."

There are a lot that are cold, but I don't think that's effective at all—I think it would be much more productive to reach out and initiate a dialogue v. emailing me.

On the Competition

50% of what we get is big market platforms, 50% are more the manager/smaller firms.

A lot is thrown out on cost.

Startup funds think they can go at it themselves in terms of distribution and then they end up having the firm bombing us [with outreach]; then they realize how hard it is.

Most are through third parties; newer managers who have known us but have spun out we see once in a while.

It peaks my interest when a manager or their IR [investment research] person reaches out because it is so rare.

Number of funds depends on category, so EM debt local currency will be small, whereas US large cap equity will be huge. Finalists are generally 7-10; we will complete a baseline screening of a good 50 firms in a crowded space.

Summary on Redefining the Competition
The competition is more than the manager next door.

Broaden the Firm's View of 'the' Competition to Include Other Product Structures, the Index, and the Market Itself

Understand Product Dynamics

Complete a Thorough Competitive Analysis

PART III

Stepping In:
Driving Content and Context

In Part I, firms gained an understanding of the institutional perspective. In Part II, firms were encouraged to step back and fully vet their value proposition, whether new or established. This included a review of the firm itself, its offering, the firm's branding and its capital commitment. Once the pre-launch puzzle was in place, firms were asked to take time to understand the institutional prospect and the competition before engaging the market. The "Stepping Back" process is complete when managers confirm the following: (1) they have the best profile and internal commitment that can possibly be achieved; and (2) they understand institutional prospects and their competition as well as they can. Conceivably, firms have now fully vetted themselves. They are now prepared to tackle the market.

In Part III *Stepping In*, firms will build out their marketing and sales effort, developing context around what differentiates them. They will make contact, completing their introductory outreach and initial meetings with prospects. Part III begins with the development of the firm's oeuvre—a content library, and then dives in to active institutional marketing and sales outreach utilizing the content library as a basis for communications. Outside of the outreach managers do, several external data sources are available to institutions when screening managers. Managers may believe institutions will only look at what they provide. This would not be efficient nor effective due diligence. Institutions typically have access to and will tap into third party data sources, including databases and online media. Part III is focused on assisting managers in putting their best foot forward as they get on the road.

In this section, managers are encouraged to carefully consider the highest and best use of available resources. The book's *Resource Prioritization Matrix (RPM)* provides a guidepost for prioritization and spending that ensures resources are committed on a highest and best use basis. This section incorporates several key steps in the institutional marketing and sales process that can make or break a manager's candidacy, including the initial introduction and the live meeting. Firms are encouraged to take their pre-launch puzzle pieces and utilize them, along with their review of the prospects and the competition, to create a content and collateral set that can efficiently get them in the door, and on the road towards asset growth.

CHAPTER 7

The Firm's Oeuvre:
Creating the Content Library

RPM Rating on Content

DE MINIMIS	CORE	PRIORITY	GAME CHANGER

According to the *Resource Prioritization Matrix (RPM)*, content is a *core* element to any effective marketing and sales effort. Without content there is no story. Nothing to discuss, agree and disagree about; no basis for asking questions or gaining insight into a manager's process. Institutions are seeking the best "fit" in a manager. How can they ascertain fit? Numbers alone are both insufficient and inconclusive. Sales professionals know this; they are eager to have something to say and send that speaks to what the manager is doing; they are eager to demonstrate how the manager can "fit". Seasoned sales professionals instruct managers accordingly, suggesting ideas and opportunities for storytelling. However, inconsistent results ensue. Why?

Good content is hard and a lot of it is needed over a long period to be successful in the institutional market. Managers have difficulty coming up with consistent and meaningful content, particularly when they are new to the industry and/or have limited resources. They tend to rely exclusively on their numbers. Numbers don't paint a complete picture. Two different managers can get to the exact same set of numbers in very different ways. Additionally, as we've discussed, the numbers are part of the past. Institutional investors want and need to get comfortable with what a manager will do in the future. Getting inside a manager's head, understanding what philosophy and process will be in play under various market conditions is what institutional investors want, and what great content can provide.

Content Minimalists v. Sensationalists

Like Goldilocks and the three bears, managers tend to fall into three camps when it comes to content. Those that produce too little content, those that overdo it, and the ones who get it "just right", producing a consistent and appropriate amount of content that is both interesting and timely. Unfortunately, in the world of money management, Goldi-locks would struggle to find that "just right" manager. Managers tend to be either minimalists or sensationalists, with the majority falling in the minimalist camp. We will focus on these approaches and their inherent challenges first, followed by a discussion of what is "just right"—what institutions are seeking and how to build an effective content library.

Minimalists

Managers who produce minimal content simply want the story to be their numbers. Performance is not a story; performance is history. After all, *past performance is no guarantee of future results*, right? Why should a decision be based on performance alone? Building the case for a manager is not only about whether the firm checks all the boxes, it is about how a strategy can work into a diversified and pre-existing portfolio; how the manager will "play" along with others in the sandbox. As a respondent articulated, institutions want and need to know: *"When the storms come, will this manager run for the hills? When the markets move aggressively, will they stay the course? And when they make these adjustments, or when they elect to ride out the storm instead, will they tell us?"* Performance does not tell this story. Managers must.

Managers who rely on performance and little else are content minimalists and this is a drag on their ability to grow market share. Institutions will invest with the firms they are most comfortable with. Gaining comfort takes time and interaction, sharing and understanding;

it takes content. Comfort is not built on historical numbers alone, no matter how lengthy the track record or strong the performance. Managers might find that this book harps on the need to look beyond performance in all aspects of product development, marketing and sales, because it does. The market has seen long-term performers cease to exist virtually overnight, and fraud occur under the watch of government regulators. The market has seen excellent strategies drown in their own fee structures and vehicle choices. Institutions want to be certain they fully understand the manager in all facets of their business and investment process; they are dogmatic about the details. Good content, well timed and positioned, can accelerate this process.

Sensationalists

Managers who overwhelm the market with external proof statements in the form of academic papers on their strategy, or links to "what he said" content from other sources in an over the top manner (often delivered with overly aggressive introductory language, too large fonts in too bright colors, and pages of run-on text) are sensationalists. This approach is unwelcome. The use of external proof statements is "backfill" research according to respondents. This research might be something institutions are quite interested in receiving, but they don't tell the manager's story. When these types of perceived proof statements are provided, managers tend to double down on them as well, submitting copious examples in list form of the same basic argument, academic white paper after white paper. Managers are seeking to gain credibility by jumping on the bandwagon of others, rather than engaging the market in their own right.

Managers who are sensationalists seek to be the ambassadors of their asset class. They constantly focus on the broader strategy's value proposition as opposed to their own. These managers focus their commentary, if they produce any, on generic global market and world events. The Armageddon scenario in which their asset class is a "must have" is the drum beat of their communications. Unless the manager is running a global strategy that directly benefits from this broader and emphatic view, there are others with more credibility who can and will tell the story better. Relying on third party proof statements, or providing overly general market news focused on broad global themes is not telling the manager's story. The firm has missed the mark, giving the market nothing meaningful to remember them by, other than a graduate class worth of reading material. It is unwanted homework and deleterious to the firm's efforts.

What Does the Market Want?

The institutional market begs for a shot right down the fairway. Respondents indicated a consistent wish for engaging, compelling and consistent communications that provide an internal view to the manager's thought process. Content that is so unique and different, so specific, that institutions can utilize it in their own internal communications to inform their organizations and clients. This type of content is not accomplished through a quarterly performance page, introductory email, overly lengthy standard presentation, or generic market commentary. It is a dialogue built over time that establishes the case for a manager's participation in the asset management process of these institutions. It is content designed to build a relationship of trust and understanding regarding what a manager is doing; a bird's-eye view into the firm— its priorities and perspectives. This chapter will outline content areas to be created or enhanced prior to a significant market push. In *Chapter 14: Adding Value Through Ongoing Communications*, a deeper discussion of content related to the post introductory period is provided. Managers who have figured it out, providing "just right" content, are ahead of the curve. It is a difficult balance to get the quantity, depth and timing of content on track in building the case for a firm's candidacy.

Reactive Content

The institutional market asks for content in many forms, regularly requesting managers jump through hoops by filling out overly burdensome, custom questionnaires and additional databases. Managers interested enough in raising institutional assets will begrudgingly comply, even though the effort may not make sense. This type of data dump will be discussed in *Chapter 16: The Institutional Research and Funding Process.* We can all thank the advent of intense regulation for the proliferation and expansion of due diligence questionnaires. A manager recently had an RFI request from an institution who is well known for working with emerging managers. The questionnaire had 445 unique questions. That is a lot of data, particularly for a lean organizat-ion. It required the manager to slice and dice their data into multiple formats and formulas, among other feats. Is this value-added? What is value-added is the unique manager who utilizes these requests as opportunities to enhance their content library. Perhaps a few of the questions present to the manager a new way to talk about what they do? Why not turn that into broader use content to inform the market?

Use Some New Words

The same key words are overused by the industry to tell the audience how firms manage money ("uncorrelated returns", "bottom up", "relative value", and "integrity" for example). Respondents repeatedly requested, *"new ways of thinking about the process."* Content requests in the form of DDQs, RFIs, RFPs or one-off exhibits can help in cultivating examples that show how the firm manages money with more detail and impact. Consider these data requests an opportunity to shore up the firm's messaging, further developing its content library. While the requests appear to be a time-consuming regurgitation of the same information in slightly nuanced forms, institutions believe there are many ways to think about investment managers and what they do, and their way is unique and important. It is unlikely this desire for 'spin' by institutions will go away. Creating an effective and efficient content library is the best way for managers to be prepared. There are tools in the market that consolidate data to feed the investment management databases as discussed in *Chapter 9: Tools of the Trade-Databases*, but there is nothing that truly serves as an effective and universal RFI. Questions will always vary just enough to require diligent review. Consider creating one Q&A database in excel or another program that permits simple and efficient sorting of data. Utilize this data repository as the baseline for all content requests, and for all marketing related initiatives. Seek to integrate more than the typical language that institutions have seen thousands of times. Find informative and creative ways to "show" what the manager is doing and why it is differentiated.

Why Do Researchers Want So Much Content?

Managers attempt to minimize the creation of good content, whether requested or proactive, both to save time and to avoid giving away "too much". They simply want to "tell" organizations what they do and let the numbers speak for themselves. This perspective is in direct conflict with the mindset of the institutional investment research professional, who has a "show me" mentality. Good content builds confidence and understanding; good content demonstrates expertise and engagement. Content effectively delivered builds the case for a manager's candidacy, one piece, and one request, at a time.

There are three primary reasons why institutions request content:

1. *Due Diligence:* As good stewards of their client's capital, and to quite literally "cover" themselves on the due diligence front, institutions want to build a massive pool of data before they commit capital.

2. *Survival of the Fittest:* There is some sense that getting a manager to jump through hoops shows their resolve. It indicates that the manager is not only eager to play ball, but that they have the back field covered in the form of resources to respond to such requests. Managers who deliver on data requests are possible contenders for allocations because they have proven they can respond in a timely fashion and with sufficient data to meet institutional standards.

3. *Fit:* Understand that it is not about whether a manager is "good" at what they do that determines who gets hired, it is about how they fit into a client's existing portfolio. To this end, institutional research professionals must understand what drives a manager's

thinking, and thus their portfolio management process to determine if it will either complement or compete with what is already in place.

An institutional investment management professional who recently changed firms provides a good example of the rationale for the deep dive requests for extensive data. In a prior role as a key member of the research team for a major platform, he was tasked with researching and identifying a wide variety of manager solutions in registered mutual fund format on behalf of his firm's client base. To this end, his team focused less on the complementary nature of managers, and more on simply "picking good ones". These managers were hired in liquid fund structures and could easily be swapped in and out of portfolios. As registered funds, they were already held to a baseline regulatory standard, and monitored by the regulators as well. There was a lot of flexibility and opportunity to select managers for this platform, due to the conceivably lower risk of each individual manager selection and need to build out a platform of options.

Now, in his new role as a senior research professional for a global financial institution, the institution was seeking to allocate significantly larger sums to a much smaller pool of managers. It became imperative, in fact the driving force of his team's decisions, to identify managers that were "different" from what they already have, yet in the same asset classes because they were seeking to build out more capacity in their offering.

For example, take two small-cap growth managers. They might have similar numbers while having completely different profiles. The researcher must understand how each manager thinks about concentration, turnover, industries and sectors, making changes, macro event impact, short-term v. long-term thinking, quality control, what factors matter and what don't, etc.

Once this baseline review of philosophy and process occurs, institutions want to "see" how the manager invests and communicates relating to these principals and processes to understand how consistently they apply them. Can the manager be counted on to have the same profile 6-36 months from now? Was there a market event that happened that the institutional researchers anticipated a certain manager would have reacted to one way based on how they defined their process initially, and yet they reacted entirely differently? Is there a component of the investment management process that the manager failed to mention in the initial review that they are actively employing? Is there an element of macroeconomics that might, or has, caused them to change what they are doing (buying or selling) despite their reported fundamental nature? These are the nuances that investment management research professionals want and need to understand.

In the case of this institutional investor example, the institution is seeking to make a more significant allocation, and in a separately managed account structure. This structure alone introduces additional levels of risk. In this professional's case, it meant that extensive institutional due diligence would be required before they could allocate, including an onsite visit to the manager by the institution's risk team, and a full operational due diligence review distinct from the investment research team's screening. The institution is not attempting to be difficult nor nitpicky. They want to understand who they are hiring and what they might expect from the manager and strategy as they move ahead so that they are not unpleasantly surprised down the road. These are sizable and long-term commitments of capital. A big aspect of conducting great research is avoiding the surprises. It doesn't mean that institutions expect perfection. Quite to the contrary, they are well trained to expect disappointment as both managers and markets tend to fluctuate.

Institutions want good and deep content, the kind that paints a full picture of the firm—its investment team, philosophy and process, and then specifically discusses how the firm has dealt with successes and failures. What lessons have been learned from mistakes and how will those mistakes be avoided or managed in the future?

Defining Content

Content is at the core of every communication provided throughout the institutional investment management marketing and sales process. Content carries straight through into good client servicing. It is the life blood of the firm's communications. For our purposes, content is considered across three metrics: (1) The Firm's Oeuvre: Creating the Content Library; (2) Content Quality; and (3) Content Substance. There is a fourth metric for content, frequency, which will be addressed in *Chapter 14: Adding Value through Ongoing Communications.*

Metric #1: Creating the Content Library

Some may consider the term 'oeuvre' to be better applied to higher brow bodies of work, such as that of a great composer or artist. Money management is art. It is the marriage of art and science. The development and successful build of an institutional investment management capability is certainly a life's work, if not several. The content library is identified as the firm's oeuvre for that very reason; to elevate its importance and to encourage managers to create an extensive content base for all communications.

The firm's oeuvre should have its own home; a content master document ideally in outline form that will feed the messaging and materials of the organization across all media. This oeuvre will serve as the basis for topical conversations in the form of in person meetings, commentary and ongoing communications. It should synthesize the various thoughts, opinions and perspectives of the team in their own words in relation to the firm's overall value proposition: who the firm is, what it does and why. This master document will provide the entire firm with the key words, ideas and perspectives that the firm was built on, that the firm believes in and wants to tell the market about, now and over time. The firm's oeuvre does not need to be an excessive document; it does need to be in writing and shared with the entire organization. Why is this content library so important to put in writing? For reasons of completeness and consistency.

Managers commit content failures all the time. They introduce themselves in one way in an initial meeting, follow up with written content that says something else, and then revise the story yet again as part of an RFI response or follow up phone call. This lack of consistency is a content failure. Delivering a consistent message, applying it in both short and long communications and across all mediums is not only part and parcel to great branding, it "shows" the institution that you are a consistent resource. The firm's oeuvre also ensures that the content delivered by multiple voices is a true representation of the firm, what it stands for and what it is prepared to deliver. A good content library will also provide a blueprint for the types of content the firm can put out in the market. What key ideas does the firm want in writing? What philosophical views and process attributes does the firm want its representatives to be talking about?

Content is often well thought out to fill an initial presentation and fact sheet, it is what follows that tends to be subpar. More information is discussed on these components of ongoing communications in *Chapters 15* and *16*, including the establishment of a content calendar. For now, think about content that goes far beyond the initial pitch to institutions. What can the firm opine on long after that first meeting that is value-added and differentiated?

By defining a core set of content to which all messaging can be applied, managers can most easily see how they can take current market events and portfolio happenings and build a story. What market events are ripe to promote these ideas? Ideally when these events occur, whether daily, weekly, monthly, quarterly or just once in a blue moon, managers and their representatives will be ready to seize the opportunity to "show" the market how these themes play out in their portfolio management, and how their clients can take advantage of them too.

A Word on Aspiration

The firm's oeuvre should provide an accurate depiction. Content is not meant to present an aspirational view of what could be done or of what one thinks the market wants to hear, it is meant to define who the manager is, what they have accomplished and what they are doing right now. Think about the resumes you've seen over the years. How many times has an interview candidate looked perfect on paper, only to later discover that their purported experience was grossly overstated? In investment management it might be argued that performance is the great equalizer. Clearly the firm is "that good" because it has the numbers to prove it. What the market is looking to understand is how the firm does what it does, and in so doing, how repeatable that process is in an uncertain future. Managers often put an aspirational view of their process and team on paper, providing an overall framework that is not exactly in line with what is happening day-to-day in their investment management practice. Researchers are adept at figuring this out. The breakdown in structure, in what is presented v. what is done, is often what causes managers to perform "differently" than expected. This variance can wreak havoc on overall portfolio results. Managers are encouraged to say what they do, and do what they say. No surprises.

Two key areas in which managers often present aspirational views of themselves are in the positioning of the team—roles and responsibilities, and in the positioning of the investment management process—screens and protocol. Put on the hat of the institutional investment research professional. Unlike most high net worth clients, institutions know what to ask and what to look for. If a manager indicates that a resource is on the investment committee, be sure they are an active member and not just the note taker. If the firm indicates that a resource is covering a certain market segment, have specific examples of their work in that area. If the firm indicates that the investment process includes a certain screen or protocol, review internal meeting notes and history to ascertain if it has been consistently applied and create examples of the application. All processes and protocols, no matter how small in the mind of the manager, must be clearly identified as a formal component of the process. In other words, the firm must take the time to map out exactly what occurs day-to-day through its investment management protocol. This includes identifying the break downs and loose wiring in the firm's process and organization before its description is memorialized so that aspects of the process are not over or undersold. Be prepared to address obvious inconsistencies, and less obvious ones. Determine in advance how the firm will position them.

A Content Outline

A good content outline will incorporate the major areas of firm evaluation including the positioning of:

1. The Firm's History
2. The Firm and It's Structure Today
3. Regulatory and Legal History
4. The Organization *(Org Chart, Titles, Roles & Responsibilities)*
5. Ownership and Incentive Structure(s)
6. The Investment Team
7. Bios
8. Departures *(Timing, Names, Length of Service, Roles, Rationale)*
9. Thesis *(Why this Strategy/Asset Class/Area of Focus)*
10. Investment Management Philosophy
11. Investment Management Process *(Steps, Screens, Protocols)*
12. Investment Management Committee
13. Investment Management Meetings *(Timing, Attendees, Process)*
14. Investment Management Tools
15. Risk Management Framework
16. Compliance Framework
17. Cybersecurity Framework
18. Infrastructure and Operations
19. External Resources *(Who, Why, What, Contact Details)*
20. Strategy Fit in a Diversified Portfolio
21. Strategy Specific Market Triggers *(If X, then Y)*
22. Track Record Analysis *(Point in Time Highlights, Lessons Learned)*
23. Team Voices *(Key Messaging Quotes from Team Members)*
24. Themes *(Overarching Perspectives Delivered in Key Phrases)*
25. Differentiators *(What Makes the Firm and Philosophy Different)*

Metric #2: Content Quality

The content itself is what matters most. Yet some institutions will not look past poor quality; why should they? How the content is presented deserves honorable mention. Be timely, clear, concise, factually accurate, and error free in all communications. Create templates upfront wherever possible; focus the firm's time and resources on what goes in them, not on constantly redesigning them (lest the branding police get called back in). Fill the templates in with the most interesting, engaging and timely (or evergreen) content the manager can write. Manage content within the following standards of high quality and efficiency.

The No-No List

What to leave out when telling the firm's story:

- ❏ No Poor Word Choices; Be Professional
- ❏ No Overly Designed Fonts (*Use standard business type sets, keep them size appropriate, and professional looking, either black or a professional color palette of dark and neutral colors—no neon.*)
- ❏ No Typos
- ❏ No Errors (*Data transposition errors are too common; have a well-defined QC process.*)
- ❏ No Old News; Nothing Outdated (*Make it evergreen where possible.*)
- ❏ No Incomplete Information (*Particularly regarding track record and fees.*)
- ❏ No "Cherry Picked" or Misleading Performance
- ❏ No Overstatement of Resources/Roles/Process Depth
- ❏ No Mile-long Paragraphs or Pages (*Utilize bullets and be succinct.*)

The Glass Is Half Full

Institutional research professionals generally indicated that the bar for materials was high and they rarely see anything that is not sufficient with respect to general look and feel. In fact, it was noted by several that this used to be an easier way to identify *"new and less experienced"* managers from the more mature firms, but the playing field has leveled as to the quality of materials screened by institutions. It seems that most managers have figured out how to put together a basic PowerPoint that includes the 'five Ps' (People, Philosophy, Process, Performance, Price; preferably in that order).

Anecdotally and perhaps "pre-institution", there is disagreement about manager's general readiness. Marketing and sales professionals see many managers, including well-established ones, who miss the mark on these basic points. Perhaps this variance in perspective regarding manager readiness can be attributed to marketing professionals carefully looking at what they receive to determine who they might want to work with, and therefore they are attempting to look closely at everything. Conversely, institutional investment researchers are getting bombarded; they are not looking at everything, and certainly not for long enough to raise a red flag this early in the process over poor branding, trite content, inadequate design or a typo. This would take a lot of time and effort on the institution's part, effort that they don't need to expend. Respondents confirmed that a good 50% to 75% of what they are taking the time to review is coming through a marketing professional. In these cases, it is anticipated that the most blatant of content quality failures have been resolved prior to submission.

Despite respondents' general comfort level with the quality of the content they are receiving, managers are reminded of the risk of poor quality content. Content that is saved, cataloged, and referred to years later. Ensuring that managers are consistent in their messaging, and professional and succinct in delivery, is likely to result in greater acceptance of their ideas and ideally the firm's candidacy. Revisit the *No-No List* one more time before moving on to ensure the firm's content quality avoids these basic mistakes.

Metric # 3: Content Substance

At this point, the firm's oeuvre has been defined and the need for high quality in its delivery discussed. What is it that managers should provide content about? Let's reverse the question: what do firms want to *show* the institutional research professional whom they would like to see hire them v. what a manager can simply tell a prospect. Good content demonstrates what the manager is doing and why it is important. Good content is delivered over time; we need markets to move and portfolios to manifest into the story told on day one to provide opportunities for good content. Consider the opportunity to share with institutional investment management research professionals three things:

1. Performance.
2. The macro trends in the market.
3. How the specific portfolio recently dealt with a market change or security anomaly and what the manager thinks about it.

If you were the institutional investment management research professional, sitting there all day, every day, getting bombarded by economic updates, performance updates and requests for "look at me", what would you find most interesting of the above three choices? What might you be intrigued enough by to click and open, or to answer the phone call? Better yet, what would engage you enough to call back? What would be the subject line and opening line that is professional and measured, but intriguing enough to draw you in? Managers presumably know the response to the above questions. Institutional investors can look up performance. They have macro trends from more dedicated sources than most managers. What they want to know about is the specific portfolio and the event the manager recently dealt with. They want to know what that manager thinks about it.

Content substance can be developed off most anything in the firm's oeuvre that the firm wants to provide real time examples of and serves to further the dialogue with the institutional researcher. These examples will change over time; the market knows that. Avoid living in fear of presenting the "wrong" answer or identifying an opportunity that does not pan out. Having an opinion, sharing how the process worked or why the manager did not act on market information, looking at what didn't go well under a microscope—this is what makes content interesting. Respondents consistently identified examples of contrarian and opinionated managers in regard to who they elected to track and read. The best way to think about content substance and whether the firm is meeting this metric is to go back and look at the last several communications sent out. Review them in their entirety from the perspective of the institutional investment management research professional. How much of the content revolved around answer number three above? How much of it was truly substantive?

This chapter covers the overall content library firms should build out in order to best define initial positioning and to prepare to communicate efficiently and effectively with the market over time. The firm's oeuvre is a living, breathing document that must be regularly referred to, updated and augmented. The firm was a long time in the making, it has an interesting history and story. Ideally, the investment philosophy and process are nuanced. By creating a content library and laying out the important aspects of the organization, opportunities will present themselves to utilize this content in conjunction with current market activity to build a case for the manager's role in institutional portfolio management.

Questions Asked

Respondents were asked the following questions in bold face text specifically in relation to this chapter. The consensus answers are in italics and immediately follow the question asked.

What content is most helpful in understanding a manager's value?
The five Ps (People; Philosophy; Process; Performance; Price) with primary focus on the first three; How the manager believes they "fit"; Impact of the current market on what the manager does/has done; Specific examples; Industry standard portfolio analytics.

Where does performance belong?
In the back; at the end. We already have it.

How important is the manager's ability to articulate how they fit within a diversified portfolio?

Critical. Ultimately, we need to ascertain fit for our own client portfolios, but understanding how the manager perceives their strategy and where it fits in a typical portfolio construct is immensely helpful.

How important is correlation/correlation analysis?

Not important. We can run that ourselves.

How important is attribution to your initial analysis?

Not important, but we often request it as a follow up. More managers should have it ready to go.

What analytics do you think managers should include in their core presentation?

Industry standard measures; expected and appropriate benchmarks; statistics including performance on an annual basis, not just rolling periods; all time periods feasible given inception date; holdings and/or market cap weights.

Words to Drive By

The following quotes provide a broader sampling of the respondents' direct feedback in relation to the above questions. Firms are encouraged to drive their marketing and sales activities with these rules for the road in mind.

On Content

[We want] a presentation deck that lays out the investment process extremely well; same process [is explained] when they come in and talk about a name—it doesn't deviate—the same over and over.

Thematically what is it that they really do; how does it fit into the context of a diversified portfolio; if their goal is to reduce risk well how do they reduce risk; what is it that statistically should happen based on their strategy.

Key differentiators v. peers are important to highlight, you are going to be a slice of the pie; you need to think about how your strategy fits into a broader portfolio. If 85-90% is from asset allocation, you need to be able to explain how you fit within the context of a total portfolio.

The pattern and history are most important; there is the narrative, there is what happened in the portfolio, and there was the market.

Transparency is key; color behind thinking is key; nobody expects the right call all the time.

On Performance Positioning

We aren't making a decision on performance anyhow; we want to see attribution—there is a tendency to want to show 1, 3, 5, 10 but we want to see annual because we can see what happened in 8, 9, 11 etc.—periods of downturn.

We request monthly data upfront; we want to touch on it particularly for abnormalities.

Standard operating procedure is that managers don't have enough performance measures and analytics for me; standard pitchbooks are standard, they don't have enough—reason why is that you don't know who the consumer is in advance but the risk is overwhelming with data. [Managers] should really have it in with the appendix, or as a separate hand out. [I] hate having to ask for a follow up, just not as contiguous a process and requires more back and forth.

Performance goes towards the back as a proof statement to what you've talked about up front; always asked for and prefer to get the book or the pdf of the book a few days in advance.

On Manager Perspectives of Fit

I hate when managers try to sell their 'unique' strategy without context on how it adds value to a portfolio—on a typical 60/40 split, how would it improve sharp ratio or volatility? A lot of times we get lost in how cool the strategy is, but it doesn't answer the key question of fit.

We can do all that [the analytics] ourselves and tease that out, but we do need managers to clearly articulate their value-added and how their strategy would benefit our client portfolios. Not enough managers do that and do that well.

Where have other people found issues and how did they find comfort? i.e. 'cyclicality risk' looks like X but actually it's not; managers who can provide a polite interpretation of the data and can give you the counter case is really good.

A very important piece of information to figure out how they are building the product and who they are tailoring it too. We will also hold the manager accountable to their response a year or two from now.

This is one of the most important pieces because we are building portfolios and each piece should complement each other. Ultimately, it's for me to figure out but I don't mind them saying 'here is where we are differentiated.'

First order is be really good at what you do and prove value. Second order is where you fit, and ideally you fit in well.

On Providing Attribution

Attribution is so nice to have to avoid having to follow up with it. How much of your alpha in the past has come from tactical decisions v. security selection? If you're bringing a book you should include that. The data is available, you might as well share it.

Being able to show that all return has come from X is helpful, but historical is more relevant; fixed income managers tend never to have it and they should as research teams can't run it without Bloomberg and don't have the tools.

We do request attribution and exposure data; we look for inconsistencies to verbal comments.

It's gotten a lot better over the years, but we still need to chase [it] down; I wish it was standardized, some give beta adjusted, some give delta adjusted, but very, very helpful and needed tool to help analyze the manager better.

It is important, but managers often make the mistake of focusing on short term attribution and should use time periods that are relevant to the investment. If you had a bad quarter you can use that but you need the investment time horizon—three years, five years and since inception.

It's very important—in some fact sheets [it's in there] day one— attractors and contributors; we have to ask for historical most of the time.

On Analytics to Include in a Core Presentation

[For one group you] could see the stock selection within sectors, attribution by security within the sector; it's not typically done this way as most want to hide who did what.

Rolling over trailing, excess v. traditional; want to see over time more than we do; snapshots are not enough.

Basic security level attribution should be in there for equity managers. [The] challenge is [the] benchmark as research may not agree to benchmark but can do multiple benchmarks. Use a few benchmarks and let the consumer decide what they want to focus on.

If it's a strategy that is supposed to be a risk reducer than show different points and times when they did that: 2007-2009 market went down X, what did they go down?

Summary on Content

Content brings the firm's story, and numbers, to life.

Create the Firm's Oeuvre
Focus on Quality
Be Consistent

CHAPTER 8

Core Collateral

RPM Rating on Core Collateral

DE MINIMIS	CORE	PRIORITY	GAME CHANGER

An effective marketing effort requires a complete set of core collateral. Managers do not always see it that way. Particularly early on, managers might believe that they can get on the road, talking to a highly institutionalized market with nothing more than a back test and a few academic papers that support their philosophy. Managers with a long history will typically have a presentation and an investor update of sorts, but rarely do these components effectively represent the manager's added value. This is a missed opportunity. "Trust me" does not work in institutional investment management. In fact, it doesn't work in any investment management realm given the regulatory environment and onslaught of options available to investors. Investors of all shapes and sizes require, and deserve, some baseline material set from which to make an informed decision. Managers who prematurely enter the market without their collateral ducks in a row are wasting time—their time and that of the market. Perhaps a well networked manager can get a phone call or meeting through a 'friend', yet without a solid baseline collateral profiling the firm, there is no likelihood of an allocation. That great introduction is now wasted. Collateral, if nothing else, provides comfort that there is some structure and substance behind the opportunity. Core collateral receives a *core Resource Prioritization Matrix* rating as an expected element of an effective institutional marketing campaign.

Core Collateral Components

Here is a profile of what constitutes core collateral for an investment manager and the basic components that should be incorporated in each piece. Firms should have all pieces in place before engaging institutions. Each piece must reinforce the same brand proposition; a review of branding in *Chapter 4* provides direction in this regard. *Chapter 12* on meetings will provide additional color on the depth and breadth desired in the meeting materials, which typically refers to the most core of all collateral in investment management—the "pitchbook", "overview presentation" or "core presentation".

Presentation

The presentation is the core of the collateral series in terms of content. The presentation is typically created through Microsoft PowerPoint slides in landscape format, or a similar application for manager introductory meetings. The content for the presentation should be pulled directly from the firm's content library, as outlined in *Chapter 7*, and supported by current performance and composite (where relevant) information. A quality presentation will adhere to the following guidelines:

Target Length: 15-25 Slides

- *Template:* A clean, horizontal template with an appropriate amount of white space to permit key content to shine (this applies to a printed presentation application; onscreen versions can have full color backgrounds provided they adhere to professional guidelines of clean, streamlined design, and do not double as the hard copy version).

- *Framework:* A Table of Contents, Presentation Overview or Agenda for any presentation beyond ten slides.

- *Slide Titles:* Clear and concise slide titles that permit the audience to efficiently ascertain key messaging and to find desired content.

- *The Five Ps:* Content covering the five Ps: People, Philosophy, Process, Performance & Price, preferably in this order. The first three Ps command the most attention and interest from institutions. The last two Ps are considered past tense and negotiable, respectively. The last P, Price, might be better thought of as 'Product', incorporating product terms in a single table, including the price.

- *Visuals:* Visuals that depict the process in action. Use of graphs, tables, pie charts and schematics to provide easy reference to the firm's core positioning. Note that copy and paste Bloomberg graphs, 'pictures' of content too small to read and often poorly replicated, and clip art are discouraged, as are multiple listings of references for further reading in bibliography form.

- *Appendix:* An appendix to house the additional content that might be referenced, but is not critical in the main body of the presentation to provide an overview to the five Ps noted above. Content appropriate for the appendix includes biographies, additional process exhibits, portfolio analytics and examples.

- *Contact Us:* Contact information for the firm including the firm's corporate website address, a main phone number, the primary contact name, and office location. Multiple office locations and contacts may be listed; it is helpful to focus on a primary contact for all ongoing correspondence to streamline the process for the prospect. Contact information should reside on the very last page of the presentation.

- *Composite/Track Record:* The strategy composite if a separately managed account solution, typically provided in the appendix or at the end of the presentation before the contact information.

For limited partnerships and private placements, a breakdown of performance by Fund should be provided to demonstrate the firm's history and results. For registered products, a simple performance table and graph is sufficient; institutions can and probably already have looked up performance in the likes of Morningstar and other databases where a Fund ticker is provided.

- ***Disclosures:*** Disclosures, which can be relegated to the back of the presentation for institutional audiences, are required. Be certain to provide an appropriate disclaimer up front and reference to disclosure page numbers. Professional compliance review prior to distribution is a necessity.

Fact Sheet/Executive Summary

The fact sheet is the most efficient way to present the firm's strategy. It serves as the strategy's executive summary. The fact sheet is typically at the strategy, not the firm, level. It is called a "fact sheet" for a reason; the norm is no longer than two pages, and preferably front and back when printed. Budget a half page for disclosures. It should also be filled with facts, not qualitative descriptions, generic graphics nor third-party references. The fact sheet can efficiently present the core contents of the presentation in a consolidated fashion while providing up to date analytics all inside of a page and a half. Fact sheets are most often produced monthly for registered products such as mutual funds, and quarterly for separately managed accounts.

The Executive Summary is the normal term identified for this overview one pager for private equity and venture strategies. The Executive Summary serves the same purpose as a fact sheet—to provide a quick snapshot of the opportunity. The fact sheet can be created in a variety of programs including Microsoft Word, PowerPoint, Publisher and several other applications. It is most often created in a portrait, or vertical, orientation. The content for the fact sheet should be pulled directly from the firm's content library, as outlined in *Chapter 7*, coupled with current portfolio analytics. Fact sheet content can be variable, although certain facts and figures are expected. Managers are encouraged to budget the real estate on a fact sheet to permit the content to best represent the strategy's strengths. In short, wasting a large section of the front page of a fact sheet with a growth of $10,000 graphic is not the best use of space. Typical fact sheet components include:

- Target length: One to two pages
- Framework: Vertical template with visual separation between content sections
- Firm Overview: Three to five bullets or sentences
- Strategy description: Three to four bullets or sentences
- Strategy objectives: Two to five bullets
- Team Profile: with portfolio manager short bios
- Analytic content:
  - Performance Table
  - Performance Chart
  - Risk/Reward Chart
  - Top Holdings
  - Sector Allocation
  - Risk Statistics
  - Fund Purchasing Information/Offering Terms
  - Contact Information
  - Disclosures *(No smaller than the smallest font on the page.)*

Commentary Template

The commentary template permits the manager to 'comment' on the market on a regular basis. It should take a consistent form that assists the firm in building its brand over time. The firm should provide quarterly commentary at a minimum, utilizing a standard template as discussed in *Chapter 14: Establishing Active Voice through Commentary*. The template should include:

- Date identification: the quarter or month the commentary is based on
- Firm logo and masthead: that promotes the firm's brand
- Interesting titles: to grab the reader's attention

- A small key: for the contents such that institutions can easily find what they are most interested in
- A firm/offering sidebar: that highlights the firm's profile and offering
- Contact information
- Disclosures

Other 'core' collateral components that might not be top priority, but should be:

Business Card

Business cards reinforce the firm brand. Include the firm's logo and provide a window into the firm's identity through the production of a professional business card. Business cards can be produced quite inexpensively through online resources. It is surprising how often managers have business cards that do not look anything like their brand as portrayed on other written materials. Why miss this opportunity to engage the market on behalf of the firm?

Website

Websites are discussed in *Chapter 10: Tools for the Trade: Online Marketing*. Technology permits organizations to quickly ascertain a manager's readiness to be in market. A simple way to check is to search for the firm online. A basic web presence is a required element of core collateral. While it might not technically be collateral, it is part of the profile managers are expected to have in place and it should be complementary to the firm's core marketing materials.

Email Address

Emails are a direct form of marketing communications. Having a firm email address is imperative to establish the firm as a viable player. Respondents noted that a generic address is a non-starter. Even for those just starting out and seeking 'feedback' before they engage, a business email is the standard. Cybersecurity procedures will often reject generic email addresses. Establishing a firm website, and particularly an email address that incorporates the firm's name, can be done within a few hours at very low cost.

Email Signature

The email signature is also worth considering as part of the firm's core collateral system. Adding a signature that professionally and consistently represents the firm, and provides address, firm website and contact phone information is an opportunity to both indicate that the firm is established, and to provide some context for location. Firms may want to consider including some personality into their signature, adding their logo or some minimal color to reinforce their brand.

Questions Asked

Respondents were asked the following questions in bold face text specifically in relation to this chapter. The consensus answers are in italics and immediately follow the question asked.

Do colors/design matter in a presentation? What colors don't work?
No; just make sure it's legible.

How important is quality/professionalism of the manager's materials?
Most meet a basic standard that is acceptable, if not we take a pass.

Do you prefer more, or less, content in a presentation?
Middle of the road; enough to be meaningful, 15-25 pages max. Make sure a second and third meeting get their own version of the presentation with enhanced content.

Words to Drive By

The following quotes provide a broader sampling of the respondents' direct feedback in relation to the above questions. Firms are encouraged to drive their marketing and sales activities with these rules for the road in mind.

On Professionalism

I've stopped meetings because the presentation is littered with typos—how do I know the research is thoughtful if this isn't?

Needs to look professional, it doesn't have to be the highest quality, just someone had to spend enough time on it that they are proud presenting it.

Have you seen [XYZ's] presentation deck? It's awful! Like someone opened up a PowerPoint and just started typing.

It only matters if it's pretty bad, other than that we are focused on the content.

Only see unprofessional from managers I would reject anyhow because it's too small.

On Design

More white space; way too much on the page.

You never want to judge a book by its cover, but there is definitely something to having your materials up to market standards; basic rainbow colors aren't going to sell.

Some of [my] favorite managers have the worst materials as to look because they don't spend money on it and that's ok.

It's all downside risk if you have mistakes in materials or they don't look good, that's five minutes of explaining why as opposed to focusing on the meeting; it's just expected to be right; it doesn't have to be fancy, hate the multi-color background, artsy stuff, [it] just needs to be right—plain white paper with legible black lettering is perfect for me.

On Preference for More or Less Content in Presentations

Lots of pitchbooks put in lots of examples or views on a trade. One or two is great, more is overkill.

Deck is appetizer to get you in the room. Basic deck to get meeting, and more in-depth deck for second and third meetings, some of the bigger firms have that down cold.

25 slides is a good length; we tend to see more on domestic equities and less on hedge funds.

More succinct is better; 50 pages are way too much.

15-20 slides for a meeting for the main body; appreciated having a good appendix with lots of data, history and bios—that's reference material. Focus on the 15-20 slides of why you are good.

On Content

[Presentation] should give full transparency into what you are doing; all the things you are doing should be highlighting your proof statement.

One manager shows visual depictions of buys and sells for stocks which makes it easy to visually see.

Managers who include a macro view—if the strategy doesn't call for that, than its bad.

Better less that looks great than more that doesn't look good.

Summary on Core Collateral

Define a consistent core collateral system that reinforces the firm's brand.

Core Collateral Goes Beyond a Pitchbook

Less Can Be More

Ensure the Firm Is Meeting Baseline Standards for Content in Collateral

CHAPTER 9

Due Diligence and Databases

RPM Rating on Databases

DE MINIMIS	CORE	PRIORITY	GAME CHANGER

Institutional investment research professionals have a variety of tools at their disposal. They have the materials managers send them and what they can find on their own. A few easily accessible components of a firm's profile include the content that is loaded into industry databases, and the content firms put online (corporate websites and social media presence). In this section, the focus is on the former, the databases, both external and internal versions used by institutional investment research professionals.

Institutional Money Management Databases

Let's begin with the classic institutional money management databases. These are massive data depositories that managers are strongly encouraged to populate with data. These databases, for a notable fee, will subsequently provide subscribers with both a qualitative and quantitative profile of the firm and its strategies, based exclusively on the data provided by individual managers. Leading into the book's research, the expectation was that the databases are critical, and they are. However, respondents report that they are critical as a backdrop to the research process, not a primary data source of it. They serve as a data baseline to provide research teams with the ability to efficiently and anonymously screen the reporting universe, and a specific manager as a candidate within it.

Databases are a *core* element according to the *Resource Prioritization Matrix*; they must be done. Yet the depth of a firm's work here was not identified as a deal breaker in most cases, only that managers meet a few minimum standards. Respondents repeatedly harped on the timely, accurate and complete updating of core quantitative data points. They were universally less focused on the qualitative write ups and seemed comfortable overlooking "missing" data. Why? Respondents reported using the databases primarily for high level, top down universe screening. As a result, a lack of timely quantitative responses will simply eliminate the firm from contention, making the institution's screening lists shorter and their jobs easier. *Thank you, Mr. Manager, for making it simple for institutions to overlook the firm by failing to input a complete set of the firm's data on a timely basis. There are more than enough managers out there in any given category to provide institutions with ample choices.*

Quantitative Data Is the Priority

Beyond universe screens, respondents confirmed their use of the databases as a "check the box" while reviewing a manager who has requested to be screened or has been suggested to them, and in whom they have some interest. In this case, they are primarily focused on the quantitative information loaded into the databases; the data on which competitive analysis is most easily run. Respondents consistently indicated gathering the qualitative details directly from the managers. Updated materials in a format that is easier to digest such as a fact sheet and presentation are preferred to database descriptions and other qualitative questions and answers.

Recheck that Box

Managers may be thinking "we've got this covered", particularly given the databases' *Resource Prioritization Matrix (RPM)* rating as simply a *core* element with a primary focus on the quantitative data. Yet respondents don't agree. Professional resources that input manager data into industry databases for a living don't agree either. In speaking with a database entry professional who provided services to a wide variety of managers over many years, the professional noted *"managers who believe they are all set almost always have inaccurate data in the databases. It is shocking, really, how many have errors. There are performance inconsistencies and missing data points that we catch all the time, even with well-established managers."* Being "in" the databases is insufficient. Firms are encouraged to go back and recheck that box. Complete a three quarter review of the data that sits in all databases the firm populates.

First, review the timeliness of the last three quarters of data uploaded:

- Who entered the data and when was it inputted?
- Was it inputted on the same day across all databases or was the updating completed over a longer period? How long did it take?
- Which database was populated first, second and third? How many databases were populated and were they all populated consistently in each of the past three quarters?
- Was a formal quality check completed and if so, when? Is this documented?

Second, print out the last set of submissions to each database populated. Carefully review them side by side on the following metrics:

- Which databases are being populated by the firm and how consistently have they been populated in each case?
- Is the data 100% accurate?
- Is the data consistent from database to database where feasible?
- Are all data points filled in completely or has the firm left out some 'less impressive' facts? *(AUM and fees are the most common)*
- How timely was the firm's data update after quarter end? *(or month end where monthly updates are expected)*
- Is the data consistent with that found in the firm's core

collateral/offering materials? *(fact sheets, presentations, and website)*

Even with a strong team in place and a sense that a manager is "covered" in this area, the exercise should be completed prior to any institutional marketing push. In most cases, managers will find either late submissions, incomplete submissions, erroneous numbers, or inconsistent data between the databases and other marketing content that the prospect will receive. Even if the institutional researcher is willing to overlook data shortcomings, and the errors do not eliminate the firm from the screening process, it's a red flag that attention to detail is lacking.

How the Data Is Being Used

Databases are utilized in two ways; as a bottom up and top down analytical baseline. Respondents indicated that they utilized external databases (or internal in the cases where institutions have proprietary databases for external manager population) to check the box, ensuring "full review" of the available options that meet certain baseline criteria set by the institution. These top down database searches are typically run with filters applied that would exclude many managers—most often based on strategy AUM, and secondarily based on fees. Alternatively, when a manager is introduced to a researcher, and the institution may have some baseline interest, the researcher will complete a bottom up screen of the manager in the databases, provided they are a subscriber and the manager data is entered. In so doing, the institution will pull up the firm's database entries and compare them to an undisclosed peer group. In most cases, the screening is focused on the quantitative aspects of the data set: the performance track record, strategy analytics, fees and AUM, according to respondents.

The market presumes that more of the data is utilized, and more frequently, than it is by institutional researchers. This presumption is based on the questions that managers are regularly asked by institutions at the start of a dialogue. Managers are typically asked *"Are you in XYZ database?"* and *"Are your responses up to date in ABC database?"*, or the most troubling *"We were searching for [fill in the blank data point] in the databases and it looks like you have not filled that in. Can you please provide that information now?"* This battery of questions is standard procedure during a research meeting, and it creates the assumption that these databases are the very basis of manager screening. While databases are an important part of the process and require careful attention, they are not the foundation of manager screening.

Focus on Content Consistency

Based on respondent answers, extensive value does not come from perfecting the qualitative responses in the databases, other than to ensure there are no discrepancies between the data in the databases and that provided in other forms. The databases are used primarily as a quantitative data gathering and profiling tool at present, albeit a critical one. In the case of a top down universe screening, where filters are applied it is difficult for managers to meet the AUM and perhaps length of track record requirements to be included in a general search, or certainly to come up anywhere near the top of a long manager roster such that the firm will be pursued by the institution solely based on their database entries. Yet, there are lots of institutions that are searching to broaden their view on a specific asset class; looking carefully at manager and strategy availability and who is showing up as a new name in a certain asset class. In addition, once a firm has reached out to an institution, the databases will typically be tapped to cross reference the data provided. Managers often have stale, missing or inconsistent data between sources. Keeping firm data updated, complete and current will support a manager's candidacy whenever the opportunity arises. In fact, many institutional research professionals noted that they like to limit the constraints on the search, at least as a first pass, so that they do see more of the universe. This is an opportunity for firms to get noticed.

Database Population Considerations

Complete a thorough review of the firm's qualitative responses across all databases before embarking on an institutional marketing and sales effort, and subsequently at least once per year to ensure that all data is accurate. Any significant changes, such as staffing and AUM levels, must be updated as they occur. Ultimately, provided the data is accurate and presenting the most up to date information on the firm, the firm's resources are best spent on the timeliness and accuracy of the quantitative data on an ongoing basis. Database population is a significant effort. It is important to factor in costs, timing, and the quality control procedures committed.

There are a variety of database options in the market. Below are a few factors to consider:

1. ***Be Selective:*** Focus on the universal databases widely accepted in the market for each vehicle type: separately managed accounts, limited partnerships/hedge funds, private placements, mutual funds, etc. There are specific vendors in the market dedicated to databases and generally for specific vehicle types; this is their business. Some have expanded to cover more than one vehicle type, but firm's may think about eVestment Alliance, Investment Metrics and PSN Informa for separately managed account strategies, Albourne, Eurekahedge and Hedge Fund Research (HFR) for limited partnerships, PitchBook and Preqin for private equity, CB Insights for venture capital, and Morningstar for mutual funds, for example. The firm's top priority should be those databases that have the widest subscriber base. Be sure the firm is updating the quantitative data quarterly at a minimum; certain liquid product and hedge fund databases seek monthly data and it is worth providing if (and only if) most of the strategy competitors are providing the same.

2. ***Prioritize:*** Make good choices about the value of reporting data more frequently, or to more databases, than is needed. Each added database takes exponentially greater coordination and resources. It is more important to have the data perfect and to spend the firm's resources performing a formal quality control check in a series of well-known databases on a quarterly basis, rather than spreading resources too thin and risking errors,

delays or missing data points. Complete a competitive analysis to determine where and how often to populate. Managers need to be in the key databases that are widely used by institutions, and perhaps a few more that are proprietary but run by firms who have demonstrated some interest in screening the strategy. The databases the firm does commit to populating should be updated fully and in a timely manner. That does not mean loading the firm's data everywhere and anywhere that will accept it.

3. ***Maintain a Core Data Document:*** Create a master template of the data the firm is inputting, both quantitative and qualitative, across all databases the firm elects to populate. This will serve as an excellent tool to support the quality control process, and as a source for completing RFIs/RFPs/DDQs and other requests for information. The firm can organize the data by database, or by subject, or by both, so that the team can quickly and easily determine where updates will be needed when changes occur within the organization and its strategies. This content document is a part of the firm's master content library as discussed in *Chapter 7: The Firm's Oeuvre—Creating the Content Library.*

4. ***Be Strategic:*** Complete the ancillary, proprietary databases of specific consultants and organizations when the firm is ready to pursue them. There is no value in spending countless hours loading a unique data set into a major consultant database that the firm is not going to sell to or be a candidate for in the near term. However, do populate the institution's system fully before picking up the phone. The first question that the sales agent will be asked: *"Is this manager in our database?"* Have a game plan related to this increasingly customized effort to ensure it works with the firm's existing resources. If the firm offers multiple strategies, populate the firm's flagship strategy first, and add additional strategies only when they become viable institutional candidates.

5. ***Outsource:*** Consider hiring a professional to populate the databases, utilizing the firm's resources to provide the initial content *and* the quality control check once populated. Database entry is often relegated to junior staff and is too frequently poorly managed. Or, it is done "on the side" of lots of other competing activities. Errors and delays are highly likely in these cases. Database population experts are surprisingly cost efficient in the bigger scheme of things. They will expand the firm's footprint much wider than it could on its own, and they will do so professionally so that the firm is putting its best foot forward.

Pricing is typically based on entering the firm's profile itself, followed by a price point for each strategy to be loaded. As noted above, where firms offer more than one strategy, money can be saved by populating only the strategies that are timely (or ideally will be in the foreseeable future) and marketable to institutions. In some cases (either provided by a database provider themselves or by the professional database population vendors who populate on behalf of firms) there are templates that permit managers to input their data once into a singular depository. From there, the data is parsed and loaded into a wide variety of databases from this single source, improving accuracy, consistency and timeliness.

Accuracy Is the Manager's Responsibility

Database population is a mind-numbing task that few people enjoy. Like the higher education admissions process, there have been attempts to create the "common app" of the institutional investment management database world. There are some related solutions in this regard as noted above. Yet many institutions, particularly consultants, cannot help themselves from insisting upon "custom" content and formatting, wreaking havoc on attempts to streamline the data entry process across databases. Unfortunately, database population is and likely always will be a multistage process.

Multistage processes inherently create more opportunities for error, even when firms have elected to engage outsourced professionals who specialize in data entry, or have invested in tools designed to streamline the process. The data still needs to be reviewed and confirmed upon entry. No one knows a firm's data better than the manager itself. Check it often. Set up a regular quality control process consisting of a rotating schedule of logging in and spot checking that the data is accurate and fully up-to-date. Anecdotal evidence suggests that often it is not quite right. This is highly problematic if institutions are screening managers based on it. Accuracy should be part of the firm's brand proposition. After all, the manager is selling investment management services. Accuracy and strength with numbers are at the heart of what managers are offering. Firms must be certain that this attention to detail carries through to the databases.

Internal Databases: Another Tool of the Trade

The ease of submitting and managing data electronically, coupled with the globalization of the marketplace, has resulted in an overwhelming onslaught of managers and manager materials for institutional investment research professionals to weed through. The sheer volume, coupled with concerns over cybersecurity, has necessitated the establishment of highly structured systems for the acceptance, uploading, reviewing and cataloging of manager data. 100% of respondents noted that they maintain some kind of internal database for the filing, vetting and storage of manager data. This means that the data the firm provides, if it makes it through to the recipient in the first place, is rather permanent in institutional research systems, easily recalled and reviewed not only months but years later.

Internal Database Submission Best Practices

Here are some best practices that the firm should employ to maximize the chances that their data is being received, reviewed and saved:

1. ***Avoid Generic Email Addresses & Confirm Receipt:***
   Send materials from a legitimate business address; follow up to ensure that emails are being received to avoid getting lost in a

never-ending spam filter. Lots of managers, their marketers and sales professionals are not getting into the system in the first place. Is your firm one of them?

2. ***Send PDFs:***
Respondents universally preferred PDFs to links such that they could easily file these materials away. Send PDFs, not links.

3. ***Follow Protocol:***
Institutional research professionals regularly request the use of an info@ address for sending ongoing updates and materials; be sure to honor that process. Managers may wish to cc the individual who they are in contact with, but always use the info@ address if that is the institutions protocol and request.

4. ***Content is Permanent:***
Make sure what is sent (and what is said) is what the manager wants to be reminded of three to five years later, as this is exactly what will happen. When they say, "your reputation precedes you" they may well be talking about that very first send of collateral. Or they may be referring to the notes the institution took based on that first phone call. Was it the best representation of the firm and what it is offering? If not, step back and refine. Firms can recover but it takes more work—so managing the input up front given the permanency of databases is critical. This does include the notes, handwritten or otherwise, taken by the institutional research professional. Institutional research professionals will recall research notes from past and present researchers, all archived and saved for easy reference forevermore. Sales agents cringe when a consultant starts the conversation with "so I pulled up the old notes we had on you in the system [from three years ago], what has changed in your investment process since then? So where did Bob go?" Perhaps, the manager has changed nothing and it's a great conversation. More likely they have changed something, whether in practice or simply in positioning,

and that old set of notes isn't representative of how the manager wants to be viewed today. In real time, the manager will need to figure out how to connect the dots and provide a convincing case for whatever changes have occurred. It is not how they wanted to start today's conversation, but its where they must start because of what they introduced several years ago. In the rush to push content out, always keep in mind the permanency of it. Keep track of what has been posted to the databases in the past. Old fee schedules, past personnel and varied investment process descriptions can all be problematic.

Questions Asked

Respondents were asked the following questions in bold face text specifically in relation to this chapter. The consensus answers are in italics and immediately follow the question asked.

What percentage of managers that you consider come from screens/database searches you run?
Very few; databases are used to ensure we didn't miss anyone and in this case, we often screen on AUM and/or fees, or as a follow up to managers we have received information on.

How important are the databases to your research process and what do you look for?
Important as a data point, but not the focus of our activity. Managers need to be sure their quantitative data is accurate, timely and complete in the databases first and foremost.

Do you utilize an external database, an internal database, or both?
Both in most cases.

Words to Drive By

The following quotes provide a broader sampling of the respondents' direct feedback in relation to the above questions. Firms are encouraged to drive their marketing and sales activities with these rules for the road in mind.

On Frequency of Database Usage:

[Our process is] 60/40—60% we drum up our own universe; 40% based on strategies sent/interesting. The databases let us look at the whole universe but then screen it down particularly in alts where some universes are particularly small; we only screen down if [the universe is] broad based.

80% [of the time] to make sure we are not missing anything; it's embarrassing when a client says, "why didn't you look at XYZ?" Typically, they weren't in the database, sometimes they came out of another firm—I don't want to get blindsided by someone we should have looked at; a lot of that is resource dependent as well. If we have three great solutions and don't have the time and resources, we won't look.

We don't look at them daily or monthly, but always for a search to make sure there is nothing I've missed out on.

No, we don't even use databases anymore, [we] didn't find use for it. Most [managers] come from referrals and researching a certain type of strategy/opportunity.

We require managers to have filled in our own database as a prerequisite for a conversation.

On When Databases Are Utilized

It's helpful but ancillary; nice to be able to go out and look in an area and see who is submitting data—see if there are any names that we weren't familiar with; relative analysis of how our managers were doing against competitors.

Realistically, even as a second reference its useful for the amount of data that is in there and the ability to sift through quickly. We are focused on the quantitative inputs in this case.

Databases are best when attacking a new asset class.

Backfilling data after we've met, heard about or [received data] from a manager rather than screening; sourcing is who knows who that's doing what.

50% are up to date, but we look past it; 'next' if it's not up to date.

On How Databases Are Utilized

If we have a client specific search we do more constrained searches; [if it is] for us we look more broadly and then cut down based on asset size and fees.

This is a good way to look at info without alerting the manager.

We do some quantitative screen on the front end, by asset class. On the hedge fund side it's the least meaningful, on the private equity side we are looking for managers in [the] top quartile and not a first fund; some [screening] on the long only side.

It's just another input; we try to be liberal in the quantitative screens so we don't eliminate a potentially good manager for reasons of size as AUM might be small, but [the] manager might be larger.

Great idea generator—not even in a space we have funds but perhaps [screening] up [the] cap[italization] spectrum from what we really want, etc.

Summary on Databases

While databases are not the cornerstone of manager screening, they are an important confirmation.

Recheck the Box—Revisit Database Content and Timeliness;
Keep Track of Changes Made

Be Strategic: Not all Databases Are Necessary Right Now;
Focus on Quality over Quantity

Consider Outsourcing

CHAPTER 10

Digital Marketing

RPM Rating on Digital Engagement

DE MINIMIS	CORE	PRIORITY	GAME CHANGER

D igital engagement is the most significant marketing advancement of the modern era. Once of limited use to traditional business development professionals, who would rather identify prospective clients through known sources or direct networking, digital engagement has become a key tool in business development as well as in corporate screening. Both buyers and sellers now utilize digital assets to assess capabilities and to market solutions. Furthermore, the accessibility of technology, matched only by globalization, has created a level playing field. Organizations, regardless of size and connections, can share their capabilities with prospects through digital marketing. Those interested in creating a presence online and in actively engaging the marketplace through technology enabled communications can build their businesses through digital marketing. There has been a paradigm shift in the financial service industry's application of digital tools in all stages of business development.

A firm's digital footprint represents its online presence, social media footprint, and the social networking of the organization and its team members. Specific elements may include the following:

1. *A Corporate Website*
   Particularly savvy thought leaders may even create their own personal brand websites to expand reach, one such example being www.stacyhavener.com.

2. *A Social Media Presence*
   The dissemination of content in the form of posts, blogs, videos, electronic publications, infographics, podcasts, and eBooks, for example.

3. *Social Media Networking*
   The organic and genuine engagement between the representatives of your firm, the content the firm produces, the content that circulates their social media feeds from other sources, and their likes, shares, comments, and connections with their network; all together, social media networking is your organization's usage of platforms and content to build connections and engage potential buyers.

4. *Paid Digital Advertising*
   The ability to target specific demographics with paid advertisements to boost brand awareness, drive website traffic and generate targeted leads.

We can cross from here into conversations about unpaid advertising, which fall squarely into a public relations game plan, often tied to a comprehensive paid and unpaid strategy that permits organizations to fully engage with key media sources and platforms driving content around their area of expertise. All organizations have the first three elements of a digital footprint, whether they are active and their footprint is awesome, or whether they are inactive and the non-existence of a footprint is what prospective buyers see. The fourth element, paid digital advertising, is a complementary opportunity that can serve to boost content and ensure it gets in front of the right people.

Digital engagement, and a cohesive strategy around it, was once considered a cutting-edge marketing technique. Now, it is a requirement for organizations seeking to compete efficiently. According to the *Resource Prioritization Matrix* digital engagement is a *game changer* due to the ease in which prospects can search for anything that an organization and its representatives have produced digitally. A simple and free Google search can reveal quite a bit about a firm, its people, and its priorities. Organizations should ask themselves: When is the last time we completed a search on our own organization? Here is a simple framework that organizations can use to assess their current digital engagement, which is best completed by entering your own firm and representative's names in the search bar. The first row is completed as an example only; the scope and type of data added will be dependent

Firm	Location	Date	Scope	Traffic/Activity/Response
Website	www.xyz.co	Last Updated on xx.xx.xxxx	Added new CTAs to home page	15 webinar registrations, 20 adds to mailing list
Website CTAs				
Website Blog Posts				
Website Articles				
Website Offers				
LinkedIn Posts				
LinkedIn Paid Ads				
Social Platform II Posts				
Social Platform II Paid Ads				
Social Platform III Posts				
Social Platform III Paid Ads				
Social Platform IV Posts				
Social Platform IV Paid Ads				
Video Assets				
Podcast Assets				
Infographics				
eBooks				
Thought Leadership/White Papers				
Tools/Checklists/Workbooks				
Other				

Representative(s)	Location	Date	Scope	Traffic/Activity
Website	www.marymary.co	Last updated on xx.xx.xxxx	Added new links to home page	15 webinar registrations, 20 adds to mailing list
Website CTAs				
Website Blog Posts				
Website Articles				
Website Offers				
LinkedIn Posts				
LinkedIn Paid Ads				
Video Assets				
Podcast Assets				
Infographics				
eBooks				
Thought Leadership/White Papers				
Tools/Checklists/Workbooks				
Other				

on the firm's and team's activities. Some elements may not apply to individual representatives and can be removed from the table; this tool can also prove valuable in tracking representative and firm activity for internal digital engagement conversations and compliance oversight as shown.

Let's Get Active Online

Digital marketing represents one of the most highly varied elements among firm profiles. Organizations may elect to avoid the limelight, preferring anonymity, and a boutique persona, sharing little online. These firms barely define their services, offering a basic website with a rudimentary design and only a few pages of real content. This can make sense for certain types of organizations, particularly those who provide behind the scenes support to other brands and prefer to stay neutral about their areas of focus, priorities, and perspectives. Other organizations go all out, with interactive online tools, videos, blog posts, team interviews, podcasts, tweets, long lists of social networking connections and a high-end, professionally designed corporate website. Technology permits firms to demonstrate their creativity and engagement online. Is it worth the effort? Will your firm benefit from an active digital footprint? Should you spend your resources here or stick to traditional marketing? Is your business model best served by a strong, dynamic online presence, or a stealth, limited scope online contact point only? The best way to answer these questions is to think about your avatar—your ideal client profiles. What do they need to see online from you?

Digital Marketing for Institutional Engagements

In the original interviews, respondents (who were institutional investment management research professionals) affirmed they typically visited a firm's website simply to check the box, seeking only a confirmation that the data matched expectations. Little else was reviewed. Not one respondent highlighted a social media or interactive marketing campaign as value-added and impactful to their process. But that was then, and this is now.

The market has changed dramatically in recent years, driven not only by the massive developments in technology but by a global pandemic. Have institutions changed with it? An unequivocal yes. And we believe this change is permanent.

During a recent webinar in which institutional allocators served as panelists, the discussion focused on due diligence and data sources. In all cases the institutions responded that they heavily rely on digital content to screen firms. Of note was an increasing reliance on databases, and on the firm's presence online. Commentary to this effect is everywhere, espousing the advantages of engaging prospects and clients alike online. Yet, most firms continue to undermine their candidacy through a lack of content, planning and execution when it comes to digital engagement. They fail to follow the golden rule: be consistent. Content on various platforms is easy to compare to that sent directly from the firm. Consistency counts: putting out consistent content in timing and messaging is key to success. However, consistency of delivery does not have to mean an overwhelming amount of content development.

One of the big misunderstandings around content development that leads to inertia is the belief that firms must continuously create unique content and they simply cannot do that, so why try at all? Quite the contrary, clearly defining the firm's ideal clients through avatar creation, determining the firm's core differentiators that will drive that ideal client to purchase, and remaining laser focused on the constant drum beat of these core differentiators is the content that will prove most impactful in business development, regardless of the medium. Therefore, it is not the uniqueness of the content that is of value, so much as the opportunity to repurpose and recreate core content to meet the needs of various audiences. Some may recall the Aristotelian Triptych: Tell them what you are going to tell them, tell them, and then tell them what you told them. This is critical in content creation and marketing. Firm's that continuously throw different ideas out, speak to general market conditions without reference to how it relates to their offerings, and maintain no structure or game plan around their content focusing solely on getting 'something' out have missed the mark on the power of marketing and in particular of digital engagement. Creating content on 'too many' different ideas leave the prospect unaware of what your firm specializes in. In contrast, a single piece of well-defined, core message driven content can make its way across the digital asset spectrum: a post, a blog, a written article, a video interview, a podcast conversation, an infographic. Digital engagement provides the perfect playground for the implementation of this Aristotelian Triptych. Revisit Chapter 7, on building core content around key messaging, to ensure your team has clarity around the firm's content creation priorities.

Content Considerations:
The Institutional Research Mindset

Investment research professionals are fundamentally fact oriented and risk averse. They are seeking sustainable solutions and good people to work with because they are looking to hire a firm for the long term. Historically, they have not wanted or needed the 'buzz' that comes from digital engagement. Social media and social networking can be just that; these are 'social' media designed to increase connectivity and to provide calls to action. Given the 100+ inbound requests for review that respondents receive in an average week via email, however, a quick online assessment has become the norm to easily screen in—and out—worthy candidates for further due diligence. What is a researcher attempting to efficiently assess via an online screening? Here are the top ten questions organizations seek to answer when screening a firm online:

1. Is this a viable entity?
2. Is this [the services/offering we want to hire them for] their core business?
3. Does their online presence match what they sent to us in the mail and what we read in the databases? Do all three sources tell the same story?
4. Do we see any red flags, regulatory concerns, or obvious missteps?
5. Do they have anything meaningful that describes their edge? Or are they simply focused on what they are not doing? i.e., Is the team out denigrating value stocks on Twitter when selling a core strategy?
6. Can we get their story by following the digital footprint?
7. Do we like them? Does it feel like a cultural fit?
8. Are they up to date or outdated?
9. Does the team demonstrate diversity of process, thought, and culture? Is the team sufficiently deep in resources and skill set?
10. Is it interesting? Do we want to learn more? Do we want to talk to them?

While it remains true that institutional research professionals are overwhelmed, they prefer data to hyperbole, and are not looking to 'get social' with firms until they have determined their viability. It is also true that digital presence does provide a virtual lens into a firm, and that institutional researchers are seeking to identify any red flags, like a good detective should, to avoid wasting time on a nonstarter of a candidate.

A great digital engagement strategy will avoid the pitfalls that social media and social networking can create. It will also ensure that firm represents its culture and priorities in a way that is consistent with the reality of the organization. In effect, your digital presence is your first date with a prospect, only you are not invited to attend. Therefore, your voice is provided by what they see, read, hear, and feel from experiencing your digital presence. Make the first impression a value-added one.

Content Considerations: The Regulatory Mindset

The financial services industry has been a significant laggard in digital marketing, driven by regulation. The regulatory environment does indeed impact the depth of what a manager can provide publicly in the form of investment management content. These limitations and the power of compliance within organizations further limits the depth of content provided, and in turn the perceived value of what is posted online. In other words, we often hear from managers 'why bother spending a lot of time and money on digital marketing that can't truly tell our story'? Traditional tools such as databases and collateral do not have these same limitations, particularly when it comes to one-on-one communications. Traditional tools provide a more consistent framework from which to compare investment solutions, given that online marketing is so varied among investment managers.

However, these hurdles should not stop firms from engaging digitally. In fact, there is so much greater capacity to tell the firm's story online, and this makes for great content. Through digital engagement a firm can tell the nuances of its story, what makes the team and offerings different, how they think, what matters to them, how they see and respond to market conditions, what they think about the future of industries and sectors, geographies, and countries. Importantly, what makes great digital content is not a set of numbers or risk management statistics, nor general market information—these items are a given to get considered. Digital engagement, and marketing in general, is about giving the market the opportunity to intimately know you and what matters to you, to know your firm and what matters to your firm, with a focus on the services and products you offer to ensure appropriate context and fit.

Dan Sondhelm of Sondhelm Partners, an industry veteran of PR and digital engagement, had the following comment to make regarding the need for investment managers to use online mediums for business development: *"The regulatory fear that many financial services firms had, keeping them from engaging online, has largely been replaced with a necessity to get active through digital engagement. The market has shifted dramatically in this way. It is no longer enough to have a simple web presence and static content online if your objective is to grow brand awareness and market share."*

The Accessibility of Digital

Readers might worry that an exceptional budget and time commitment is required to be active online. This is not the case. Today's marketplace provides a wide variety of access points, both paid and unpaid, to advance the firm's digital presence. Who has the largest voices in the industry when it comes to digital presence? Institutional research professionals talk endlessly about the 'contrarians' and how much they enjoyed reading articles, opinions, perspectives, and the newest rants from highly engaged, nationally known social media finance leaders who make a business out of their commentary. Economists, strategists, true investment contrarians and global business leaders all fall into this category. Most firms will not make the cut, but their digital footprint will be found, researched, evaluated for cultural fit and meaningful content and their teams engaged around what was found online. Regulation is no longer a viable excuse to avoid an active market presence in a digital world.

Individual Engagement: Politics and Party Cups Aside

College students are told to avoid photos with a party cup in hand. These photos can magically appear on social networking platforms and can come back to haunt them in their job search process. Think of party cups as the investment firm's content. Several facets of a firm's brand identity can be challenged by these unnecessary party cups. Social networking can quickly and permanently change a firm's likelihood of being considered in a search. For larger firms, with hundreds of employees and broad infrastructure, the risk is mitigated; it will not surprise anyone that a bad apple or two exists among the ranks. Plus, it is much less likely that a firm screening a large company has the capacity or interest to due diligence such a broad employee base.

For smaller organizations that can show their entire team on the website and typically do, a simple LinkedIn and Twitter search can be done in minutes. The screening process for institutional investors is easy; a few clicks in the form of a search will produce a wealth of information on most anything or anyone.

Institutional researchers are getting younger, as are staff members; this is a welcome reality as younger employees bring energy, fresh ideas, different ways of thinking and doing. One of these ways is digital. Regardless of a firm's profile, an active internal dialogue and rules for the road are critical regarding the firm's online presence, and that of its representatives, to ensure the conversation remains professional and avoids the many pitfalls of party cups, both visually and in words.

Party cups aside, culture is a key component of defining the firm's digital engagement strategy. In a recent interview, a CIO of a major trust company noted they had hired a new firm two months prior and 'had to let them go.' Why? It was not a good cultural fit. More online probing would have identified these cultural differences and avoided wasting both time and resources on what was an inappropriate fit. Organizations have the opportunity, and the responsibility, to utilize digital footprints as a source of information in due diligence, as both buyer and seller. There are digital resources out there that can help organizations create master game plans or simply establish a presence, engage the team around content and active participation or simply ensure the firm's brand is well represented and monitored online. The scope and depth of the digital engagement strategy is entirely up to the firm.

Avatar Awareness: Take Time to Understand the Audience

You may have created avatars of your ideal clients, but has the firm taken time to consider the avatars who are tasked with identifying managers for their clients? Institutional investment research professionals have their own preferences for social media usage and messaging, as we all do, but they have client perceptions and belief systems to contend with. Personally, they might love a manager's most recent rant on the latest political story or economic news out of China, but they may have clients who would find it in poor taste. Researchers are screening to understand a manager's investment management philosophy and process as well as to avoid any surprises that could create issues down the road. Cultural fit is one of these issues. Whether a manager or their representatives are posting, tweeting, or blogging, understanding the collateral risk is imperative. In addition, staying focused on core messaging to describe the firm's philosophy, service offering, and how its solution set adds value considering these avatars will increase the likelihood of a perceived good fit, and the opportunity for meaningful consideration. In the interest of developing content, increasing 'likes' and 'shares,' organizations often drift from their core story. Define your message, understand your avatars, and implement a consistent digital presence building connection with the marketplace around the core elements that best represent you.

Social Media Rules for the Road

There has been a surge in activity among managers across all aspects of social media. For managers committed to growing their social media presence in a meaningful way, here are a few rules for the road in social media and network engagement broken down into two categories:

1. **Active Content:** Content that is real-time, such as in the moment posts, tweets, likes, shares, comments and connecting through online social media platforms;

2. **Static Content:** Content that is preplanned (and preapproved), such as videos, podcasts, webinar recordings, thought leadership pieces, blogs, and e-books.

Active Content

Active content is the quickest to disseminate, but it often lacks the filter and forethought needed. A tweet here and a post there; a request to connect on LinkedIn or a shared viewpoint posted on Facebook can all seem like benign activities. Active content can be engaging, timely, more candid, and efficient compared to its static counterpart. However, it has the greatest risk. A firm's social media policy should provide clear guidelines for active content, particularly given the regulatory environment. Dan Sondhelm of Sondhelm Partners states the importance of offering a variety of digital formats: *"Users generally have a variety of digital asset interests, just as we all have different interests in other areas of business engagement. For example, professionals will look at brief posts but never stop long enough to read an article, others are only interested in true thought leadership pieces provided and hate the quick hits. Still others want video and podcasts so that they can hear the presenter's voice. Varying your forms of digital engagement ensures you will have the broadest reach and keeps the content interesting."*

Technology blurs the lines between business and personal as well as friends and colleagues. Live content can be posted 24/7 and 365, and it is. It is impossible to know who shares one's views and who does not. Until a manager has made it up the road to AUM, and is managing within range of their full capacity, well known to their clients and fully aware of who their end investors are, why risk it? Protecting the firm's reputation and avoiding the creation of unnecessary red flags is everyone's responsibility. Having a clear social media policy will assist in maximizing the firm's presence while minimizing unnecessary risks.

Static Content

Static content, more permanent and involved forms of social media, includes videos, podcasts, blogs, and e-books. Static content is growing. Managers want to demonstrate technological savvy and seek creative ways to differentiate themselves in a crowded market. The two most accessible, diverse, and commonly employed are discussed below: video and blogs.

Video

The use of video is a common tool for managers seeking to dip their toe into a prepared form of social media (while you are at it, you can create a podcast from the same content for your base that prefers to hear your latest market thoughts vs. watching you on screen). However, most videos are ignored by institutional investors. The problem lies not in the medium, but in the content. Often the quality and typically the inefficiency of engaging with the content renders most videos a waste of time and resources. But this is changing; creating an engaging video is the key to success.

We happen to be big fans of video, so let us discuss how to make it meaningful. The challenge for those committed to video is in determining what is value-added to provide in video format and managing the scope and format of the content. Creating a video to check the social media box, and then forcing it on the audience by making it the centerpiece of a website or an outreach campaign is a mistake. Video can be an engaging and informative way to draw in the viewer, but the viewer must be interested in being engaged in this way. Institutional investment management research professionals are not looking to be entertained. "Just give us the facts, Jack!" If you are game to try video, here are some speed bumps and opportunities on the road to video-based engagement:

Speed Bump #1: The viewer is required to watch and learn at the pace and order of the video. There is no effective way to select what you would like to see. This is especially true in the case of videos more than a few minutes in length. If viewers are unable to quickly find exactly what they want, they will likely fast forward at random or exit the video altogether.

Opportunity: Consider a more dynamic user experience that permits the user to select clips based on topic areas of interest, keeping the topics concise and each clip no longer than 1-2 minutes. Provide a limited and efficient menu of intriguing topics and catchy headings. Just as a well-structured navigation makes websites themselves user friendly, consider incorporating user driven navigation when creating video content. Short clips are what made YouTube famous. And now there is Tik Tok.

Speed Bump #2: Video has a personality all its own, whether it employs characters or real people, flashy designs, or stagnant content.

Videos might be catchy, but they often do not add any real content to the conversation. They are typically more form than substance; a form that is not often a match to the culture and personality of the viewer. Ironically, they are rarely a match to the personality and culture of the manager on whose behalf they were created. A video might represent thinking "outside the box" by a creative agency, but it is not adding anything to the institutional review process. To the extent that a video is more aspirational than actual in its depiction, it may not be adding anything to the understanding of the manager either.

Opportunity: Video can be complementary when used to engage the audience on direct aspects of a manager's philosophy and process that are difficult to express on paper. Video can engage our visual and verbal senses; video can provide a 'show' as opposed to simply telling a story. Video can create a powerful connection between the presenter and the viewer, mirroring a one-on-one dialogue. Here are examples of how video can work:

1. *Face Time:* An in-person interview with a portfolio manager discussing a specific element of the manager's philosophy and process can be extremely impactful. The manager can display their passion and place emphasis on key differentiators. The institutional research professional can see and hear the manager directly. Ideally, it is a candid depiction of the manager and how he/she thinks. Think Barbara Walters and skip the monotonous intros. Pick a few key elements of the process and story that the manager is most enthusiastic about. Create video clips that dive right in, focusing exclusively on what differentiates the firm.

2. *Show v. Tell:* A tour of a property, company, factory, or country in which the manager is investing can demonstrate an opportunity set in an efficient manner. Why does everyone love HGTV so much? Humans love to see things for themselves. Video is a terrific way to provide institutional research professionals and

investors with a direct view into why an investment was made. Particularly for managers focused on real estate, private equity and venture, commodity related investments, ESG and impact investments and far away investments, video has the unique ability to show, rather than tell.

3. ***Complex Process Visualization:*** A visualization of an investment process, providing an inside look at the building blocks that get investments in and out of the portfolio is worth a thousand words. The more complex and broader the strategy, the more valuable a visual and efficient walk through can be. This should not be confused with simple presentation slide 'builds;' these are overkill and unwelcome. What institutional investment research professional needs to watch single bullets of content slowly appear, one after the other on the screen? Paint can dry faster.

Blogs

Managers have something to say, and they want an easy and efficient way to say it. Thought leadership through white papers can be so daunting that nothing gets produced. Blogging is certainly a sign of the times and an opportunity to share perspectives and ideas. It is also short, which is a plus. Managers who do not like the blog concept can consider the application of a series of brief articles, or one page Q&As in this same category. This is short, written, key idea vignettes designed to share current thinking. From an overall content perspective, it is our belief that managers should focus first on decent quality commentary, delivered on a quarterly basis (commentary is discussed in Chapter 14: Establishing Active Voice with Commentary) before blogging to confirm the core element of quality commentary is in place. If it is, then blog away. In fact, the commentary itself can and should prove valuable in producing blogging content by taking key themes and timely ideas to work into efficient, bit size blog posts. Firms often worry too much about redundancy. Keep the Aristotelian Triptych in mind.

Blogging Framework

If blogging is in a managers blood, and they are committed to the medium at an early stage in their development—before they have established an institutional client base, careful thought should be put into the tone and content of blog posts and related thought leadership content elements, including articles, market briefs, commentary, and white papers. For managers with a fully engaged marketing and sales effort, running on all cylinders and deep in momentum and stride, blogging can be a nice add. For those that have not framed out their offering and marketing fully—who have not delivered well on the basics—blogging is best placed on the back burner. The goal is to get the basics right (core digital presence, monthly/quarterly updates, core materials, commentary), and then to add more dynamic content, which blog posting can be, later in the process. If the firm does elect to blog, the below framework is useful in defining parameters and establishing objectives. Note, this framework works well for content creation to be used in social media applications as well:

1. What is the firms goal?
2. Who is the audience? What avatar(s) are you seeking to engage through your blog?
3. How will this audience be proactively notified when content is added?
4. If the firm has multiple audiences, is there a risk of alienating one over the other based on the types and depth of content? *(Will it be too basic for one and too technical for another? Will it be controversial to one or overly mundane to the other?)*
5. What might the audience want to hear about?
6. What type of posts could be risky?
7. Is the firm an expert in the areas in which it intends to provide a voice?
8. Will the blog have a theme and if so, what will be the focus?
9. What parts of the firm's investment process would be supported by pushing out content about them?

10. What market events create opportunities for the firm and strategy to produce content?

Questions 8-10 will permit the manager to create a listing of potential topics and touchpoints. Communication on these topics and touchpoints should be in line with the goals defined for the blog or social media application. Ideally, the market will provide opportunities to post content about these topics over time. Managers who elect to post content must have clear guidelines and resources defined regarding each application. Once introduced to the market, commit to a certain frequency of posting, depth, and scope of content.

Avoid the Urge to Push the Firm's Social Media

Several respondents commented on managers who put them on the spot about how much research and content review they had done prior to a meeting or call. These respondents universally noted they did not appreciate being quizzed on what a manager had provided in any medium. Managers often become committed to the forum of social media if they are active in it and have taken time to create the content, believing others can and should actively engage with them on it. Just as manager interest and involvement in social media is widely varied, so goes the institutional investment management research population. Managers are discouraged from pushing their social media content and presence on institutional investment management research professionals. Making the market aware of how the firm is electing to communicate is good business but making social media a homework assignment for research professionals is not.

Social Media and Social Networking 101

Regardless of a manager's current online presence in social media and social networking, here are some factors to consider:

Core Presence Online

Digital presence establishes the firm and its representatives as legitimate entities in the market. It gives a face to a name. It is easier to reject a set of numbers than it is to reject a personal photo and a heartfelt profile. Certain managers and firm representatives prefer anonymity, but it is suggested each have a basic LinkedIn or other business-related social media profile, and that representatives seek to build connections over time. The profile should be kept up to date. It does not need to be treated as a product sales tool, and for many who are regulated it cannot be; keep it professional, factual, and straightforward. The goal is to clearly establish the who and why of the individual and organization.

While institutional research professionals may have LinkedIn profiles of their own, it is off-putting to be extremely aggressive in attempting to connect with these professionals online. Respondents repeatedly noted that while some connectivity is appropriate, many managers and marketers take social networking to the extreme and fail to respect boundaries. Imagine an aggressive vendor who is constantly bombarding you on LinkedIn. Would you be more or less likely to buy from them?

Avoid Overactive and Potentially Controversial Online Persona

Returning to the party cup image, think about what certain words and perspectives mean. Firm profiles rarely create the dilemma that individual ones do. Consider the institutional research investment professional reading the words of a firm representative. Managers and representatives should review their own posts and profiles in this light. As researchers receive information, they must ask themselves:

- Is this a person/team we can introduce to our clients? Is this person overly opinionated about non-core and potentially controversial subjects and will/could our clients be offended?
- Is this person focused on the right things; will managing the portfolio be the primary focus?
- Is the investment management business the top priority? Or are they wealth managers first and foremost?

- Are they serious about being in the space, passionate about the markets, and engaged in the industry?
- Is this person/ commentary positive? (No one wants to be around negative energy.)

When pursuing institutional investment management business, keep in mind these organizations are serving a wide variety of constituents. It is important to avoid postings that can aggravate the market before the firm has had the opportunity to tap into it.

Keep Up with Social Media Trends

There will always be new players in the space who are vying for attention. What will be the next Facebook? What disruptive technology will impact us next? Keep an active, running list of social media and social networking applications; be sure the team is aware of when and how the firm's social media policy applies. If there are areas where it does not apply, and professionals are entrusted with self-monitoring, monitor to ensure this remains the case and is an active dialogue within the organization.

The Great Website Divide

Websites remain a great divide in the world of investment management marketing, even in a digitally driven market economy, immediately identifying the manager as a 'have' regarding branding, focus and professionalism—or a 'have not.' Corporate websites are a dead giveaway as to the resources and focus areas of a firm. Here is a profile of the 'haves' vs. 'have nots' in the realm of manager websites:

The 'Haves': Firms in this camp have created a professional site experience which reinforces their brand and defines what they do. The site speaks effectively to a broad-based audience including institutions and provides a solid profile of the organization. Sites are not necessarily extensive, overly complicated nor high-end, but the 'haves' have checked the box by providing an efficient corporate website that raises no red flags.

The 'Have Nots': Firms in this camp have failed to pass the smell test. In short, the sites stink and create unnecessary red flags, often during a 30-60 second site viewing experience. These firms do have something out there on the web, but it raises more questions than it answers. Sites range from an 'under construction' landing page, to a simple contact page, to a more robust site with details, but the entirely wrong ones. These 'have not' sites are poorly designed. The site promotes other ancillary business focus areas of the firm over the firm's core investment management capabilities, speaks directly to retail audiences about financial planning, and/or demonstrates a lack of core focus on investment management. Often sites are badly dated and fail to provide any calls to action, engagement, or content. Alternatively, they can be so cookie cutter and generic, sourced by generic content providers, and therefore lacking any ability to truly differentiate the firm, its approach, its team or its offerings.

Website Rules for the Road

Let us start by being realistic about the pitfalls of a website that are easy to avoid if seeking institutional investment management market share or any other market share. When a potential investor or research professional does come to check the box, the site must avoid creating any unnecessary red flags. Here are basic best practices for investment management company websites:

1. *Do have a strong web presence* and make sure it is consistent with the brand identity of the firm. The site should work with, and not against, the story being told to the market in person and in writing.

2. *Do not direct institutional investors and research professionals to a website that touts a wealth management practice* and that focuses on financial planning. That is not what the institutional prospects were told the firm is focused on, and not what the firm is proposing to do for the institution. It may even compete with the institution's services if the institutional prospect maintains

its own wealth management client base. The market understands a wealth practice can be helpful in paying the bills as a firm grows but directing institutions to a site that is a contradiction to the skill set being offered to them (institutional investment management, not financial planning) is inherently problematic. A good wealth manager is worried about downside protection, tax planning, and life planning in a vastly different way than a dedicated institutional investment manager. Institutional investment research professionals know from experience that high net worth clients, and thus high net worth priorities, can have a direct impact on performance and what the portfolio is likely to look like.

How can this be reconciled? Begin by having clarity of purpose. If a manager can only support one site, be sure the home page provides a broader message of the firm's value proposition, philosophy about investment management (not about financial planning) and brand, and subsequently and efficiently permits institutional investors to click directly to an investment management capabilities section (related to the strategy(s) marketed). Institutional investment management research professionals do not need to hear anything about hopes, dreams, and taxes; they solely want to understand the managers investment management acumen.

3. *Avoid overly gimmicky, retail-oriented messaging and site experiential content,* at least in the sections where the primary content directed to institutional investors resides. This is particularly important if the content requires the visitor to click on and wait for an extended video to run, for example. The audience often will not click on it anyhow or will not stay long enough to get any value; at this point the site experience has given them nothing to remember the manager by except wasted time and frustration. Managers often think they can force the watching of a video or a focus on certain content by the layering of it within the site's navigation. Right out of the gate, firms

overpower their valuable home page real estate with a focus on the wrong content and too much of it; content may or may not be relevant to the visitor. The beauty of the web is being self-guided by design; the user can quickly navigate through content interesting to them. This flexibility is a double-edged sword. The user can just as easily exit, move on, and/or shut down. Avoid providing a reason to do so.

4. ***Do make the content work by telling the story clearly, precisely, and efficiently.*** Be bold and crisp with wording choice and positioning; make sure the site has an efficient user experience. The site should not be a regurgitation of the firm's overview brochure. It should engage the viewer with key messaging and core content that defines and differentiates the manager, as succinctly as possible.

5. ***Do not waste money overdoing it.*** Quite a bit of time and money can be spent on technologically advanced web applications. Unless the investment offering can seamlessly be invested in online, or the manager has an interactive tool that supports the investment management review process built into the site, extensive site design may not be the best use of capital. Keep it professional, effectively branded, visually appealing and up to date. But do not spend a substantial chunk of the budget on unnecessary bells and whistles.

Website Structural Guidelines

Websites are an assumed component of any firm's infrastructure, along with business cards and a company specific email address for business correspondence. Websites are benefiting from online applications and resources available that permit managers to easily create an efficient and cost-effective online presence and website development is a suitable place to spend resources on a vendor who does this for a living. For under $10,000, a firm can have a custom site built with basic functionality and appropriate security. A 6-8 tab navigation with 10-12 core web pages of content covering key contact information, team, firm philosophy, and positioning is all that is needed. To confirm that a site is competitive enough, visit five competitor sites (competitors managing a similar strategy in the same vehicle structure) and carefully review the depth and breadth of content, along with the level of professionalism (look and feel) of the site experience. It is important to be in the ballpark in terms of overall site experience. It is better, all things being equal, to spend additional budget dollars on engaging through social media and social networking, particularly LinkedIn and Twitter among other business-oriented sites.

In the case of liquid strategies including mutual funds and exchange traded funds, beyond the above referenced minimum infrastructure, the direct feed of daily performance content is the norm, along with the availability of PDF downloads or links for fact sheets, presentations, commentary, and the prospectus.

When it comes to institutional research professionals, they are seeking to confirm a firm's existence and consistency of messaging, and to pull down collateral materials in the form of PDFs where they can. Respondents indicated they are looking to confirm their client will not play a secondary role to a primary wealth management business. They want to hire an investment management specialist and not a jack of all trades.

Keep Digital Engagement in Check

When it comes to online marketing, social media and web presence can be significant consumers of a firm's overall budget. It is important to maximize all unpaid media opportunities. First, create multi-use content and manage post and engagements to a manageable number the market will appreciate without feeling targeted. Yes, it is quite possible to overdo it on social media and websites, having so much 'engagement' that the market tunes you out.

Alternatively, the mere thought of getting online can be so overwhelming that managers are frozen; they are held captive by their own fears of doing it right, doing enough or in determining what to say. Neither path is a good outcome.

Regarding institutional marketing, managers should create an efficient corporate website that effectively represents their brand, and then focus on other aspects of the overall institutional marketing and sales effort. The firm's resources should be spent protecting its brand, educating its representatives, and avoiding the use of social media and social networking in ways that could harm the firm's chances in the marketing and sales process.

Proactive social media and social networking on behalf of the firm and its representatives should be well planned and executed within the context of the firm's budget and priorities. Solid, methodical planning can ease the overwhelming feeling that can come from seeking to address a global, digital society. Be sure your team has implemented basic weekly, monthly and quarterly tracking tools to show the strides you have made, and where additional opportunities to expand will benefit your prospects and clients most.

Find Your Voice

You may hear this concept talked about as story development, differentiators, personal brand, and a myriad of other marketing buzz words. In short, keep it brief, simple, and most importantly interesting! Do not be boring! Bring your own edge to the dance, whatever it may be. Define what matters to you, how you differ and then find your voice within that difference. Bring your best game, not your competitors, to your engagement efforts. It is not about quantity. Those we remember are clear, concise, and interesting!

Your Digital Toolkit

The following tools provide a framework for efficient digital market engagement and oversight:

---

1. Firm Social Media Policy—A formal social media policy is useful in ensuring compliance and protecting the firm's brand. Formally defining social media presence, its goals, and objectives, who can post and what type of content, as well as how social media will be monitored are required internal protocol of any firm seeking to grow assets in the institutional space.

---

2. Digital Marketing Plan—A thoughtful digital engagement plan that builds on the core expertise, messaging and traditional marketing of the firm is paramount to efficient and consistent communications. Take the time to formalize your digital engagement strategy, ideally in tandem with your traditional marketing and sales strategies.

---

3. Communications Calendar [Featuring Traditional and Digital Engagement Activities]—Ensure the team is working from an active communications calendar, communicating regularly to the team regarding posts, content development, events, social media pushes, video creation and web updates to continue to build out the firm's footprint quarterly and annually.

---

4. Digital Update Email—Maintaining a regularly scheduled email communication to the internal team to review posts made and posts occurring within a 1-4 week period can prove pivotal to team engagement. Busy professionals often fail to log into social media to see what the firm is doing. Engaging the team around the firm's social media activities increases reach and improves messaging consistency.

---

5. Digital Engagement Metrics—The marketplace has developed a myriad of analytical tools and resources to permit organizations to track the success of their digital engagement efforts. At the most basic level, increasing followers, shares, likes, and visits are straight forward. However, through SEO and Google Analytics, CRM and email marketing related applications, and technologies designed to engage visitors offering next steps, further conversation and calls to action, organizations can more effectively assess what is working

and share these results with the organization to help drive further content and product development. We will provide one critical warning to those managing budgets and assessing initiatives accordingly: avoid judging an effort too quickly. Creating momentum in a campaign takes time. There is competition in the marketplace for screen time and other organizations providing your ideal customers with content and opportunities to engage at the same time. Give each effort a minimum of six months before determining whether it worked and ensure your definition of 'working' incorporates increased engagement, not necessarily closed sales.

6. Oversight & Training—Completing the framework exercise provided at the beginning of this chapter will assist in defining where the firm is today, both as an organization and regarding individual representative activities. Take the time to define this baseline, set goals, and then determine training and oversight needed to implement your digital plan effectively and efficiently. Digital engagement should be an active element of each individual salesperson's business plan, and the firm's overall business development strategy.

Summary on Digital Engagement

Digital engagement is a critical element of effective business development. Ensure your firm has a clear plan for active and consistent digital online presence.

Maintain a formal digital engagement plan that includes measurable goals.

Ensure the firm's website is efficient in representing the firm's capabilities.

Engage the team in expanding the firm's reach online through their own compliant social media usage.

Measure results to ensure engagement maximization; adjust the plan regularly to take advantage of new opportunities.

CHAPTER 11

A Successful Introduction

RPM Rating on Introductions

DE MINIMIS	CORE	PRIORITY	GAME CHANGER

Finally, the introduction. The firm is ready to dive in to the deep end of the pool. This is the exciting part, after all that hard work to build a team, brand, the best offering possible, and the infrastructure to pursue institutional investors. The firm is ready to make a formal pitch to an institution. Those great numbers are ready to go. This should be easy!

This is a great time for managers to keep their eyes on the bigger picture, remembering the depth of competition discussed in *Chapter 6*. While the firm has been in the weeds, building a track record, and creating the perfect story, institutions have been actively allocating around the world. Institutions can see much farther and wider from their vantage point. Keep in mind the sheer volume of inquiries the typical senior level institutional investment research professional receives. A reported 10-30 new introductions per week on average, coupled with another 50-75 "updates". The competition for attention is fierce. The firm's introduction is a *game changer* according to the *Resource Prioritization Matrix*.

Why Waste a Good Introduction?

Managers may perceive that if they are referred in at a senior enough level, and/or if they can position their "value add just right" with institutions, the institution can and will overlook major flaws in their candidacy. Rarely will this strategy work. Premature outreach is likely to waste valuable time and resources; the firm's and the institution's. Ultimately, the institution's requirements are just that; exceptions are rare. Small variances outside of the guidelines will be tolerated for the perfect "fit" and for spin out teams that are well known in the market, while significant anomalies will not. Introducing too fast, and too aggressively, can in fact delay the ultimate opportunity set. Managers may get their screening and a perceived "at bat", but it will result in a subpar rating (where institutions employ rating systems, particularly common among consultants) and a dubious set of notes in the institut-ion's internal database that are difficult to overcome one or two years from now when the firm *is* a viable candidate. It is difficult to get a mediocre rating, and a poor first impression, overturned. A review of *Chapter 4* in the section *The Natural Progression of Institutional Assets* is valuable in understanding where firms should introduce and when.

Whether connecting in through a referral, having a 'carrot' the firm believes it can dangle in front of the research professional in the form of a name to drop or a connection to be made (more to come on this game of who knows who in later chapters), or whether it's a frozen introduction from nothing at all (aka "cold"), the institutional research professional doesn't care all that much. As the front-line screeners of what is and is not a viable candidate and value-added to their existing portfolios, institutional researchers are more interested in ascertaining quickly what the firm does (in case they have an immediate need for it) and whether the firm is worthy of their limited review time.

The world is built on connections. Imagine if institutional research professionals felt compelled to engage with every manager who knew someone in senior management, or new clients of the institution? That would make for an extremely messy asset allocation. It is indeed their job to be the gatekeepers, avoiding decisions without merit and maintaining a focus on the institution's overall priorities and requirements. Managers too often think of connections as escalation points. Unlike the customer service phone call that isn't going well in which a consumer asks to speak with the manager, in institutional investment management this escalation backfires more often than it leads to an opportunity. Keep this in mind, particularly if the manager's starting position is that they have got a hook and that hook should give them special attention. Ultimately, no matter how aggressively or patiently a manager knocks on the door, it is going to come down to qualification and fit; and whether there is 'room at the inn'.

The Nine Lives of an Introduction

The market norm for an introduction is electronically based and accompanied (perhaps) by a phone call. The introduction is always in a format that is easy to punt: easily trashed, forwarded to friends and colleagues, stored in databases forever, or simply ignored all with the click of a button. This is not what most investment managers wish to hear because they generally believe that their strategy is *so* unique and *so* interesting and performing *so* much better than PIMCO (fill in the blank for manager du jour). Managers deduce, from their own internal analysis and perceived strength of the numbers, that if they can just provide the perfect pitch as they perceive it, assets will come. That perfect pitch means getting the positioning right, and including the right information such that the investment research professional can't help but want to move the ball forward right now, regardless of what else is going on. Where managers and institutions will differ is in their definitions of the perfect pitch—the right positioning, information and timing.

Be Efficient

It is imperative that managers provide an efficient introduction. One that permits the investment research professional to ascertain if this is an area of current interest and if the firm is a viable candidate right out of the gate. The introduction is a *game changer*; it sets the stage for how the firm is perceived in the market and first impressions die hard. Don't make the institution do any weeding today. Give them a clear view of who the firm is and what it seeks to provide. Specifics on introduction efficiency will be provided below.

The Goal of the Introduction

The goal of the introduction is quite simply to get on the radar; to launch the review process and ideally to get a call or a meeting. Consider the introductions the firm has sent out. Go back and look at them; *print them out*. Think about the clarity, depth and breadth of what was sent. Critique the introduction against a variety of variables to be discussed below. What managers might find is that their introduction could benefit from a major overhaul, or at least some meaningful tweaks.

The Introduction Wish List

Not surprising, the consensus among respondents was that succinct introductions are best. That did not necessarily mean less, however. A high-quality introduction will include the key elements needed for a research professional to quickly ascertain if this is a strategy—in a structure—that is timely and worthy of their review. Specific requests were made for:

1. Clear and descriptive subject lines
2. Avoid sending too much or too little—a simple fact sheet or primer and perhaps a presentation to start—not the kitchen sink; not a set of abstract articles, and not solely performance
3. Email body bulleted/numbered
4. Include the below specifics within this basic order and in no more than two paragraphs, or preferably one bullet per topic:
   - Team background and firm ownership
   - Firm and strategy assets under management
   - Offering profile *(asset class, strategy, structure)*
   - Length of track record
   - Key terms
   - Brief statement on differentiation

- Any factual specifics on closing dates/relevant timeliness of opportunity
- Performance

The respondents were mixed on their interest in receiving a phone call before, during or after materials were sent. Some felt it was important to "put the firm on the radar" and encourage a review of the materials. Others acknowledged that they rarely answered their phones and found email to be sufficient. As it is "their job" to review managers, institutional research professionals generally do, and certainly will communicate if an immediate call/meeting is of interest. Lack of a response, of course, typically means there is no immediate need nor interest. Regardless, the manager, or better yet its professional sales resources, will eventually need to pick up the phone and get in front of the research team real time. This is where the finesse of great sales professionals comes in, whether internal or external, to understand the specific organization and to determine who responds best to a call and who does not. Revisit *Chapter 5: Understanding Prospects* regarding identifying the right prospects.

The phone call is certainly considered a best practice in sales, regardless of the product; it's typically necessary to ask "for the order". Managers want to secure a more legitimate and timely review, as well as feedback on the level of interest in the opportunity. The target market is getting hit with 100+ inbounds in an average week. It is the rare email that gets an immediate response of "we can't wait to hear about this manager, get them in here, we are definitely IN!"

Top 12 Introduction Show Stoppers to Avoid

Below is a brief list of highlights identified by respondents regarding what "not" to do with introductions, or anywhere else in the process. Several of these highlights are covered in *Chapter 7: The Firm's Oeuvre— Creating the Content Library*, as they relate to content quality. They are so important that we will review them again here:

1. Do not send a data dump of words, extending beyond the visible screen.

2. Do not send an overwhelming set of attachments.
3. Do not write extended paragraphs full of superfluous and generic language.
4. Do not act too friendly with someone unknown *(i.e. "Hey buddy" is not for someone the sales professional, or manager, has met only once if ever).*
5. Do not provide "cherry picked" performance which is not only a regulatory issue, but an obvious red flag.
6. Do not lead with performance. *(While it should certainly be a key point in the body of the introduction, it shouldn't be in the subject line, nor the first bullet.)*
7. Do not allow typos.
8. Utilize a standard and professional business email format and type face—do not use huge letters, overly stylized fonts, all caps or neon colors.
9. Don't expect that the respondents will click on and watch a video.
10. Don't try to be 'cute' with the introduction to stand out. *(This is an institutional investment management research audience; this is their research time, not their YouTube time.)*
11. Don't follow up within minutes of sending it; give time for review.
12. Don't send the introduction separately to multiple people on the team.

Playing the Field

Another question respondents were asked was regarding marketing directly to field consultants or through known clients, before or simultaneous to reaching out to research. Is this practice welcome? Interestingly, the feedback was mixed. This may be a sign of the times; with fewer resources dedicated to the research process, respondents generally agreed that having a client or field agent introduce opportunities with some knowledge of the manager is value-added among larger consultant firms, but was not as positively received among wealth advisory firms. In the case of wealth advisory firms, researchers tended to receive such 'leads' from clients without the knowledge or expertise to evaluate managers. The research teams felt "cornered" into having to complete a surface level screening of a manager that was clearly not a good fit to appease the client, with no likelihood of an allocation.

Perhaps pursuing both avenues might be the best application of resources; reaching out to the research professionals and letting them know that you have also touched base with XYZ field consultant. Or, that the firm has a relationship with and was referred by ABC client who "may also" bring this strategy to their attention. Regarding large consultants, in many cases it is critical for the sales effort to include reaching out to field consultants rather than simply a single research professional, however this should be carefully timed. Managers and their marketers must be confident that this is an appropriate strategy for the institution, that it meets or is very close to meeting the institution's guidelines, and that the timing is good for this enhanced outreach. If it is simply an exercise in guerilla marketing, the firm will be quickly relegated to the recycle bin.

Questions Asked

Respondents were asked the following questions in bold face text specifically in relation to this chapter. The consensus answers are in italics and immediately follow the question asked.

What initial material do you want to receive from a manager as part of an introduction?
A well-designed email accompanied by a fact sheet, and perhaps a presentation.

Many managers send too much—what key points should be included in an introduction?
A bullet pointed listing of the main attributes of the firm and its offering, including size, length of track record, and any timely details related to closings, capacity constraints, etc.

What should managers lead with/prioritize?
Not performance; a clear definition of the offering and a concise list of their differentiators, as noted above.

What is a door opener? What will peak your interest?
A differentiated strategy, a spin out team, a timely idea, an excellent and lengthy track record well positioned.

What is your view on managers marketing to field consultants/clients in order to gain research prioritization?
Mixed; it can be ok if done professionally and if research is fully engaged. Clients who do not understand investment management due diligence are not the best candidates to push an idea through. Reaching out to the institution's senior management to bypass research is ill-advised.

Any particularly memorable introductions come to mind?
Certainly, but most are not memorable enough in that they are not clear, concise and easy to screen.

Words to Drive By

The following quotes provide a broader sampling of the respondents' direct feedback in relation to the above questions. Firms are encouraged to drive their marketing and sales activities with these rules for the road in mind.

On Initial Material to Send

A well drafted email, succinct, good two paragraphs.

A fact sheet to make sure the portfolio has the construction needs we look for, we have a very specific mandate. Could this fit?

Zephyr/Morningstar fact sheet is not enough; a pitchbook is better. I can do the Morningstar part on my own.

One to two-page fact sheets are useless; [we] need qualitative explanation of what they do, it is not about performance as that is a given. If you have a need you'll look deeper and if you don't you don't.

Traditional strategy the deck is helpful, nontraditional ask for standard DDQ.

We like everything up front, we catalogue it; we want a clear presentation, performance, fees, terms; nothing fancy, brief description of strategy, any points of differentiation against others that do the same thing, one pager is ideal for this; book on team, the five Ps.

Email is most important; executive summary format most useful. Explain track record/strategy/team.

On What Content to Include

[The] strategy and team is [the] quickest way; summary point— not a data dump. A quick snapshot.

I'm a detail oriented person, but at [the] outset [I] need to make a quick determination as to relevance. Go with more as opposed to less so [the] individual can determine if there is enough to reach back out. Sometimes a strategy doesn't fit neatly into a box and might have multiple applications. Sometimes it requires a conversation—so two answers.

Don't use big stats, like lowest volume in ten years. [We] need more specifics on strategy and more depth of information, not a quick stat.

What is differentiated; what makes it high quality, unique. [The] answer could be more team and history, not just the numbers.

The AUM is most important—when you do not see it, it's buried and buried for a reason.

Despite the fact we know we shouldn't, everyone looks at returns first. Return targets/deliverables is key right up front.

On Format

Typos are a big hurdle; it should never happen.

Overly fancy is an issue; too slick on the graphics.

We don't want to have to scroll. If we do its too long.

Don't attach tons of files or links in an introductory email. We just need the basics.

On What to Lead With

Don't lead with performance, I have no idea what fund you are talking about and how to benchmark that.

How do you differentiate your strategy from others in the market, how do you address risks up front. There is more risk for newer firms, what are the points that will offset that?

[I want the] background of the strategy, where does it fit in the firm's line up, buy in from key stakeholders in fund, are PMs invested in the strategy, is the firm invested in the strategy? Strategy specifics, track record; [I] do not want to hear about the Morningstar rating. What is the strategy, what is unique about it and how does it fit, how is it used; track record is secondary.

Intro email must define [what they are doing] within first two sentences; the intro email should be short.

AUM is important only to meet minimum but for us we like really small, not even seeded [managers]; snapshot of record, time and space, info on team and experience.

On Door Openers/Closers

[You] need a subject that grabs my attention; very specific—Private $300M oil and gas on shore.

Be able to read it on your phone; three points only.

People are getting away from buckets and instead looking at opportunity costs, such as what is this strategy v. what I can do myself, i.e. liquid strategies v. illiquid, and risk budget. Managers need to understand these trends.

If it is generic other than [my] name, I skip [it].

What is meaningless is the stats; the annualized return, high sharp ratio, low beta, etc. I'm looking at materials because there is obviously something attractive; [I] prefer to see the qualitative piece. What is the opportunity set now, what it is going forward—pure stats and numbers don't do anything.

On Managers Pursuing Other Points of Entry

It can be helpful if they come from a reliable source.

We have limited resources so getting referrals is useful.

When they try to go around research it never works.

Managers who reach out to our senior management team to force a meeting. They may get the meeting, but they aren't going to get our assets.

We have a process. Managers need to respect that.

On Making It Memorable, in a Good Way

[It is] much more helpful to send a teaser—one pager, then follow up with 'what we are doing and why we think we are better'; give people a chance to digest.

Why is this investment relevant? What does it do for investors/end clients?

[It is a] mistake to put things out there right after great performance, we realize managers and styles are going through ups and downs. A lot show their great one-year number—I want to see what they did in [20]15 to sustain a draw down; consistency. Explain in two minutes or less or you lose the audience.

A one pager, why unique, management team, what role do they see it filling in a portfolio, is it absolute return, market based returns? A lot of managers with a lot of strategies and a lot come in from someone they know like a client or some relative—the amount of volume [of managers to screen] is a lot even with a warm intro so a cold intro must really put your best foot forward.

On What the Institutional Researcher Is Thinking as They Review

We are trying to find the red flag first.

If preliminary checks are satisfied I will look at pitchbook if one is attached to see profile and experience of team. Is there performance that can sell?

We are looking for specific things. We want to see quickly if it meets the requirements we are looking for; we are trying to find something very specific. [Right now we are] looking for concentrated portfolios/number of holdings; [we are also] looking for managers in a certain size—$1B and up is too much for small-cap.

Always have the perspective that we have a lot more downside than upside.

It is on them [the manager]; you've got to be compelling. [The] number one thing I tell managers that I talk to is to presume clients are fully invested at all times; [it is] not always the case but should presume that, so you need to justify kicking someone out. What is going to cause me to take action?

'Uncorrelated returns' is nothing. Everyone says that.

Summary on Introductions

The introduction of a manager sets the stage for the firm's candidacy. Most introductions meet the minimum standards; those that do not are unlikely to recover.

Don't Waste Good Introductions; Wait Until the Firm Is Fully Prepared
Be Efficient; Reach Beyond Research Only if the Timing and Offering Are a Fit
The Firm Gets One Chance to Make a First Impression; Structure the Introduction to Meet Institutional Needs for Key Information

CHAPTER 12

Face Time: The Live Meeting

RPM Rating on Meetings

DE MINIMIS	CORE	PRIORITY	GAME CHANGER

Managers presume that getting the meeting, the opportunity to present the firm's capabilities in-person, whether live or virtual, is the big challenge. This certainly can be the case. However, it is the job and thus the skill of sales professionals to get meetings. It is also the job of institutional research professionals to *take* meetings. Through the ongoing review of investment managers, the research team informs their views and indeed generally seeks to reinforce them over time. Meetings provide the most human of elements to the institutional investment management research process, and for this reason they are considered a *game changer* according to the *Resource Prioritization Matrix*.

Meetings can be a real show stopper or a first step, depending on how well that initial interaction goes. Can a manager recover from a poor meeting? Yes, they can. Over time. A long time. And it is quite rare indeed (as internal databases will hold the research professional's meeting notes on the firm and that subpar meeting for many years to come). In a world of overwhelming and intense competition, it is easier for institutions to simply say "next" rather than giving it another shot. Removing negative perceptions is challenging; institutions have long memories and unlimited choices. Managers are in a buyer's market in the investment management space, not a seller's market at most times and for the majority of asset classes and vehicle structures. *Managers must operate always as if they are in a buyer's market because they typically are.*

What Does the Meeting Mean?

Meetings are meant to inform the research professional about what the institution is signing up for if they were to hire a manager. Here are the questions that institutional research professionals are asking themselves when meeting with a manager. The questions are centered around separating *this* manager sitting across the table, from the thousands of others that the institution has met with over the years:

- What is behind these numbers?
- What is this team all about?
- Can we see their passion?
- Can we learn from them?
- Will our clients benefit from this manager's participation?
- Do they bring something unique and value-added to the table and can they articulate what that is?

These are the highbrow considerations. There are also some infinitely more basic ones that institutions are asking. After all, this is the human element of manager research. Managers must consider these fundamental drivers in the decision-making process, and in how they present themselves:

- Can we work with them?
- Do we want to be in the same room with them?
- Are they presentable?
- Do they seem trustworthy, organized and focused enough for our clients and our portfolio needs?
- Do we like them?

The market uses words like passion, integrity and humility to describe managers they like. In addition, there are unspoken words about how managers are perceived. These words are typically unsaid and matter most. They are the lead balloons of the interaction. Those moments when someone in the room cringes, most often the sales professional, sometimes the manager themselves. Yet with the adept skill of stoicism—the institutional investment management research professional simply takes a mental note. In fact, it is almost universally the case that meetings are perceived to have "gone well" by managers. Then they wonder why, if the meeting went so "well", isn't there any follow up? Why nothing immediate happens? Institutional investment research professionals and experienced sales professionals understand that the meeting is simply a step in the process, and an early one. "Nothing" can happen for one of two reasons:

1. ***It went well, but it's only the first leg of the marathon:*** The manager performed well, and the institutional investment researcher has some interest in tracking the firm, but this is a marathon and not a sprint. It is the normal process and just takes a long time. There is no need for immediate next steps. The institution now has the manager more clearly and visually on their radar and they will actively review what the firm sends and what they say going forward. The institution will keep the firm in mind for potential opportunities; the firm is on a culled short list, but is not guaranteed anything. If there was genuine interest and the manager meets the basic requirements, the institution will start to think about where (and when) the manager might fit in their portfolios and programs. Of the 100+ inbounds the institutional researcher gets in the average week, they are more likely to check in on a manager and to read what that manager sends if they walked away from the meeting with some interest. The firm has been "tagged". For the manager, ongoing communication now becomes more critical. That's the good and bad news. The firm will now have the opportunity and necessity to build the case for their participation in the institution's line up, one follow up at a time.

2. ***It's not a fit:*** It was a courtesy meeting rather than a real opportunity OR the firm didn't fair all that well in the meeting. If it is the former, this is still ok; it puts the firm on the radar and gives the manager a shot at changing that narrative. If it is the latter, there were aspects of the meeting that did not go well enough for any immediate follow up. Unfortunately, it only takes one aspect that is a miss to throw the conversation off track. The institution has said "next" to themselves most likely, but might cordially keep in touch.

Institutional Researchers Own the Poker Face

Institutional investment management research professionals rarely let down their poker face when things aren't going right. However, they are making active decisions throughout the meeting about whether a manager could potentially be a fit and is worthy of further review. It could be as simple as "This is interesting, but this manager is really just too small; we look forward to seeing how they grow and perform over the next few years. Now we have a great baseline from which to start to watch them." It could also be a bit more complex and difficult to communicate, such as "This manager does not have their act together. We would never get them past the investment committee." And yet there is no clear "objection" that the institutional researcher can perceive of providing. In this case it is often the little things that occur, visually and verbally, throughout a meeting that will drive this reaction. Like steering a ship, managers cannot easily change the direction of big things now that they are actively in the marketing process. Such things as time in market, brand awareness, performance, offering and term issues are not easily changed. What managers can address are the little things that might be standing in the way. We will focus in this chapter on those things the manager can control in order to maximize the meeting opportunity.

The Meeting's Objectives

What is the goal of the meeting from the manager's perspective, particularly a meeting of an introductory nature? Ultimately, it is to get through the gate and to advance in the process of institutional asset gathering. Meetings are an opportunity to generate the following:

1. ***Enthusiasm***—about the firm and strategy

2. ***Engagement***—with the institution as a potential partner

3. ***Knowledge***—of the firm's offering(s) and process

4. ***Comfort***—with the firm's team and its approach

5. ***Consideration***—of how the manager's offering could fit into the institution's portfolios moving ahead

Firms are encouraged to build the presentation and the presenter remarks around these five priorities with the objective of advancing post the meeting. To accomplish these objectives, there are many landmines to avoid during the meeting. This is, after all, a game of survival. Can the manager get through the meeting without raising any red flags, leaving the institution with enthusiasm about the firm and strategy, engaged by the prospect of working together, educated about the firm's offering(s), comforted by the manager's representatives, and considering where the offering might fit? It is a tall order yet entirely feasible with good planning.

Let's Meet

Let's unpack the meeting to ensure the firm meets its objectives when the team gets this unique opportunity to connect real time. The goal is to raise no red flags; delivering content that only advances the manager's cause. Aspects of this topic are likely to seem nitpicky if the manager does not appreciate nor understand the importance of presentation. Review it regardless. Even if it does not apply to the firm overall, it likely applies to someone on the manager's team, or someone else that has been hired to represent the manager's brand. Improving the meeting results is one way that firms can improve the odds of institutional success without major firm or offering changes. The firm's goal is to put itself in the driver's seat, leaving the institution with a positive impression and a desire to work together.

Managers miss cues and opportunities, often several times within the introductory meeting. A significant percentage of meetings *"could have gone better"* when respondents are asked to comment on their experiences with introductions. For managers who believe they are "beyond" this topic, keep the poker face in mind and take some time with it. The firm only gets one shot. Perceived "good meetings" that don't lead to next steps in a reasonable period, presuming the manager and strategy has had sufficient time in market, are potential indicators that the presentation could be improved.

First Impressions

It is not unusual for managers to miss the mark in the live meeting setting for some rather benign reasons that could have been avoided. What can managers control in the live meeting? They can control how they look, what they provide for materials and how they interact. Managers and marketers are encouraged to think strategically about their dress and physical presentation when offered the chance to meet research professionals in their offices. In the truest sense, the firm has one chance to make a first impression. This may seem trite, yet dismissing the importance of presence and presentation in the live meeting, when the firm has worked so hard to get this face time, is a major miss by managers.

When the Institution Is "Known"

Even when the manager, marketing or sales representatives know the institutional prospect well, if the firm is new to the institution, the institution must be treated as new to the manager. This is particularly important if the connection is with the sales professionals and they are outsourced agents; their relationship with the institution may have gotten the meeting, but the long-term commitment and connection is to the sales agent and not to the manager. In this instance, the manager is the transient component of the relationship. The institution is screening and considering hiring the firm, not the sales professional.

Perhaps if the manager or their representative was getting together with the institutional researcher just to chat markets and outside of the office, more room for error and providing a 'casual' presence would be acceptable. In the formal meeting process, however, the firm is asking the institution to entrust significant assets to the manager's care and to present the manager as the "best candidate" for a specific mandate to the institution's clients. The firm is assuredly smaller and/or less known than lots of other firms the institution could hire to do the same job. Why create the opportunity for red flags? Why open the door for a "next" vote before the firm gets the opportunity to share its philosophy and process? Why not look the part the firm is telling the institution it is prepared to play?

It's an Interview: Act Accordingly

While the work place has become more casual, and research professionals are often dressed in business casual, the manager and their marketing representative is there on an interview. Careful consideration in knowing the manager audience, and not taking it 'too' casual nor being 'too decked out' is important. Perhaps the modern era and the virtual world we live in have permitted a casual acceptance. Ultimately, we believe dressing professionally still matters, and may even set you apart. Having a very good, quality suit that is in a classic color and not risking the odd colored shirt, the disheveled tie or dress is meaningful—after all this person or team is going to spend the next 45-60 minutes starring at you. What image does the firm want to portray? Haven't we all had interview candidates come into our own offices with literal stains on their tie, an overly flashy outfit or a harsh combination of pinstripes and bright colors? What message did this send? Quite literally, taking the time to have a streamlined and organized appearance promotes the manager as a streamlined and organized candidate. Managers must also consider the environment they are presenting in. A manager visited a global bank in New York City for a meeting with senior investment research professionals. The portfolio manager arrived in a gray pinstriped suit, under which an oddly royal blue colored dress shirt was placed, supported by a bright purple sheen tie. Institutional investment research professionals are just that, they are professional. This dress was not a match to the climate nor culture of the prospect. While there was no stated response to the manager's dress, there was no second meeting either.

Presentation carries forward to the representative's briefcase and materials. A binder full of dog-eared and disorganized papers? Coffee stains? No pen and paper—really? A jumbled compilation of random business cards the representative needs to weed through to hand one of their own out? Not having the presentation primed and ready to launch on screen in a virtual meeting? Not knowing what comes next on the slides you have on screen? Does this demonstrate organization? The institutional investment management research professional(s) are trying to determine if they should bestow upon the manager the ultimate responsibility of managing their client's capital. Make sure the manager's visual representation matches the manager's work ethic and value proposition. All representatives of the firm who could possibly be placed in a client or institutional prospect facing situation should own at least one nice, clean and crisp looking professional outfit. Invest in a decent work bag and be sure that it is organized and ready to easily find business cards, notebooks, pens and materials. In other words, look the part the firm wants to play.

There are the exceptions to this rule; the absent-minded professor, the eccentric intellect. The firm is discouraged from believing it will be one of them. The manager who gets hired to run large pools of institutional assets with no capacity to be "presented" to the institution's client base is an anomaly. Managers cannot afford to bet their businesses on anomalies. Institutional research professionals indicate they are "above" this discussion; they indicate they don't care much about presentation. However, anecdotal evidence certainly suggests that the managers who are most professional (even if eccentric) are those that get hired.

Keep it Simple

Looking professional and organized does not need to be costly, and signs of overdoing it can be equally as problematic. Representatives simply need to represent the firm well. This does not mean they have to hide their personality. Representatives must understand that whatever they bring to the table in visuals, words, and actions is a reflection not just on themselves, but on the firm that hired them, its culture and priorities. Perhaps this seems to be "someone else's issue" and the firm is in great shape in this regard. Or perhaps that little monkey is tapping you on the shoulder, whispering names of professionals who are going to be/have been in the room and for whom there is even the slightest chance they aren't holding their own regarding presence and presentation. Encourage the entire team to read this brief reminder.

"Be Prepared" Is Not Just for the Army

Now the meeting is secured, the team is appropriately dressed, and the firm has the unique opportunity to spend one-hour with the research professional(s) from the target institution. Meetings are a *game changer*. They are expected to be solid, but anyone can have a bad meeting, a bad day, a bad moment. As a result, they tend only to be a game changer if the manager raises red flags through their presence and presentation that did not exist prior. Investment managers often will say, "well, if we could just get in front of XYZ, we could show them why we would be a great fit." Research professionals have done their homework (if it's a worthwhile meeting in the first place) and they already have a preconceived notion of whether the strategy and team is a fit and timely. They know whether this is a courtesy meeting, if they are genuinely interested, or it is something they wish they could do, but don't have a mandate for at present. The bulk of this chapter is about what happens once the team is inside; now that the firm is taking up someone else's time, and has spent the manager's resources to get there. There is little sympathy and no patience for a lack of preparation. Firms shouldn't have any either.

Take a Seat: Let's Get the Party Started

From the moment the team walks in the door what happens? Where do managers and marketers falter, what works regarding format and content and what questions do research teams like to ask for which managers should have answers before they enter the room?

Sit Strategically

Most managers and sales professionals intuitively understand the value of productive seating arrangements and do a great job in terms of identifying the best placement of team members. The primary presenter should sit across from the research professional(s), and there should not be a distracting view behind the primary presenter. Secondary presenters sit on either side of the primary presenter. Marketing and sales professionals who are not anticipated to be key contributors to the dialogue by design, are wise to sit between the manager and the research professionals, in clear view of both, as if the referee on no one's 'side'. In the live meeting, one is the sales agent's manager client, and the other is their investor client. This seat location gives the marketing and sales professional a bird's-eye view and the ability to jump in strategically, without being a visual distraction to the main event. If this is not possible, sales professionals are encouraged to sit at the end of the row, to the side of the secondary presenter(s). For virtual presentations, have a corporate background defined in advance and be consistent.

Introduce Everyone

If more than one person is attending the meeting, be sure that everyone is appropriately introduced. Permit and encourage the institutional research professional(s) to do the same. Everyone wants to feel heard and loves to find connections which often occur when backgrounds are discussed; this is human nature. ***This does not mean, however, that managers should waste valuable meeting time taking a long trip down memory lane.*** Simply that everyone in the room should be introduced and their primary focus and any highlights of background should be noted (particularly if the manager has prepared well, having looked in advance into the background of the research professionals through their firm's website and on LinkedIn or another relevant social networking site, and identified any natural connections of schooling, places of employment or residence, activities enjoyed, etc.) This pre-planning is not to suggest nor encourage name dropping, which is ill-advised by research professionals (especially calling out senior people in the researcher's own organization). What is well received are experience related connections. This is a connection worth making before diving in, provided it is brief and to the point. That common nod and smile the team will get when relating to a place, experience or outside interest with an institutional research professional will certainly set the meeting off on the right foot. Make the connection and then get to work.

Virtual PM Participation

Research professionals understand that if the manager is with them, they are not working on the portfolio at that moment. They respect managers that want to be in the office perfecting their craft. Institutions understand that if they were the client, they would want the manager's time spent on marketing to be limited. Yet, they won't invest without knowing the manager. Managers are strongly encouraged to get face time with institutional prospects at least once and ideally as early in the process as possible. The meeting can in effect "start the clock" more formally than just a phone call or sending materials, certainly when the request comes from the manager and not from the institution. However, where and when this is not possible, dialing in a portfolio manager (PM) can be effective. Institutional investment management research professionals indicated a great deal of comfort and acceptance for dialing in PMs. It was not their first choice, but a viable one, per respondents.

In this case, however, it is important to plan for what the portfolio manager will address, ideally being introduced up front and then muting the phone line until it is time to talk. The PM should plan to speak to her/his philosophy, process and portfolio examples. Those in the room should cover the rest of the meeting, leaving the investment core to the PM and completing the remainder as interactively as possible. A prepared plan of attack, with a team member in the room assigned to recapping for the portfolio manager and prompting the manager into the dialogue is imperative. Firms can improve the efficiency and results of a virtual PM by ensuring there is an active counterpart in the room guiding the conversation. This appointee should determine when the manager is asked to jump in v. leaving this interplay to chance. In addition, see important comments related to conference calls below, which would apply to the PM who is dialing in.

The Value of Product Specialists

Managers get excited about the notion of a "Product Specialist" who can be the presenter: a colleague who wants to do the dog and pony show, representing the firm while the manager remains laser focused on the portfolio. Sounds good, right? Larger institutions tend to have the product specialist position in place, yet the reviews are lackluster. Respondents noted a comfort level with product specialists as stand-ins for a portfolio manager only in two instances:

1. For updates when the institution has already had the opportunity to meet and interact with the portfolio manager.

2. When the product specialist is extremely knowledgeable and actively engaged with the portfolio management team.

The first of these criteria is more often met than the second. Respondents noted that most product specialists, estimated at 75% or more, "are not knowledgeable enough to carry a meeting". They understand and support the need for the role, yet repeatedly indicated that the product specialists they have interacted with are, overall, underwhelming. Institutional investment research professionals have limited time and specific questions. For firms that elect to utilize a product specialist model, a few suggestions to make this role as effective as it can be given respondent feedback:

1. ***Product Specialists Should be Active in Internal Investment Meetings***
   The product specialist(s) should sit in on internal investment committee meetings and other investment oriented team meetings as often as possible to ensure their full understanding of the firm's philosophy, process and current portfolio. If this is not possible, portfolio manager(s) should have a call with the product specialists no less frequently than bi-weekly.

2. ***Product Specialists Must Practice the 'Pitch' Extensively with PMs***
   The product specialist should practice extensively with the portfolio manager(s) to ensure their understanding of the team's desired positioning and information disclosures. This should include a broad-based Q&A and detailed review of specific portfolio positions, timing of trades, etc.

3. ***Product Specialists Must Bring Portfolio Analytics with Them on the Road***
   Whether the manager or the product specialist will be presenting, both should have the complete portfolio breakdown on hand to efficiently answer as many questions as possible during the meeting.

4. ***Managers Still Need to Show Up***
   Ultimately, the institution is hiring the firm, it's portfolio managers and investment team to manage a significant pool of assets. No other resources can replace the portfolio managers during the due diligence and onboarding process. Showing up and building a direct relationship can be pivotal for managers seeking institutional mandates.

Start Where the Prospect Is

Once the typical chitchat is out of the way, ask how the institutional research professional would like to use the time and how much time there is for the meeting. Managers will benefit from starting where the prospect is; addressing what the institution wants to address, when they want to address it v. forcing the prospect through a format and timetable that is the manager's own. Before diving in, go ahead and provide the materials burning a hole on the manager's end of the conference room table with the assurance that there is no expectation of reviewing them page by page. Respondents repeatedly requested "a conversation", and much less page turning. Managers tend to fall into two camps: those who hold the materials hostage until the very end, requiring the researcher's undivided attention without the benefit of visual aids, and those who pass materials out immediately and say, "let's start on page two". Neither extreme is preferred.

Give Up the Goods

Managers who withhold the materials, typically do so thinking it is best to wait until the research professional has asked something that requires referring to a specific page or section. They know that a page by page review of the deck is unwanted and they fear losing the research professional in an individualized exercise of thumbing through the materials while the manager is trying to present. Alternatively, managers who give out the materials they have brought to the meeting right away tend to be overly reliant on them, wanting to cover most, if not all, of their contents.

Research professionals indicated a preference for receiving materials up front, unless they have brought their own printouts (often already marked up) to the meeting. Go ahead and hand it over. Trust the discussion will be interesting enough to keep their attention and use the materials to the manager's advantage as discussed below. Research professionals are also particularly good at thumbing and listening simultaneously. The presenter should not permit this to be a distraction nor a crutch. Keep moving and stay on point. Managers are typically good at this as they are passionate and excited to be talking about their firm, philosophy and process. As is the case with most things in a live meeting, rolling with whatever happens will always provide the best outcome.

Time Management

Time availability deserves special attention. Institutional research professionals are "busy" (aren't we all) and they often book meetings back-to-back. Confirm that the meeting is set for the standard one-hour, and that the manager comments will be kept to 30-40 minutes right off the bat. Encourage the researcher(s) to jump in with questions at any time. The more interactive the better; respondents consistently indicated a preference for a dialogue over any formal presentation. Keep in mind, however, that the firm has a set of content it does want to present, whether simply through a conversation, through the formal presentation, or a combination of the two. Additionally, many humans are visual learners and they may not have reviewed any materials previously sent. Do not permit the open dialogue to limit the information exchange.

Have an agenda, if not in writing than certainly in mind to ensure that nothing significant is missed. Managers can often go on tangents; while the discussion is good in many ways, key elements of the firm's offering are missed. Follow up can happen later, and it is most critical to use the time as the institutional researcher desires. Nevertheless, the manager has the responsibility to deliver what it came to provide. A formal agenda helps to ensure this, but it can be accomplished through a simple check list that the manager has at the ready as well. A quick glance at the list near the conclusion of the time allotment will ensure nothing significant was skipped.

The one-hour slot may be standard, but sometimes research professionals have less time. Researchers may lead off the discussion, particularly if this is more of a courtesy meeting, with "we only have 30 minutes". This is always hard to hear, coming across as quite harsh and dismissive. After all, the manager worked hard, paid money and took their time to get there. Don't let it throw the conversation off course. Simply dive in quicker and move more efficiently, getting to the heart of what the firm does and how they do it. The firm should have a prepared elevator speech anyhow, and pivoting to this as a high-level review, then focusing in on the investment process in the time allotted is an efficient model with or without the time constraint. In short, managers should always present as if they are under a reasonable time constraint. This does not mean rushing; it means remaining cognoscente of the time and specific content the meeting format is meant for. Content the institution cannot simply read on their own to gain a broader understanding of the manager, its philosophy and process.

When Time Is Limited

When the team is notified that the time will be shorter than expected, it might be helpful to say, "given you are short on time today, which we certainly can appreciate, let's jump right into our philosophy and process if that is ok with you? We can always circle back on our firm's history and team when you have more time or later in the presentation if you want to, does that sound good?" This acknowledges the institution's constraints as a good partner would, demonstrates efficiency with the manager's time and the institutions, and puts the manager back in control of the meeting.

The 30-minute mark can come and go anyhow, provided the research professional leading the charge is interested. Do not let this unexpected and often unenforced limitation throw the meeting. Roll with it and tighten up the content delivery. The manager's ability to be flexible is a sign of the team's capacity to manage change and deal with disappointment right out of the gate. If the research professional is truly tied to a 30-minute window, the meeting goes well, and the manager was respectful of the time limitation, the manager is more likely to get the follow-on meeting which is the ultimate goal—to keep the ball rolling.

Be on Point

In speaking with one senior research professional from a major consulting firm, she describes a scenario in which she takes a preliminary meeting with an investment manager at the strong suggestion of a colleague. While she finds the numbers exceptional and the story quite compelling on paper, when the manager came in he was *"meandering"* and couldn't stay on point. This was not enough to eliminate the firm from consideration. However, in a follow up discussion with her colleague about whether to consider this manager further, after jointly reviewing the numbers and the portfolio fit for which both agreed this was a good candidate, she mentioned to her colleague that the manager was "meandering" in the meeting. The colleague immediately replied it would not work, the client they had in mind would not tolerate that presentation style and was keen to meet all the underlying portfolio managers.

This scenario is not unique. In fact, as one might imagine, this is a rather benign complaint. More significant ones relate to physical appearance, organization of presentation, content and spoken words, focus in meetings, inappropriate conversations about taboo subjects like politics (one better really know one's audience and who their clients are in this case) and culture, inappropriate technology interruptions and lack of general preparedness. Be on point from beginning to end.

Practice Makes Perfect

Enough books have been written about preparedness; managers know that they need to be prepared. Presenters should not be looking at the content in their own presentation, and troubleshooting standard questions, for the first time in a live meeting. This occurs too often. Know where content falls within the presentation; memorize page numbers for key pages, and the content in those pages. Despite rounds of presentation review, updates to content and discussions of the audience, it is surprising how often managers seem thrown off by their own content. Perhaps this is because institutional investment management research professionals are adept at asking questions and looking for the places where they have seen managers fall before, in the same asset class, at the same firm size, in that same room.

Managers will often say "we've got this" and "we are all set". Yet, in meetings managers have uttered such words as "hold on…let me review this" and "I think we have that here somewhere, let me see", expecting an infinitely long pause to be acceptable as they dig for what they weren't prepared for. *The Hail Mary is not in the pages of the presentation*. The ball has already been thrown. The game is over. Managers cannot afford to waste their own precious meeting time while they regroup and study, perhaps reading for the first time what is on their own slide.

Another common failure, despite the best attempts at preparation, is the portfolio manager who says, "I don't have the answer to that question—we will have to get back to you". This might be ok for a very technical and time specific question, but it is not ok when asked generally about a holding listed in the manager's portfolio, about why something was bought or sold, or how the team and process works.

Portfolio managers must have portfolio examples, along with portfolio holdings and characteristics in front of them when presenting. These exhibits can be kept confidential but should be within arm's reach. Know the content, inside and out. Every person who will be in the room and whom may be asked a direct question, should have completed the following protocol before any meeting:

1. Full review of the materials that have been sent to the institution prior to the meeting *and* those that will be presented in the meeting.

2. Prepare any additional exhibits or 'internal use only' printouts that might be needed as reference tools to answer questions about the portfolio and its holdings, timing of trades and rationale, etc.

3. Practice the presentation and Q&A with a live audience and/or with a phone audience at least twice before the first live meeting and again when the core materials, story or examples change.

4. Look up the institution and the institutional researchers the firm is scheduled to meet with to understand their background, the institution's mission and structure. Seek to make the firm's comments as relevant as possible to the prospect.

The Meeting Framework

Managers can get caught spending way too much time on elements that are unnecessary in a live meeting. Avoid areas that are undifferentiated, areas that the research team can easily review on paper (and probably already have). Where the portfolio manager went to school is a check the box; the detailed history of how the firm's partners first met X years ago is a quick statement, not a saga. Most importantly, it is not worth the time away from the core topic—what the manager is doing in the world of investment management, and what it is proposing to deliver to this institution right now. The most important question of all, why this solution is better than what the institution already has or could have, must command the lion share of the time. ***It should not take 20 minutes to get into the meat of the presentation.***

A manager was starting up in the market and had scheduled some webinars to introduce their approach and strategies. In timing the agenda, a full 20 minutes was spent on the history of the organization and how the partners met to kick off the call. On a webinar no less! Even interested parties will have a hard time not hanging up, or more likely shifting their attention away from the call all together; 20 minutes can be a lifetime on the phone. This lengthy intro didn't help the audience understand what the manager was doing and how it would work in client portfolios. It was in effect a waste of time and a lot of it; it got the manager no closer to raising assets.

It is always appropriate to ask if there are specific questions, or areas the researcher would like to focus on. If it is background information they are most interested in, then the focus is warranted. If nothing is immediately raised as a top priority, stick to an efficient framework with four or five preselected pages that the firm will specifically refer to within a hard copy deck or on screen/tablet, no more and no less. Whichever way the manager elects to run the meeting, the meeting should never start with "let's turn to page two". Here is a general framework to keep a meeting on track. Time the presentation repeatedly to ensure that the right amount of time is being spent on key areas. Attention spans are short, thanks to modern technology. The firm's story isn't intriguing enough to overcome that for very long no matter how good it is.

Sample Introductory Meeting Framework

I. ***Agenda/Meeting Priorities Confirmation:*** Two minutes—either brief review of planned agenda confirming it meets expectations, or request for the institution's priorities for the meeting.

Goal: Ensure buy in on content to be covered; introduce the notion that the manager is a team player, here to serve the institution and its clients, focusing first on where the institution is.

II. ***Firm Overview:*** Five minutes—firm roots/history, time in market, core competencies, organizational profile (not an AUM focus), client profile, capacity.
Goal: Efficient history and update on organization.

III. ***Team Overview:*** Ten minutes—team members, how they work together, how the manager's day-to-day process works.
Goal: Establish depth; demonstrate experience; give the team a voice.

IV. ***Philosophy and Offering(s) Profile:*** Ten minutes—what the firm believes in and what product(s) manifest that belief; a brief reference to performance and attribution pages in the appendix (generally one product and only one product should be the manager focus in a single meeting; derivative products are appropriate if they are an active part of the story and investable by institutions).
Goal: Effective positioning of the firm and what matters to it; explanation of what product(s) the team has available in which to manifest the manager's views.

V. ***Product Fit:*** Five minutes—how clients are using the strategy; where the manager perceives the product to fit in a diversified portfolio; benchmark comparisons.
Goal: Assist professional(s) in understanding where and how the product can fit in a diversified portfolio to help support the case for its value and complementary nature.

VI. ***Investment Ideas/Current Market Views:*** Ten minutes—specific perspectives and investments and how they fit; lessons learned and a minimum of three case studies/investment examples

that inform the institutional researcher(s) about the manager's process, showing varied examples and outcomes.
Goal: Clearly define the role of the product and where others are using it/considering it for an allocation in light of current market conditions.

VII.   *Q&A:* Five to twenty minutes—have prepared two additional examples to cover if no immediate questions are asked.
Goal: Relationship building; establishing a direct dialogue and open forum for asking questions.

VIII. *Recap:* Summary and review of next steps.
Goal: To advance the discussion.

Note: Performance is not referenced as a primary category in the above outline. That is because the firm wouldn't be there without it. It has already been reviewed. If the researcher has questions they will ask. It is suggested that managers merely acknowledge the performance in the appendix or at the end of the presentation. Performance should not be a significant focus of the manager meeting time.

Red Flag: Multiple Products

What products the firm has is a dicey conversation when the firm is trying to present more than one at a time to institutional investors. For large firms with a wide variety of products, institutions generally expect to see a single page exhibit which profiles each available offering across a basic range of metrics. The risk of the multiple product focused firm is particularly significant for smaller organizations. The notion of showing multiple strategies is overwhelming and raises more questions than it answers. Yes, the manager's AUM breakdown and overall story will cover the fact that they have certain offerings, ideally presented in a visual pie chart for quick reference without the need for a product by product review. If the manager starts down a rabbit hole of product offerings with "this one is actually closed" or "this one is for our high net worth investors" or "this one is brand new"—none of this is helpful!

In addition to the constraints of time, institutional research professionals are adept at knowing what is "realistic" for a team to manage, and what is most relevant. Work with the marketing and sales team to ensure that the firm is focusing on what product is its best foot forward, avoiding the natural obsession to throw everything at the wall to see what sticks. For marketing and sales professionals, the challenge of managing a portfolio manager's expectations on how much can effectively be shown is real. Fight back the urge to give in. It will not im-prove the manager's sales in the institutional investment management space, it will detract from them.

Monitoring the Manager's Perspectives and Attitudes

Presenting to institutional research professionals can not only be daunting, it can be quite frustrating. The research professionals are often younger, sometimes significantly so, than the manager. They may be less experienced than the manager thinks they should be, without the perceived ability to give meaningful feedback or to move the needle in any significant way. These concerns of managers may, or may not, be valid. Managers tend to react in two ways to research professionals they perceive as either too junior or ineffective. In some cases, they elect to pursue other institutional contacts at the same organization in a concerted effort to expand their presence. Getting to the decision makers rather than to the junior research staff is of course the goal and often a necessity, yet starting with the research analyst assigned to the specific manager, asset class or structure is required. When a manager attempts to circumvent the process and in so doing, offends the institutional research professional, no matter how junior they are perceived to be, the manager is shooting himself in the foot.

The other response of managers who are frustrated by the process is delivering a negative tone. Managers must do their very best to stay as positive as they can no matter what is thrown at them. Carefully consider tone and wording to ensure it is not overly judgmental or exacerbated. Avoid the desire to question the research professional; they don't like to be put on the spot and they don't need to be. The institution is not the one interviewing. The manager is. The manager is a subject expert and that is the persona they need to project; professional and polite, always positive, upbeat and engaging. This can be challenging at times. Managers generally do a good job with it, but there are times when frustration bubbles up and it is apparent. Managers must manage their own expectations, and be cognoscente of how they project their frustrations in relation to the institutional asset gathering process.

Top 10 Meeting Moments to Avoid

Top 10 answers that will not generate the desired outcomes from respondents in a meeting:

1. Dull, monotone, boring and overly scripted presenters.
2. *"I don't know."*
3. *"We don't really have a limit/rule about X, Y or Z."*
4. *"That's a great question, I should have [data] in front of me, but I don't."*
5. *"We don't disclose that."*
6. *"We don't have anything 'formal' on that, but it's basically what we do."*
7. Meandering, never ending answers; flipping through the deck looking for content.
8. Lack of specific examples.
9. Inability to address any statistic or holding related questions.
10. "Yes" or "No". *(This is a great start, but should always be expanded upon; meetings are not the time for a game of 20 questions.)*

How long did the firm wait to get this meeting? How much effort was poured into getting in that room? How is the team not prepared for any possible question that could come up on the manager's own process and portfolio?

Virtual Participation Dos and Don'ts

Sometimes face to face is not possible. Virtual participation and meetings, and occasionally dialing in the PM, will be a part of the sales process. These exchanges count as meetings in the minds of research profession-als. Decorum is required in an effective conference call because the manager does not have control; there is no assurance that the manager has the researcher's undivided attention. Here are a few rules for the road:

1. ***Meet Mute:*** Conference call participants, including the present-ers, need to have an appreciation for, and active use of the mute button. Background noise is problematic; the sound of computer screens clicking and beeping, people in the background, kids and dogs, and other phone calls coming in are all distracting. Even the primary presenter is not immune from at least some of these background noises no matter where they are. Actively utilize mute and unmute to manage the background noise on a call. Once on mute, don't forget to turn it off when it is time to speak. How many times have participants waited patiently for someone to answer a question only to hear them say "oh so sorry—I had myself on mute". As benign as it sounds, this is a poor use of everyone's time and may mean the presenter, who asked for the meeting in the first place, is not really paying attention either. A conference call is a meeting; it is an active dialogue and should be treated as formally and focused as an in-person meeting. Presenters should have a hand near the mute button; active and efficient use of this feature goes a long way towards maximizing the efficiency of a call. Those not presenting should always be on mute.

2. ***Make It Interactive:*** Thanks to the advent of modern technology, the majority of us are easily distracted and expect information to be delivered instantaneously, and in bite-sized segments we can efficiently digest. Plan accordingly. For a conference call based meeting or a webinar, increase the agenda's interactivity by building in even more dialogue through active Q&A. Throughout a conference call, the presenter is constantly at risk for having the audience drawn to something competing in the

room they are in, on their cell phone, on the very screen next to the manager presentation, or out the window. Make certain the presenter is not distracted by these things. This is the manager's time; maximize it. Plan for exactly what questions will be asked to engage the audience, what content will be shown to draw their attention to the screen, and how frequently the content will be rotated. Managers will often park on a single screen and talk incessantly. Regardless of the value of the content, this monotony and lack of engagement will lose the audience quickly. Yes, the box will be checked and the "meeting" will have been had, but going through the motions is all that has been accomplished.

3. ***Dogs and Kids Need Not Apply:*** We all get the work from home concept; business has continued to move in this direction. Working remotely is a gift for those who can take advantage of it effectively. No matter how much we all love kids and dogs, however, they are a distraction at the very least, and a redirection at worst. As many of us have dogs and kids, when we hear them in the background we logically start thinking about our own kids and our own dogs…why aren't we working at home? What are they doing right now? Do they sound similar? Could we work with that going on? It's a slippery slope that the presenter can't afford. Plan conference calls when these background noises can be extremely limited if not eliminated in their entirety. It might be cause for some nice conversation, but it won't move the needle towards getting the firm hired.

4. ***Timing Matters:*** Plan calls for effective business hours. Avoid scheduling during the lunch hour when the audience might literally be more interested in having their lunch—or what is for lunch—than on chatting with the manager. Friday late afternoon conference calls are also ill-advised if maximizing the audience's attention is of interest. TGIF syndrome is real. Yes, there are those professionals who claim, "I never eat lunch" and "Friday afternoons are my best time". For the common denominator of

professionals, skip these times anyhow. This conference call is the firm's time and the manager deserves undivided attention. Schedule conference calls wisely.

5. ***Avoid Hold:*** Managers should never say "hold on" during a conference call in which they are an active participant. Even managers are not immune from a "must do" small task of "checking something" or "addressing something". This is not acceptable and will result in a quid pro quo in the form of lost attention. Remain diligently focused on the call, from beginning to end.

6. ***Define Next Steps:*** No different than a face to face meeting, the firm needs to clearly define and encourage next steps. This is more easily accomplished in person. Unlike a live meeting where there is a natural transition out of the content and out of the room, conference calls often end abruptly due to time or interest or both. Managers must attempt to efficiently recap their value-added and to suggest next steps. A recap should be prepared before getting on a call. The most obvious next step is to discuss the possibility of face time in the future. Whether the conference call was the solution due to the institutions schedule and interest, or the manager's schedule, the most efficient next step is to meet in person. Be sure to raise this notion before hanging up the phone, ideally setting a target time frame for this interaction. It is always appropriate to end by inviting the institutional researcher to visit the firm's offices. Everyone appreciates a warm invitation; it sends the message that the firm is ready to host and believes a site visit will demonstrate its capabilities in meeting the institution's needs.

Questions Asked

Respondents were asked the following questions in bold face text specifically in relation to this chapter. The consensus answers are in italics and immediately follow the question asked.

What is your favorite meeting format? Book? On screen? Conversation?
A Conversation, with a book.

How important is having some handout?
Very.

When do you want the handout in a meeting?
Right away.

Who needs to be in the meeting for it to be of value to you? PM? Firm rep?
Prefer the PM, particularly because the alternative is generally not knowledgeable enough.

Does dialing in a PM work?
Yes.

What was your worst meeting experience? Any manager 'don'ts' come to mind?
Tons. [Read on.]

What questions do you like to ask?
See responses below; they aren't about performance.

Words to Drive By

The following quotes provide a broader sampling of the respondents' direct feedback in relation to the above questions. Firms are encouraged to drive their marketing and sales activities with these rules for the road in mind.

On Meeting Materials

Pitchbook is key but I don't like to be lead through it, I've already reviewed it.

I like the pitchbook, [I] take notes in it; I do prefer a PDF in advance so we can store it and I can review it.

For an intro I find a book is really helpful particularly if I'm not familiar with the firm, that's a critical piece of the due diligence. I want to spend a lot of time understanding how the firm operates.

We much prefer a book and a conversation rather than a formal page by page.

I don't like the mini books, they drive me nuts. And I find a projector or iPad distracting; stick with the regular book.

We like to see a three-ring binder of research reports so we can just scan through; it helps mold the investment process.

Large firms should have a single overview/matrix.

On Meeting Format

I like to review a book before a meeting and then prefer a conversation and prefer to steer it away from a monologue; better conversation results in people buying in. Manager should plan to reference no more than five pages in a deck; the more interactive with the manager the better.

I still prefer the printed book but [we are] trying to get away from paper, when [XYZ Firm] came in last they actually had iPads in the room and the presentation on it and the pages that were relevant to what we wanted to talk about; they had enough iPads for everyone in the room, that was a pretty good use of technology.

Yes, the old-fashioned pitchbook is good so long as it's not an encyclopedia; flip to different pages. Technology is hard to disseminate or so watered down by compliance and marketing that it's not a real flavor for what's going on.

Some managers will bring in real output of models, or portfolio management which is useful if done well; sometimes a fine line if its in 4-point font and you can't really see it and they are taking it back, other times they are really prepared to explain it. [This content is] good for a subsequent meeting, good for on-sites.

We just had a meeting and the manager started with 'please turn to page 64....' UGH!!!

On Meeting Participants

95% of firm reps don't know the strategy well enough; we need the PM.

There are good firm reps but for me even at an intro meeting its best to meet with the PM to cut down two meetings into one meeting—the PM is the one you'll be backing and you need to have a sense of trust and comfort with the PM so why add a barrier.

Ok with product specialists but not with consultant relations person because they don't know enough; [we] want someone from the investment committee.

Intro meeting doesn't require the PM; IR person is fine, marketing person, analyst all fine.

Don't necessarily want the PM, more active the strategy the less I want to see the PM; a good institutional rep is fine for 95% of it, plus PM is not always easy to talk to anyhow and taking away from [their] own strategy if they are talking to me.

On Product Specialists

First brush it's ok but if the institution is interested enough to inquire than you need access to a PM.

Run the gambit of skill set and you might as well be talking to the PM, others are not as strong, at some point in the due diligence process we want to talk to the PM, but initial meeting it's not necessary.

I have a lot of respect for people that are true product specialists but very few firms have this unless it is a very large firm.

Product specialist only works if they were once on a team, if they were once an analyst.

On Dialing in PMs

Works if PM is in London and the manager in NY, all else being equal its better face to face.

Works great; analysts are driving decisions and PM makes final— so we want to talk to both. [The] best meeting is in their office to see more of the team anyways.

More effective face to face because engaged in a conversation, see body language, I can see the manager reaction, etc.

PM can't really be on the road, in meetings/marketing—1 in 4 product specialists are actually good; good for first meeting only, then meet onsite to meet PM.

Conference call is a wash; a bit awkward, but if PM is really good at it then it works out ok, but not always the case, better once we know them, and are close to having them online.

WebEx loses you very quickly; I can do many other things at the same time.

On the Institution's Meeting Goals

You have to listen to what you are being told and look for what is being hidden, what are they avoiding and that is where I want to steer the conversation. I'm digging for coal, not gold.

I ask tough questions to see how they react; biggest knocks are aggressiveness and high expectations that come out through the way that they communicate.

I want the handout at the beginning, so I know I have it.

Exhibits are best—worst meetings are sitting there flipping through the pages of a presentation deck. I want to see specifics.

As much as possible before that call happens its critical to find out what is important to that investor. What does the gatekeeper really want to know v. what they have shared with you, this comes on with marketing—we've already heard the story so really just needs to be more of the meat, more specific examples, most interesting— how do you think? What do you do? Why is portfolio positioned the way it does? What are some of the mistakes you've made in the past? Give a greater look behind the curtain. Basically humanize it, don't talk 'at' it.

Have a dialogue that is constructive; what do you [the institution] REALLY want to know? How do we best use the time for you? It means you are making it matter to me AND using PM time the best.

On Questions Institutional Researchers Like to Ask

The organizations goals/direction; how long-term incentives are aligned with clients. I'm amazed with how little transparency there truly is in terms of how people get paid; the structure is set up to fail—it is not set up for the success of clients, just gets the head of the firm very wealthy.

Focus on what delivers performance to the client. If it is the analysts how are they structured and how are they paid; not just their titles.

Retention tools, because professional turnover is a very hard sell; it tells me how the team might manage the portfolio differently depending on that.

Qualitatively, where does the firm spend their money; does the value manager take cheap flights or stay at the Ritz?

Five-year plan is huge—it's a business before an investment firm; [it takes] a legitimate, logically backed process, patience and a lot of working capital.

Some of the most interesting are when managers aren't doing well— we want to ask about that, what happened and what was learned.

Specific examples that show the process and tell me if they really know their holdings, why they are in them and why they got out and what was happening in the market when they did.

Summary on Meetings

An introductory meeting can make or break a firm's candidacy.

Understand the Meeting's Objectives; Meetings Are an Important First Step Regardless of Immediate Need
First Impressions Last a Lifetime; Raise no Red Flags
Be Prepared; Bring the Firm's "A" Game

CHAPTER 13

Tech in the Room

RPM Rating on Use of Technology in Meetings

DE MINIMIS	CORE	PRIORITY	GAME CHANGER

Technology has infiltrated our society. Thanks to the global pandemic, the move to virtual and digital communications has only accelerated. However, as live meetings return (we are humans after all), the role of integrating technology into the live meeting setting is worth careful consideration. Does the institutional investment management research professional appreciate the inclusion of technology in live meetings? Most commonly applied using an iPad or computer-based presentation, the use of technology is *de minimis* at best according to the *Resource Prioritization Matrix*.

Factors to Consider in Technology Use for Meetings

Respondents were either neutral or negative regarding the use of technology in most cases; where technology was *"not a plus"*, it was a distinct negative. Why impact the limited face-to-face time the firm has been granted in a potentially negative way? Managers and their marketers would be wise to consider the following in determining if technology can and should play a role in their live meeting agenda:

1. *The goals and stage of the interaction:* Later stage and follow on meetings are the best place to consider integrating technology, when the manager wants to shake things up and provide a deeper view into what they do and how they do it, having the basic underpinnings of a relationship with the prospect already in place.

2. *The technological savvy and usage of the prospect:* Sales professionals may consider asking institutional research professionals, as a component of their meeting preparation, if the researcher is open to/interested in technology use in the meeting. If there is a specific component of the process that is ideal to show in this way, it is useful to highlight this upfront.

3. *The technological savvy and usage of the manager/marketer:* In this case, both the creation of the content interface and the professionals tasked with delivering it should be carefully considered.

4. *The value of using technology in relation to the strategy being presented:* Is it a highly technical, quantitative strategy, or a hands-on, fundamental approach?

5. *Is technology critical?* Does it permit the firm to present something it could not present otherwise in a face to face meeting?

Technology's Application in Meetings

Where could technology be a differentiator in the room with an institutional research professional? The use of technology as a dynamic visual aid could keep the meeting interesting. However, it requires a separate element of focus; a divergence significant enough that it may inherently take away from the point of meeting in-person. The research was anticipated to be mixed on the topic of technology use in live meetings, and it was. However, the large majority were negative reviews based on today's technology with three key exceptions:

1. The manager and/or marketing team brought a whole set of iPads, enough for everyone in the room to have their own to play along with *and* the presenter(s) were adept at using them. The presenter(s) had a very specific game plan for the use of technology. They knew exactly which slides would be shown and what interactive presentation content would be reviewed.

2. The manager and marketing team utilized technology to actively show key elements of their process, in the form of real time data and live screens. The technology took the form of the old three ring binder "databook", series of crumpled spreadsheets, and "too small to read" exhibits, bringing the manager's data to life and permitting the firm to demonstrate their process real time, including its efficiency.

3. Computers and iPads were generally considered "ok" for note taking and the occasional opportunity to "bring up something of interest", but only when the user was adept at keeping the technology on the low down, quite literally. Respondents noted that they did not appreciate having a large computer screen in their face. Nothing is surprising about this market feedback. The meeting has been called in order to have an old-fashioned conversation. Only the most adept use of technology in live meetings adds value.

Other than these few exceptions, the respondents were generally inclined to reject the value proposition of tech props in today's in person meeting. Technology is making new strides daily. Technology's value in meetings is subject to change. In several cases, respondents recalled managers who had attempted to work with technology. A few even considered this *"advanced"* and gave these managers *"credit for trying"*, but most offered examples where the technology failed to work. The screens were *"too small to see anything meaningful"* or the content was *"still static at the end of the day and it was nothing more than an electronic pitchbook"*. In each case referenced, the activation and integration of the devices during the meeting felt *"disjointed and less productive"* than meetings without it.

Where Technology Matters Most in Meetings

Who might technology work well for? A special shout-out to quant managers, and multi-strategy managers who can utilize technology to quickly and adeptly demonstrate a variety of process and data screens. In these cases, technology can permit the research professional to "see" inside of the manager's system and process.

There are certainly some strategies that are heavy on content for which technology could be used to synthesize the discussion down to key elements more efficiently and interactively. There are also scenarios in which the proprietary nature of models is most easily shown on screen, and where a manager can provide a researcher with a 'hands on' look at an investment up close, using technology. However, for a firm marketing a fundamental, long only small-cap growth strategy, is technology really needed? Managers will first want to determine if their strategy is a "fit" for a technology based presentation, and then determine if the representatives of the firm *and* the prospects are up to the task before proceeding. If technology is determined to be critical, firms must focus on training and execution of the content in a technology based format to ensure it works as well on the road, as it does in the office.

Questions Asked

Respondents were asked the following questions in bold face text specifically in relation to this chapter. The consensus answers are in italics and immediately follow the question asked.

How does technology work in meetings? Are on screen presentations better or worse than books?
Jury is still out with a consensus towards worse.

Do iPad based presentations work?
Ok, IF an iPad is available for everyone in the room.

Words to Drive By

The following quotes provide a broader sampling of the respondents' direct feedback in relation to the above questions. Firms are encouraged to drive their marketing and sales activities with these rules for the road in mind.

On Technology Use in Meetings

Ten years ago it was weird when someone had a computer but now it is ok if integrated; I don't like the back of a laptop in my face.

An online/web based tool if it makes sense can walk through trading programs, tour of space, organization within an office more efficiently than paper.

Sometimes firms try to integrate technology, which is impressive, but it doesn't always work well. The presenter has to really have the technology down.

On Whether Technology is Additive in Meetings

It doesn't give research the ability to switch pages, etc. There is also a risk that you are talking about things we don't want to talk about.

[It] makes reference documents/points more readily available but it can be a huge distraction in the meantime.

I still like having something I can write on, it makes it more permanent for me; still [prefer] the more traditional deck.

Both distracting and useful, from the manager's side I like it if it is transparent, not when it is forced.

On Tablet Use in Live Meetings

Surprisingly fewer than we thought are using technology; it is very effective as it allows the manipulator of the iPad the ability to track what you want them to track. But it only works if they are adept at using it real time.

More people are bringing in iPads and showing things. Quant-[itative] models will show on the iPad which is very helpful; show me, don't just tell me.

[An] iPad is fine; I take notes on my printouts.

Very few have come in with iPads. I don't like it as I am a writer; maybe there will be a place for it someday.

Gimmicky [in reference to iPad presentations].

Summary on Technology Use in Meetings

Technology drives so much of our time and attention.
It can add exponentially to the presentation of content at certain times.
However, it is rarely value-added in the live meeting setting,
particularly for initial meetings.

Determine if the Strategy Is a Fit for a Technology Driven Presentation

---

Evaluate the Technological Savvy of the Firm's Presenters and Prospects

---

The Goal of the Meeting Is to Meet Face to Face;
If the Firm Is Committed to Integrating Technology, then Spend Sufficient
Time on Mock Trials of its Use in Meetings to Ensure Efficiency

---

PART IV

Stepping Up:
Staying The Course

In *Part III Stepping In*, firms were tasked with building out a content library and establishing their presence in the market. Initial outreach and the meeting process were reviewed. Managers are highly motivated and amenable to implementing marketing and sales plans up until this time. Creating initial materials, making introductions and meeting new people is enjoyable for most industry professionals. Next, firms must survive the hardest part; the waiting game. Managers believe they have made their case, and they have certainly begun to do so. They believe institutions should be moving ahead with allocations, and wonder aloud "where is the AUM?" Patience is a virtue. Appreciating the depth of competition is an important factor in maintaining manager patience and fortitude.

In Part IV, the focus is on "Stepping Up" in institutional investment management marketing and sales. Stepping up means staying the course, and continuing to deliver on the value proposition presented to institutions during the introductory phase of marketing. *The ability to deliver over time is what separates managers who thrive, from those who simply survive.*

Several important elements of an effective marketing campaign are covered in Part IV, including producing meaningful commentary, having an active voice through ongoing communications, and managing resources. Efficiency is enhanced through an understanding of the institutional investment management research and funding process, which will be reviewed in *Chapter 16*. This section is dedicated to understanding the long run; what firms must understand about the institutional process, and what they can and should deliver over time.

It is in Part IV that managers often fail; the stress and economics of the effort begin to take hold and managers stop producing content and start making premature changes to resources. Managers work hard to establish themselves, to build a track record and team, and to identify and fund the right resources to support the firm. It is human nature to question these resources, and the manager's own resolve. Part IV will encourage managers to step up in the realms of content creation, active marketing and resource commitments, while staying the course despite an anticipated lack of institutional responsiveness at this stage. If the activities of stepping back and stepping in reviewed in the first thirteen chapters were accomplished inside of a 3-12 month window, the stepping up activities will generally consume the next 12-24 months. Yes, 12-36 months is the normal period for institutional marketing and sales to take hold, and to produce results, presuming the firm's overall game plan is delivered effectively without fits and starts, underperformance, significant changes or too many mulligans. Managers may get a few early wins from known connections or sheer luck and good timing, but reaching a firm's desired capacity is a multi-year process.

CHAPTER 14

Establishing Active Voice with Commentary

RPM Rating on Commentary

DE MINIMIS	CORE	PRIORITY	GAME CHANGER

Firms have good momentum heading into the marketing and sales process initially; they can work through tedious sets of introductory materials without much difficulty. It is the exciting part of kicking off a new initiative and telling the manager's story that creates the momentum. Every time the firm engages a new resource, they will energetically reposition and retool, but still dedicated to the initial—or newly defined—roll out. Unfortunately, firms often engage in multiple marketing efforts before "getting it right". Perhaps this extreme focus early on leads to manager fatigue when it comes to marketing and sales efforts postlaunch. However, it is precisely these marketing and sales efforts postlaunch that differentiate managers. Commentary is a key element of postlaunch marketing. In speaking with respondents, commentary is identified as a *priority* item in the *Resource Prioritization Matrix*. Well implemented commentary can get a manager noticed.

The hard work of marketing and sales begins post the initial roll out, and this is where managers consistently fail. It is challenging to regularly come up with educational and well thought out commentary that builds on the firm's initial positioning. It is hard work to stay in front of the right institutional research professionals, so the manager becomes known, connected and fully considered when an opportunity arises. After all, this process can seem so one-sided. The firm reaches out, provides good ideas and excellent performance, and then the game begins; the game of hurry up and wait. This outreach, the firm's time consuming and "thought-provoking" commentary, gets little to no feedback regarding what's working and what is not, what is value-added and what is getting tossed in the recycle bin, if it is making it into the researcher's inbox at all. Cybersecurity protocols have resulted in intense fire walls and firms should understand that often their materials are not even reaching their desired audience. Are these institutions reading what they receive? Maybe not. But not for the reasons managers may think.

Referring to the statistics on manager inbound inquiries, which average 100 per week in most cases between new opportunities and updates, how can the firm stand out? How can the manager be one that "gets read" when it comes to commentary? Will sending monthly or quarterly numbers alone accomplish this? This chapter focuses on commentary as an industry standard element of ongoing communications. *Chapter 15: Adding Value through Ongoing Communications* will continue the discussion, focusing on additional opportunities including ancillary write-ups and continued face time that is value-added from the vantage point of the institutional investment management research professional. Commentary is covered as a standalone chapter because it is the traditional form of ongoing communications the market has come to expect, and one that can move the needle towards institutional interest over time. It is also a component of the marketing and sales process that is subpar in most cases, according to respondents. This creates an opportunity for managers looking to stand out.

The Commentary Conundrum

Commentary, often wrapped into a performance update, is the most widely accepted expectation for ongoing communication by managers and research professionals alike. In many cases these updates are sent, or forwarded, to an expressly designed inbox meant to capture this data on behalf of the entire universe of manager candidates who are sending it. In all cases, institutional research professionals are accepting this data and filing it at best, trashing it at worst. How can a manager stand out from the crowd and assist institutions in understanding what the firm does differently? How can the firm utilize commentary to explain when, where and why their offering will help client portfolios?

Managers need to provide their performance, while simultaneously making the case for their offering beyond the numbers. At the same time, institutions are inundated and often commentary is repetitive. The market only has one set of dynamics at any given time. To the extent managers are limiting their commentary to broad market conditions, the content is not value-added to institutions who have access to much larger organizations' views on the same. Institutional researchers have access and receive commentary from a broad array of market participants, including a series of economists and global macro specialists. Institutions don't need broad market commentary from a fundamental, small company growth manager, for example. They have it from a better source. Unless a manager has a notably contrarian view to share, avoid rehashing obvious market news.

The reason managers utilize limited commentary space to overview broad market conditions is rational. Managers are attempting to appease two audiences with the same material—those that are already direct investors with the firm and may rely on the firm for a broader market review, and those who are target prospects of the firm and have multiple access points for market commentary. The reason institutional researchers are not likely to read most manager's broad market commentary is also rational. The sheer volume of content bestowed upon institutions each month and each quarter is simply too great. Why would a research professional select the firm's commentary to read over the 100s of others they receive throughout the quarter and particularly the bottleneck received approximately three weeks after quarter end? This is the commentary conundrum.

Whose Commentary is Getting Read?

Respondents collectively lit up with joy when discussing commentary, particularly good commentary. This is not surprising, after all they are data geeks. They love to read and understand, they love to debate themselves, and they are motivated to build a case for their views. Commentary fuels this most engaging piece of their work. Whose commentary is getting read? At the top of the list is commentary from managers in the institutions' portfolios followed by the biggest names in the industry. Next, is commentary from managers who are carefully being tracked by the research team and monitored for potential allocations. Finally, are those whose writings they find particularly *"interesting"*. This last category, writing something "interesting", is where firms can stand out and get read. Managers can provide "must read" content no matter their size or strategy. Typically, they do not. Stop thinking standard commentary; stop focusing on a macro update unless the firm is a macro manager. Does the manager truly believe they can add value here? Respondents say no.

Respondents indicated that they attempt to read most of the commentary they receive. They discussed pooling the commentary together and taking it with them on their commutes, on planes and to lunch. Institutional research professionals indicated that commentary serves as a primary tool for learning and gaining insight into manager perspectives. However, commentary is prioritized for the sake of time and resources. Institutional research professionals expect firms interested in being read to prioritize as well, drawing attention to key content that is differentiated. Firms are encouraged to highlight the unique content areas dedicated to their strategy, utilizing a small key or table of contents, such that the most relevant commentary sections can be easily found in a multiple page write-up. Here are the characteristics respondents valued most.

Meaningful Commentary Characteristics

1. **Timely:** preferably not along with the rest of the world's commentary. It is ideal if managers can get it out ahead of the pack,

particularly when it includes performance. Alternatively, perhaps a mid-quarter send or later if the commentary is designed to cover a specific timely topic and does not multitask as a performance update (think market briefs—these are covered in greater detail in *Chapter 15*). This type of commentary permits the manager to discuss a specific event that occurred in the markets and/or in their portfolio last quarter, or even last month.

2. ***Specific:*** discuss how the markets are impacting this strategy; explain whether the strategy is taking advantage of or getting smacked by current market conditions to help inform the reader about how the investment process works, when the strategy might perform well and when it might struggle. Hiding in the corner when performance is down is not useful and is obvious in the eyes of institutional research professionals. When the manager is underperforming the firm should be diligent about speaking up, providing explanation and openly discussing what is impacting the strategy. Specific commentary does not require extensive pages. Individual names or points in time can be interesting if short and succinct. Pages upon pages on an individual name or market trend were discouraged by most respondents. Do not hide from the negatives on a name by name basis either. Keep in mind most institutional investment research professionals believe when the manager is struggling is the absolute best time to be in a conversation, and under consideration. Any good student of the market would understand this. Buying high and selling low is a rookie mistake. Institutions, or at the very least the institutional research professionals who support them, understand strategies will ebb and flow, and the right entry point is not at a performance high. Commentary is an excellent way to build the case for an allocation right at the time when it feels most unlikely; when performance is at its worst.

3. ***Consistent:*** commentary is the manager's opportunity to give their strategy and their firm a voice in the heads of institutional research professionals. The markets, and the manager's process, provide daily opportunities to communicate regarding the firm's approach and how it fits

into a broader portfolio construct. Daily commentary is not suggested; what is suggested is that managers have more than enough content to pull from in identifying a theme, a trade, an example of what makes the manager different in any given month, or quarter, whether to the negative or the positive. Use these examples to deliver consistent commentary no less than four times per year, and make it meaningful.

4. *Opinionated:* Be opinionated; specific points of view are more interesting than regurgitated, generally accepted market trends. Step out of the box and express the manager's opinions supported by the strategy's market experience. Yes, stepping outside the box runs the risk that someone disagrees with the manager's perspectives, yet institutional investment research professionals consistently referenced enjoying most the commentary they received with something meaningful to say, especially if it was contrarian. They universally acknowledged preferring managers who were "real"; those who came out and spoke about what wasn't working or what didn't work, sharing views that were intriguing and supported by their research. Respondents appreciated managers who were honest and forthcoming. Consider the value of having a catchy subject line or title to kick off a commentary. Let the institution know what they can learn within the firm's few pages right from the start, so the researcher prioritizes the commentary as a must-read. Big trends can be of interest as well, when accompanied by the manager's viewpoint regarding how they may impact the strategy. Additionally, commentary provides the opportunity to integrate broader voices from the investment management team into the dialogue. Firms might consider asking each investment team member to provide certain aspects of the commentary, or to take turns being on point, and being featured, in the commentary. Investment team members may have differing opinions in certain areas and strengths in others. Commentary provides an opportunity to showcase these perspectives and strengths over time.

5. *Brief:* Institutional investment management research professionals confirmed two to four pages is the target length, beyond that it is best to consider it a white paper and to provide it off cycle (outside of the

standard commentary delivery expectations of a few weeks past quarter end). "Brief" also refers to structuring—focus on key word use, titles and the segmentation of commentary so research professionals can quickly and easily find what is most interesting to them. Commentary should have a visually appealing template that is consistently applied to advance the firm's brand; it should not look like an academic paper. Commentary is meant to be a quick read of the manager's current "comments" on the market and the strategy. After all, in a few short weeks it will be old news.

What Not to Send

At the risk of being repetitive, let's review what is generally a waste of time and effort in commentary provided to institutional investment management research professionals.

1. *Market Overview:* Repeating the same global macro update everyone else covers, when the firm is not a global macro manager. If the firm has a private wealth audience as well, it may need to provide a general market backdrop for this audience's benefit. In this case, consider two separate versions in which the first page differs by audience. Be sensitive to this consistent feedback from institutions by clearly labeling sections. Have a small key or sidebar callout right on the first page as to where specific content is, so it can be quickly accessed by institutional prospects who wish to skip right over the firm's general market review. Ask the question internally before the commentary is finalized: "If institutions give our commentary a two-minute review, where do we want them to spend that two minutes?" Don't waste it on what they already know, and what they certainly have already from much more qualified sources.

2. *Window Dressing:* Commentary that is more fluff than substance, more regurgitated stats than actual commentary to be read and considered. The stats can be important and are nice to summarize in a brief section, or better yet profiled in a dedicated performance update. The purpose of commentary is to "comment".

3. *Generic Overviews:* Commentary that does not focus on the firm's specific area of expertise; commentary that is too general and could have been written by any type of manager in the same asset class. Instead, write about what the firm does. Show the team's expertise through the consistent application of focused commentary which discusses specific anomalies, trends or names impacting the portfolio. Go back to the firm's content outline discussed in *Chapter 7* to identify key themes that impact the strategy, and focus on them as they play out in real time. Use the platform to be specific, not generic.

4. *Inconsistent or Late:* Missing quarters or delivering commentary so late that the content is stale is counterproductive. Institutional investment management research professionals are constant readers and they come to expect certain pieces and timing from their suitors. There is a rhythm to what they do and there should be a rhythm to the manager's process as well. If the manager writes about something quite interesting, but it was relevant one or two months ago, it is a waste of everyone's time—the firm's time in writing and the institution's time in reading. Be comfortable with brevity, giving comments without requiring the ideas to be overly couched or structured. *Consider scheduling a standing internal meeting with the team, 15 minutes should do it, in which everyone is required to bring one idea that could be the basis for the firm's commentary in a given month or quarter. Then act on it efficiently and deliberately. Make the firm's content relevant.*

5. *A Novel:* Enough said. Brevity is a skill worth learning.

Questions Asked

Respondents were asked the following questions in bold face text specifically in relation to this chapter. The consensus answers are in italics and immediately follow the question asked.

How important is commentary?
It is expected, and we get a ton of it, but most of it isn't that useful. It is too generic.

What was the last great commentary you read that you remember and what are you most likely to read?
See quotes; something interesting and different than the 100s of other commentaries we are weeding through; something with a point of view.

What commentary do you trash immediately?
Too long and nothing value-added in those extra pages; macro based commentary from anyone but a macro manager; we do try to read most of what we receive.

How much commentary do you get?
More than we can read; hundreds.

How frequently do you want to be updated? Monthly? Quarterly?
Quarterly is generally sufficient, but please make it interesting.

Does the update need to be personalized?
No, but it helps. Give us a reason to read it. Point us to the most meaningful section(s).

What is the ideal length of commentary?
Two to four pages.

Words to Drive By

The following quotes provide a broader sampling of the respondents' direct feedback in relation to the above questions. Firms are encouraged to drive their marketing and sales activities with these rules for the road in mind.

On Commentary Length, Timing and Content

Less than three pages [unless it is providing a major market wide update of substance].

Three pages; [we] don't need multiple pages on an individual idea.

Anything more than a front or back page monthly is too much; 30 page quarterly letters are just too long, I don't have time. At least format in a way that allows for good headlines and key takeaways.

Long as it needs to be—everyone falls within three to ten pages; longer than eight pages better be really interesting, and a lot are; [I] like individual names but I don't care about that. I find the thematic is most applicable to me; the one exception is event driven where they tend to be so bottom up focused that there ends up being single name talk and that makes sense.

On Commentary Content Preferences

Thematic is best, big broad themes over individual positions; two pages if you can do it is best.

Brevity on macro stuff is key particularly for managers where that is not their thing. I get it that you want to have a little context.

I trust that they know what is most important for me to know, like a stock that went down 20% and affected the portfolio.

Would prefer managers get into the weeds on one security, or on one thing or on a few names—really dig in and show how you think, not just what you think. [I want to] understand attribution in the same fashion—what were the major contributors and what were the detractors.

On Favorite Reads

[I like to read the] well known figures [like] Oakmark, Greenlight, and GMO.

I like JP Morgan's overall market review as it is a great frame of reference, but I also like some more obscure names that tend to be less 'PC', or have something very specific to say. They keep it interesting.

[XYZ firm], his are more thematic, he will get into names in [his] book but it's really only a little on his portfolio and market, then two to four pages on a big theme in his portfolio.

Mauldin is good when I just want an economics review. It is helpful that the focus is entirely on the bigger picture without a specific portfolio bias.

[I like to read about] big thematic issues—but you just don't make money on the big thematic issues. So, some examples of some things that went right and what went wrong in a portfolio during some time of stress and what the manager was thinking at that time.

Summary on Commentary

Commentary is the most widely accepted form of ongoing communications by institutions and investment managers.

Make it Poignant: Create "Must Read" Content that Is Differentiated and Representative of the Firm's Unique Expertise Based on Current Market Dynamics

---

Be Consistent: Provide Timely Content at Regular Intervals that Is Delivered in a Format Institutions can Easily Scan, Finding What Matters Most to Them Efficiently

---

Be Opinionated: The Purpose of Commentary Is to Comment

CHAPTER 15

Adding Value through Ongoing Communications

RPM Rating on Ongoing Communications

DE MINIMIS	CORE	PRIORITY	GAME CHANGER

Ongoing communications are much broader than commentary. Ongoing communications will include everything from topical white papers and market briefs outside of the standard commentary que, to follow-on meetings, calls and direct requests from prospects. The work of the manager is to stay in front of institutional prospects in a meaningful way. There are few things more frustrating to engaged sales professionals than the manager who provides only quarterly numbers without context, and then wants to know where the business is. What sales tools are provided here? How do these numbers engage the institutional research professional across the table or across the pond? How do numbers alone keep a manager top of mind? What digital engagement is occurring to keep the manager's name and core message active?

Dead-End Conversations

Imagine the phone call made by a sales professional who only has a manager's numbers to present:

"Hi, Lauren, how are you today? Great? Great! Well, I'm calling about Manager Blue's numbers. Did you get a chance to take a look at them? Yes, we agree they are wonderful. What is behind those numbers you ask? Well, it's hard to tell. But Manager Blue sure is great. They are performing better than the peer group, don't you think?"

This is a dead-end conversation. There is no substance of interest; no story being told. How should we interpret the numbers? Performance can be easily screened in databases; numbers do not justify a phone call. There is nothing value-added about regurgitating data points. What is in this phone call for Lauren? For those that answer with "we've got commentary to go with our numbers", review *Chapter 14* and ensure that it is differentiated, providing a lot more than just some performance analytics and a macro economic outlook. If it was, the sales person would surely be referencing it on the call. The sales professional wants to be providing something of value because they understand it is what gives the numbers credibility, and what gives a manager the best chance at keeping the dialogue alive. Compare the above phone call to another made by a sales professional who is representing a firm that understands the value of ongoing communications:

"Hi Mike, how are things going? Great? Great! Well, I'm following up with you on that fantastic piece that Manager Green just put out, the one we sent you last week. Did you get a chance to review it? Well, it provides an in depth look at how Manager Green sees the influence of interest rates on technology stocks and how it has informed several of the firm's positions in the portfolio. Would you like to set up a call with Manager Green to discuss this in more detail and to get an update on the firm and portfolio?"

Something Tangible to Talk About

The firm's ongoing communications program is dedicated to building relationships, educating the market on who the firm is and what they do. Ongoing communications define what matters to the firm and how the manager, and offering, is likely to respond day in and day out to various market conditions. Great ongoing communications provide tangible content to the sales team, something of substance to follow up on and a reason to schedule another discussion. The institutional investment research professional is looking for ideas and content that they can utilize to help inform their views, and to educate clients. The firm's opportunity is in providing this value-added content. Great ongoing communications creates a dialogue, and for this reason it is a *game changer* according to the *Resource Prioritization Matrix*.

An Ongoing Communications Review

Here is an exercise similar to the one suggested in *Chapter 4*, in relation to the firm's brand. Produce the last several quarters of information sent out on behalf of the firm excluding the introductory materials (fact sheet, presentation, etc.). Include commentary and anything else presented or distributed such as white papers and videos. Are the ongoing communications provided offering content of value that differentiates the firm beyond its numbers on a consistent basis? Include presentations given to existing prospects at follow-on meetings in the review, along with anything produced in any media that was shared with a prospect or client. Produce a minimum of one year and ideally two years of what has been actively utilized in the market beyond the introductory materials.

First, consider how much ongoing communication the firm has delivered. Does this exercise result in a variety of touchpoints or was there very little produced? Ongoing communications should be just that—communicating ongoing. The manager is seeking to build the case for their candidacy. That requires active communication on an ongoing basis not only in responding to direct requests but in providing value-added content through all interactions that differs meaningfully from what was provided at launch.

Second, do the communications speak to the audience; are they targeted, timely and personal? Managers are competing for attention. They are competing with the significant amount of noise in the market, and the varied priorities of time and resources within institutions. Poor, repetitive or non-existent ongoing communications can waste a perfectly good introduction. Ensure that each interaction, whether proactive or as a follow up to a request, is unique and meaningful.

Ongoing Communications Rules for the Road

Here are a few rules for the road in the firm's push to add value through ongoing communications:

1. ***Be Responsive:*** From the moment an introduction is made, firms must be at the ready to respond to requests for additional information. No matter how big or small these requests are, managers are expected to be prepared with a formal process in place for responding. Who's on first? What is the protocol for data requests? Is there anything in 'stock' ready to go or is everything custom? Respondents acknowledged that managers were generally prepared in this regard; ongoing requests from institutions were responded to in a reasonable manner of time (48 hours for data requests that are straightforward, two to three weeks for longer questionnaires and more detailed historical analysis). Where there were exceptions, managers were eliminated from consideration as responsiveness is a requirement of the process, before and after hiring.

2. ***Be Prepared:*** Managers who are prepared have an easier time managing multiple requests, which is common in the feast or famine game of asset gathering; the process is smoother when an inventory of exhibits, content and materials are at the ready. Have a content library in place before pursuing the institutional market as discussed in *Chapter 7*. This content library should manifest in a few key pieces that are valuable in the ongoing communications process including:

   • A generic due diligence questionnaire (DDQ) that can and will be used as the base document to complete requests for information (RFIs) or requests for proposal (RFPs).

- Exhibits demonstrating various aspects of the firm's investment process that are more detailed than what should be included in an initial presentation.
- Attribution analysis regarding the portfolio and its holdings.
- A white paper supporting the thesis behind the strategy.

3. *Make It Personal:* Institutional investment management research professionals are human beings. They have interests and perspectives, likes and dislikes. Technology has created a phenomenon in the investment management industry just as it has across most industries; marketing can be automated. Institutions get this and for the benign task of sending updated performance, which is dumped into a database anyhow, generic is just fine. Yet, when it comes to the key prospect list, institutions the firm has met with and would like to do business with, making it personal is in the firm's best interest. The document itself will surely be generic, but how it is sent can be quite personal and respondents indicated that matters. Respondents confirmed that while generic can be ok for certain types of updates, the more personal the communication is the more likely they are to spend time on it. Adding a custom message to the introduction of a generic piece not only assists the institution in feeling connected and perhaps more committed to reviewing it, it provides a natural 'next step' in giving the sales professional a reason to follow up with a phone call based on their individualized note.

4. *Change It Up:* Institutions are seeking different ways to look at the same old markets. Managers are passionate about their philosophy and process, however that rarely translates into how they elect to communicate. Change it up. Find some aspects of the portfolio or approach that provide an angle for adding unique value, and talk about them. Managers often believe they must have an air tight thesis and extensive research before they can opine on a topic. The result is either no content, or way too much content all at once. Change it up by providing brief but

meaningful viewpoints on highly targeted aspects of the portfolio and portfolio management process.

5. ***Affirm Fit:*** The firm has made the introduction; it has provided an overview of the organization, its offering(s), its philosophy and process. Now the wait begins. Ideally the manager provided some sense for where they fit in a diversified portfolio within the introductory meeting as discussed in *Chapter 12*. Respondents consistently indicated a desire to understand where—and how—the manager's strategy would fit. Regardless, now is the time to demonstrate that 'fit' by providing content based on current market dynamics that reinforces how the manager could fit into the institution's current offering. Numbers alone do not provide this explanation. Institutions are seeking to create a dynamic, integrated and holistic portfolio. Managers who can provide consistent and regular reminders of how and where they can add value based on changing market conditions will be top of mind when the institution needs to make a change. Those who have simply provided their numbers have done nothing to position themselves as a portfolio contributor; they are not "known" to the institution and nothing has occurred to build understanding and a relationship.

This discussion of fit is not meant to be literal in ongoing communications. For example, a manager should not be hammering "we fit right here" or "we would be such a better fit than XYZ manager". Each institution's portfolio and viewpoint differs, as does their capacity to implement changes in certain time periods. What managers should focus on is building a case for how their strategy would add value to different asset combinations and under differing market conditions. This is ultimately how they would 'fit', but is positioned within a broader context, leaving the institution with the room and opportunity to define the specifics.

6. ***Be Strategic:*** Managers miss opportunities that are critical. There are certain market conditions that lend themselves to a great story told by global macro managers, there are other market conditions that beg for small company, fundamental growth specialists to sing from the rooftops. Be thoughtful about what market conditions are at play, what is likely to be most critical for institutions to be reading about, and seize the opportunity when it is a match for the firm's offerings. When it is not the firm's "time"—not because the offering is under performing but because there is something much bigger happening in the world to which institutions are fully engaged—step down from the podium. When it is the right time: when the market is ripe for the strategy the firm offers, when performance has been down but the manager sees massive opportunity, when the stars align to demonstrate exactly why the firm's philosophy and process makes perfect sense—jump on it!

7. ***Give Content:*** Managers talk about transparency, yet rarely are. Transparency sounds good in theory, but is difficult to deliver in practice. Managers believe they have a "secret sauce"; true transparency requires managers to show it. A change in perspective is necessary for most managers to deliver the level of transparency desired by institutions, and by their own sales and marketing teams. Here is the change in perspective needed: a manager's content is not the great lost treasure. It is important, valuable, informative and the source of great opportunity, but it is not worthy of the vault in which it is often placed. Let it out! Give content! Be charitable and thoughtful in communicating with the market.

   Managers often believe that they either need to hide their proprietary process, or the 'dogs' in their portfolios. Neither is productive in the goal of adding value through ongoing communications. The market loves dogs and knows that they exist, in every portfolio. Be direct and thoughtful; share the great ideas that the firm is thinking about, and examples of lessons learned when things didn't go well. Have confidence that the content will help to establish the firm as a thought leader and good partner. The firm's content will not create a competitive advantage for someone else, as many managers fear. There are lots of factors that impact how well a manager performs. Sharing small and specific details of the firm's process does not dilute the proprietary value-added that the firm can provide once hired. Sharing small and specific details is how solid relationships, and mandates, begin.

8. ***Share Meaningful Milestones:*** Regarding the sharing of milestones, respondents did not indicate a desire to be updated every time the firm gets a new client, hires a new resource or grows its AUM by $1M. Major milestones are necessary to communicate, both the good and the bad. More benign updates can be relegated to the quarterly commentary under a "Firm News" section that is easy to find. Share meaningful milestones that are relevant to the prospect, for example portfolio growth that has caused the AUM to cross a notable threshold that the institution indicated was a criterion for their investment.

9. ***Own the Calendar:*** When is the best time to provide proactive ongoing communications? When it comes to reactive data requests, the answer is easy, as soon as practical. For proactive communications, however, more strategy is required. There is a rhythm to the investment calendar and some best practices in sending ongoing communications. An obvious component of which is the avoidance of "typical windows" when institutions tend to be bombarded by updates and commentary. According to respondents, managers should send pieces which are truly value-added and not inclusive of a performance update "off cycle" so that they have the best chance of being read. Don't waste good content. Maintain a calendar that suggests content ideas and distribution plans throughout the year, adjusting the calendar quarterly as marketing conditions and opportunities change.

10. ***Get Face Time:*** Managers want to avoid unnecessary travel. That is in part what makes them great portfolio managers; the dedication they have to their craft. Managers want to minimize time away from their portfolio, and minimize costs. Unfortunately, there is no substitute for face time. The more technologically advanced marketing and sales becomes, the more valuable in person contact is in making a connection. Seek to meet in person with key prospects no less than once per calendar year, preferably twice. Respondents indicated a need for four to six touchpoints before making an allocation. Even on a twice per year schedule, firms are looking at two to three years, which is the norm. It is the firm's job to make these touchpoints happen and to ensure that they are relevant and meaningful enough to make an impact. A year may seem like a long time, but it passes quickly. Establish a quarterly calendar of trips the manager is committed to, and ensure a portfolio management representative can hit all major locations at least once per calendar year. Meetings do not have to be long nor overly cumbersome. Meetings should be interactive, topical and timely. Ongoing meetings require ongoing communications tools and collateral; the overview presentation is in the rearview mirror. Map out what a good second meeting presentation and agenda looks like given the strategy. At a minimum, have a unique and updated set of examples to share.

11. ***Give the Team a Voice:*** Ongoing communications are an opportunity to share the wealth; a chance to expand the industry's understanding of the firm and its resources. Firms should consider actively engaging their team in the process of creating ongoing communications. While there is typically a limited set of firm resources who are best equipped to conduct face to face meetings with institutional prospects, most members of the team could add value to a robust ongoing communications program by providing content. Institutions benefit from seeing the depth and breadth of a team. Consider engaging analysts, traders and portfolio managers alike in the task of creating meaningful

ongoing communications. These team resources can be featured as a component of the firm's communications program, credited formally with the creation of certain ongoing communications pieces or content.

12. ***Have a Game Plan:*** No less than quarterly, discuss what best ideas, portfolio holdings and market trends would make the most compelling conversation pieces and create exhibits around them. This keeps the conversation fresh and interesting. Respondents indicated a great preference for managers who brought something timely and topical to the meeting. Take advantage of their natural curiosity. Stand out from the crowd with something better than the numbers and the analytics that surround them. Think stories and market anomalies.

13. ***Get Known:*** There are a myriad of resources available to firms who want to get the word out about what they do and how they do it beyond their in-house efforts and online presence. Firms can engage industry professionals in their initial and ongoing communications efforts who can move the needle efficiently, with the expertise to drive effective messaging. Consider hiring a public relations organization to assist in spreading the word about the firm. A good PR resource will help drive interest and traffic, place the firm into publications, and generate street credibility. Firms such as Gregory FCA, Interdependence, JConnelly, Inc., and MacMillan Communications, Inc. are examples of firms who do a fair amount of work in the financial sector. Managers can seek to gain coverage in financial publications including *Emerging Manager Monthly* and other publications from Financial Investment News, *FA Magazine, Pensions & Investments, Barron's* and *Investor's Business Daily,* among others. A simple google search will identify a variety of industry publications to pursue for potential article placement, interviews and industry event updates.

14. ***Get Connected***: Consider connecting through associations that assist with best practices, networking and industry reach. The GAMMA, 100 Women in Finance, AIMSE, NAAIM, and NAPFA, all offer excellent opportunities to network and enhance efficiency in the financial industry. Take advantage of groups related to industry designations, such as the CFA Institute and the CAIA Association. Attend conferences to make connections and to get the lay of the land, for example, Schwab IMPACT, Morningstar Investment Conference, TD Ameritrade's annual advisor conference, Opal Group sponsored events, SALT (the SkyBridge Alternatives Conference) and events from the Family Office Exchange (FOX), Family Office Club and the Family Office Networks. Get connected in the industry to expand reach and ideally minimize the timeline associated with marketing and sales. Additional resources are provided in the *Resource* section at the back of the book.

Create a Portal

Managers can ease the communications burden of delivery and access by establishing a portal in the cloud. Several solutions are in the market, such as SecureShare and ShareFile, among others, that permit password protected access to a manager's growing suite of ongoing communications. Take advantage of these opportunities to gain efficiency. Managers can also improve their internal efficiency in relation to content and communications management through such applications as Box and DropBox, both online, cost efficient solutions for managing and exchanging data.

Get Present

Ongoing communications is not simply about what the firm sends, it is also about showing up. Managers prefer to avoid travel and face time. While they welcome discussing their portfolios, they find the process of getting on the road grueling. Showing up is half the battle. The value of conferences and industry events can be debated and is by most firms. The cost for participation is extremely high, and often the perceived value is quite low. Managers do need to manage their budgets and avoid spending too much on unnecessary travel and events. Betting the farm on the first year's sales effort is a mistake. However, a complete lack of presence is a mistake as well. Managers regularly avoid the cost of industry events and conferences, keeping their sales professionals away from them too. Unfortunately, the competition is attending these events. Being a constant no show will limit the firm's growth.

Imagine Manager Orange who attends two to three conferences a year, does her best to circulate materials and to ask for meetings and product consideration by attendees of these events. Manager Orange takes advantage of networking opportunities. This manager is not taking up a multi-booth suite, sponsoring cocktail hours or spending excessive dollars on the conference circuit with monthly attendance, yet she is showing up enough to be recognized. The sales team is liked and appreciated for the effort. Investors feel a connection and begin to track the manager more closely between interactions. The budget is sustainable.

Now, imagine Manager Brown. He has great performance and sends the numbers religiously after each quarter. His team is excited about the growth they see in the marketplace and the opportunities they perceive in various channels. But Manager Brown loathes spending capital and does not believe in attending industry events, supporting networking opportunities nor taking the time to be an active voice in the industry. Investors see these great numbers and there is some intrigue, but they just saw Manager Orange again at a conference and spent some time with the team and liked what they heard. Even though the numbers weren't as compelling, they feel comfortable with the story and look forward to spending more time with them. They understand Manager Orange's thesis and approach and believe the market will turn in their favor; it is a perfect time to invest.

Managers must be present to win mandates. Institutional research professionals are human beings. They want to feel connected and comfortable with who they hire. Sending materials is not enough. Showing up occasionally makes a big difference.

Be Social

Digital engagement has skyrocketed as the market seeks efficient ways to connect. Make sure the firm has an active social media and digital presence strategy. Show off your team, tell stories, make connections. Ensure your strategy is active week-to-week, month-to-month and quarter-to-quarter.

Questions Asked

Respondents were asked the following questions in bold face text specifically in relation to this chapter. The consensus answers are in italics and immediately follow the question asked.

Note: As commentary is an aspect of ongoing communications, a few of the questions and their answers are repeated from *Chapter 14*.

Does responsiveness to requests for data matter? For example, 24 hours v. two weeks to respond?
Yes, but managers seem to be within range generally; a few days to a week depending on the scope. A few weeks for a detailed due diligence questionnaire.

How frequently do you want to be updated? Monthly? Quarterly?
Quarterly is generally sufficient, but please, please make it interesting.

Does the update need to be personalized?
No, but it helps.

How often do you want to physically meet with a manager?
It varies; generally one or two times per year.

What milestones matter for managers to communicate

real-time?

Staff/team changes, significant AUM changes in either direction; changes that make the firm a viable prospect for us given our guidelines.

Words to Drive By

The following quotes provide a broader sampling of the respondents' direct feedback in relation to the above questions. Firms are encouraged to drive their marketing and sales activities with these rules for the road in mind.

On What to Send

I trust that they know what is most important for me to know, like a stock that went down 20% and affected the portfolio.

[I liked] a rates long/short manager talking about the credit unwind that is happening—one offs are better; standalone pieces, special pieces.

A regular read is [XYZ] blog, [it] tends to relate back to what they do, called "around the curve" and posted every two weeks. It looks at a country, or something that's changed in politics.

[I like to read about] big thematic issues—but you just don't make money on the big thematic issues. So, some examples of some things that went right and what went wrong in a portfolio during some time of stress and what the manager was thinking at that time.

On When to Send

If there is something interesting that happens in the market where the manager has expertise/insight, they should produce something specific during the "off-season"; "peak season" is the month after quarter end, "off-season" is two months past that—great time to give views/specific thoughts on something; real conviction, knowl-

edge.

Institutional update presentation a few times a year to refresh memory and get an update on the strategy; a lot of them won't send it if you don't physically meet but often I don't have time to meet and want to review over the weekend with a beer.

Send [something] the third month of the quarter. Things slow down a bit, people have caught up with their tasks and are more available.

On Responsiveness to Requests

Should be very quick, two to three days.

Ask the manager [how long it will take] and expect them to hold to that number, but if you don't send it and you don't stay relevant I am moving on; out of sight, out of mind.

We appreciate managers who have the packet ready to go, know the deeper dive questions, say they have it 'ready to go' and send it quickly—that is best.

Managers should be upfront about how long it will take, a week is reasonable, but they should set expectations.

We are interested enough to put in the request—how long do you let the fish stay on the hook before you give it a yank? Ok to use a junior person for that if it can be done quicker that way.

We understand that they have clients that are paying them already for work. We understand it can take a while, however we do notice that firms with marketing partners and those that are small are more responsive v. bigger firms that have lots of competing pri-orities or firms that don't understand the institutional space and aren't prepared.

On Personalization of Communications

As long as it speaks to what is going on and to the strategy it's ok, even though it feels better if it's personal; it doesn't really matter.

If it's personal I'll read a paragraph, if it is not I'm reading the first two lines.

On Frequency of Ongoing Meetings with Managers

If they are a manager for us every 6-12 months; if they aren't [we] can go longer.

We are pushing people off, request something only if moving forward; we can cover with go to meetings—prefer to do a conference call.

Semiannual.

One to two face times; four to six times before an allocation.

At the end of the day we want to sit down with the PM; some IR people are great, but some are not.

On Milestones and Value-added News to Communicate Real Time

Any major process changes.

Turnover, business issues, changes in terms; we don't need the growth updates.

Helpful to remind about closings.

If manager is on hold for size then I need to know when AUM grows; if I need 12 month track record reach out after 12 months. [If] staffing is open, call me when they are filled.

Change in process, team or significant change in assets we should be notified, at very least highlight in an update email we would receive. Don't bury at the end of the quarterly update.

If you are going to update a client, you should update the consultant.

Summary on Ongoing Communications

While commentary is the most common form, ongoing communications are much broader than a quarterly newsletter. Effective, timely and consistent ongoing communications can help managers stand out.

Give Marketing and Sales Resources Something Tangible to Talk About
Get Connected: Identify Timely Opportunities to Reinforce Differentiators
Show Up: Invest Sufficiently in Firm Presence to be Seen and Heard

CHAPTER 16

The Institutional Research and Funding Process

RPM Rating on Understanding the Institutional Process

DE MINIMIS	CORE	PRIORITY	GAME CHANGER

Managers are in the weeds, focused on their own firms, strategies and business development timelines. To get through the exhilarating yet grueling process of firm and track record building, managers cling to two assumptions. First, *"if we build it, they will come"*. Second, *"any institution can be moved to allocate at any time, if the numbers and story are compelling enough"*. These assumptions are erroneous and detrimental to the process. Institutions have their own organizational priorities, strategies and business development timelines that serve as primary drivers in their investment mandate decisions.

Understanding the institutional funding process is a *game changer* according to the *Resource Prioritization Matrix;* it is critical to factor in to an effective institutional marketing game plan. Not only must firms consider the institution's unique funding process, but also the overall market sentiment at the time of engagement. These revelations are not intended to encourage managers to sit on the sidelines. On the contrary, respondents spoke repeatedly about their interest in seeing new strategies, teams and opportunities developing in the market, despite their inability to implement them in the near term. Institutional marketing and sales is a marathon, not a sprint. Managers must be in the race to win. Like a marathon, having a game plan to get through the 26 miles, managing expectations and sticking with it make all the difference.

The Main Road to AUM

While there are exceptions to every rule, and unforeseen obstacles on the road to asset growth, a typical framework for how institutions conduct research is helpful to keep managers on track. There are a few aspects of the process that managers can control to shorten the road, including confirming the firm meets institutional standards, proactive outreach, and having a series of common due diligence materials prepared in advance. There are more aspects of the process that managers cannot control. Maintaining an understanding of the institution's process and expectations is imperative to avoiding the frustration, and often self-imposed manager screening delays, that are otherwise inherent in the process. *These steps, and the timeline assigned to them, presume there is interest; this is a typical scenario when the manager is a good "fit" and there is an identified need.*

Start Driving

Institutions only have so much capital and bandwidth; the research and funding process can get hung up anywhere along the way. Most managers will get caught in the very first step of the process, *Opportunity Identification*. This can be the longest component, matched only in duration by the last step, awaiting an *Allocation*. Unsure of timing and fit, managers will often delay entering the market. Firms are cautioned from holding off on marketing until the timing is 'just right'. Institutions want to get to know managers over time, typically measured in years, before they are likely to identify a manager as a top candidate for an institutional allocation. Quarters pass quickly, and institutions are interested in seeing how managers respond to a variety of market conditions which play out over time. There are exceptions to the rule, but those exceptions are generally saved for spin out teams where the portfolio manager was known by the research professionals, if not the institution itself, prior to an allocation. Regardless of how long the initial opportunity identification or the ultimate allocation takes, the typical process for institutions is as follows. Ultimately, institutions are searching for the right "fit" throughout the process. **Activities in bold represent manager opportunities to differentiate themselves beyond the numbers.** These activities each serve as a distinct opportunity to win or lose an institutional mandate.

The Research and Funding Process

1. ***Opportunity Identification (Open Ended)***
   New investment ideas or replacement searches can come from a variety of sources. They can come from the investment committee, clients or the research team. Timing of opportunity identification is open-ended. Institutions will consider market trends, as well as existing asset allocation and portfolio holdings in determining their priorities at any given time. **Inbound inquiries** from managers can lead to an opportunity identification.

2. ***Candidate Screening (One to Three Months)***
   Once a search has been confirmed, institutions will follow a predictable process in reviewing their options. They will review a combination of the inbound inquiries they have received from managers in this asset class, the **databases** (both internal and external), managers identified through their **network** and through **client referrals**, and **managers with whom they have met** over the previous few years.

3. ***Due Diligence (Two to Four Months)***
   A listing of candidates has been identified and institutional research professionals will now complete an analysis to determine if the manager meets **investment expectations and operational requirements**. Investments, then operations are typically the order of screening, however either can be cause for elimination from consideration. In some cases, institutions will have dif-

ferent teams who complete the investment due diligence v. the operational due diligence. Therefore, an investment research professional can like a manager and believe they are a great "fit" for the portfolio, yet the manager fails to meet operational standards. The due diligence process is often built around a **DDQ (Due Diligence Questionnaire), RFI (Request for Information) or RFP (Request for Proposal).** If the manager meets all necessary screening criteria through the investment and operations review, an **onsite visit**, where it is required or desired by the institution, would be the next step in the process.

4. *Finalists (One to Three Months)*
Candidates who are the best "fit" for the opportunity, and whom have passed the institutional researcher's review in terms of investment management and operations, are presented internally as part of a short list of candidates. This **presentation** can be made to any one of the following constituencies: the research team, investment committee, product committee, individual clients or the institution's board. The manager may or may not be invited to participate in this presentation. Before the presentation is made, managers will be asked to commit to **terms related to the mandate** to ensure that they are a viable candidate given the institution's proposed fees, capacity needs, portfolio or operational requirements, and reporting requirements.

5. *Selection/Approval (One Month)*
A successful outcome can be either platform approval, in which the manager is now a candidate for future mandates (in short, they are considered an "approved manager" at this time), or selection for a specific mandate. The later means immediate funding in most cases. Either way, **contract finalization and onboarding** including potential required **trade resources, custodial relationship establishment** or **operational commitments** are put in place.

6. *Allocation (Open Ended)*

   Managers can be approved on a platform but there can be no mandates, nor funding, for any period from a few months to a few years. During this time, managers are expected to be proactive in providing **commentary, firm and performance updates,** and in responding to **ad hoc requests**. When a specific mandate is defined, and the manager is selected, they will begin to see capital rather quickly, however the institution reserves the right to take as much or as little time as they want to allocate the full mandate to the manager. Managers must be at the **ready to receive and to allocate these funds.**

Market Timing Is Something

Timing of a firm's push into the institutional market can be pivotal. Consider the overall timing in relation to current market trends, the competitive landscape and the likelihood of allocations into a specific asset class and vehicle structure. For example, hedge fund of funds; institutions have been exiting, not adding, to positions in this structure. In this case, a manager's opportunity set is likely limited to a combination of existing buyers who are already committed to the space but want to swap out an existing manager, and those buyers who are small enough to need the fund of funds oversight and guidance despite the market sentiment. Therefore, a targeted effort focused on existing hedge fund of fund investors, and smaller institutions who lack the resources or expertise to manage a pool of underlying hedge funds on their own and/or do not have a consultant to assist them, is the manager's best bet. By keeping market timing in mind, managers who carefully track market trends may best define their target market and messaging. As stated previously, however, managers are discouraged from shying away from marketing all together during "the wrong time". Market timing considerations are best applied to *where* to market and *how intently* to push a specific idea or strategy, not to marketing all together.

Identify the Most Likely Buyer Profile for Today

A myriad of other examples like the hedge fund of funds example above can be found across asset classes, strategy (i.e. passive v. active) and vehicle structures. As a component of the firm's internal review process outlined in Part II, firms are strongly encouraged to map out the likely buyer profile given the current market environment before embarking on a multi-year, resource intensive institutional marketing effort. Reining in a broad based and costly effort in order to focus on a target market segment that is less likely to be fixated on the latest trend (for example passive v. active), or reducing expectations and pairing back marketing to the core elements during periods of little activity, can permit the firm to market more efficiently and for a longer period. A focus on the best buyer profile can reduce frustration and the likelihood of making unnecessary game plan changes. Changes are often made because managers want to believe they are doing "something" to address their marketing and sales goals, and swapping out resources or making other programmatic changes feels "productive". Sometimes they can be correct. More often firms make changes only to continue to bark up the wrong trees, at a time when their strategy is simply not in favor. There is always a buyer out there; seek to identify the most likely buyer profile for today in defining the firm's target market and game plan.

Understanding the Investment Calendar

Once general market timing is assessed, and a likely buyer profile is defined, firms can focus on the prospects themselves. What is this institution's process and timeline? Respondents were asked about their funding and due diligence process in general; allocation timing and required steps. Respondents were also asked if there were better times of the year to market generally, and times when it should be avoided regardless of strategy. While there were some variances, there were lots of similarities across institutions, independent of their size, client base and investment vehicle preferences.

A pattern regarding the institutional investment management research process did emerge which is intuitively known to seasoned professionals, but easily forgotten in the day-to-day drive to stay in front of prospects. ***The standard 12-month calendar has a rhythm to it that is worth careful consideration in mapping out an institutional marketing and sales effort.*** There are four quarters in the year; each quarter has a series of predictable activities that should be factored into the game plan. Firms may remember the calendar best when defined as a game of red light/green light:

The First Month Post Quarter End: Red Light

The month after quarter end is the most difficult for institutional research professionals to focus any attention on new ideas, or even on good content from existing ideas. This month is all about collecting results, tabulating them and reporting them to clients. Institutions are meeting with their clients either to share market views and to take credit for a quarter well played, or to defend a portfolio that didn't net out as hoped. A well-diversified portfolio should not have 100% of its holdings moving up in lockstep by design, so there is always something to discuss and explain. This, in effect, is the institution's "client time". These months: January, April, July, and October, are best to avoid for new product positioning.

They are also tough months for other reasons. January is the kick off to a new year, it is year-end reporting and goal setting time for most institutions. April is tax time. July is the most common vacation month as schools generally end in June in many places, and start up again in August in others; July might be the 'deadest' month of the year. October is least problematic of the four, but does have the kick off to the final quarter of the year and perhaps the last big month to "sell" in order to close business, as well as to consider tax advantaged game plans prior to year-end. In short, these are hectic months. As a result, they get the red flag in institutional marketing and sales. The only exception is in delivering the firm's performance update in a timely manner such that the institution can see the results and factor them into their own reporting. In terms of sending materials and asking for feedback on them in these red-light months, however? It is best to avoid them, or to manage expectations of responsiveness at the very least.

The Second Month Post Quarter End: Green Light

The most ideal time to reach out was consistently identified by respondents as the mid quarter month. This translates to February, May, August and November. Previous quarterly reporting is largely done. At this time last quarter is well understood, and the next quarter is only half way baked, leaving lots of room for big changes and little need to opine on the current quarter just yet. Size of the institution is relevant here, with smaller organizations requiring their research professionals to play a sales and marketing role which will impact the mid quarter months. Managers may be competing a bit with an institution's own sales cycle, which is best implemented within the same mid quarter months. For institutions with distinct investment research and sales resources, this is not a factor. The middle month periods do have their own challenges baked in: potential weather issues in February making travel a bit dicey, summer vacations and back to school in August, and Thanksgiving break impacting a lot more than that third Thursday of the month in November. There is always May! ***Nevertheless, these mid quarter months were consistently highlighted by respondents as the best time in the quarter to reach out with new ideas.***

The Third Month Post Quarter End: Yellow Light

The last month of the quarter was not as popular among respondents as was expected. Quarter end was a bit ill-advised when discussing the "ideal" time to reach out on something new, or to share something the firm wants read. Why? Most redemptions that occurred based on the previous quarter end are now ready to be reinvested and institutions are focused on the final details of these allocations at this time. Additionally, institutions continue to be out marketing themselves at this point, whether they are seeking assets to manage or to oversee, now that the dust has fully settled on the previous quarter and they have gotten "caught up" with existing client communications.

The third month of a quarter also means a potential whole new scenario to present on the investment side of the equation, and yet the quarter isn't quite done. Depending on how volatile the asset class has been over the quarter, the manager might not be prepared to provide the level of color desired at this point, and certainly research teams know that. Therefore, the third month post quarter end gets the yellow light; proceed with caution but do proceed if you missed the middle month time frame. Quarter end months are March, June, September and December. Except for December, these are all great months to market in. March Madness brings a natural dialogue among professionals, June is a 'feel good' month of generally great weather and the kick off to summer, and September is 'back to school'. December can be a great month to garner some year-end meetings as institution's think about their next year plans, particularly the first two weeks of the month. Additionally, it is a festive time. Firms can use these themes to their advantage as they seek to engage the institutional market.

The Calendar: Month by Month

When establishing the firm's institutional investment management marketing and sales game plan, keep in mind the following month by month calendar. The calendar has been separated by quarter to encourage firms to think about a quarterly communication, at a minimum, ensuring managers are fully engaging in the institutional process:

Market Timing	Q1	Q2	Q3	Q4
Red Light Months	January	April	July	October
Green Light Months	February	May	August	November
Yellow Light Months	March	June	September	December

A Potential Game Plan for Calendar Optimization

When might an institution have the most time to consider an opportunity fully? That depends. It is all relative to the specific institution, their needs and priorities. Yet there are enough commonalities among respondent feedback to carefully consider the calendar when planning outreach so that the firm has the best chance of full vetting. Plan A might be to make sure the firm has a game plan associated with the middle month of each quarter regarding outreach and requests for review, including a live meeting. Plan B may be to pursue institutions in the third month of the quarter, at least for the first three quarters of the year, prioritizing March, June and September, followed by the mid-quarter windows of February, May, August and November.

Why Swim Against the Tide?

Firms and their marketing professionals might argue that this research process and calendar conversation all feel like a convenient excuse to limit responsiveness on behalf of institutions. Indeed, it can be. Regardless of the reason, the goal is to maximize the firm's brand recognition through its outreach, to gain face time with the target audience and to provide educational value to institutions such that the firm is perceived to be a resource. Why not be strategic and send that white paper the first week in February when folks are snowed in, done with Q4 reporting and with not much else to do but read it and consider the firm's candidacy? Firms who elect, for any number of reasons, to ignore the natural rhythms of the calendar, must be cognoscente of this at the very least. It is not uncommon for managers to find great frustration in the lack of responsiveness from a prepared outreach despite the timing of its send. This can create unproductive animosity among the sales and marketing team, and among the institutions that the firm is seeking feedback from. Respondents universally expressed frustration with firms who do not take the time to understand, nor respect, their calendars. Doing so is an easy way to avoid the crowds. Swimming with the tide is much easier than swimming against it.

Institutional Processes Will Vary

Respondents were asked about their funding process; when they set their own investment calendar (this varied more than expected) and what steps were required before funding can occur (also quite variable). Is an onsite required before funding? Is meeting the portfolio manager required? Not surprising, the less liquid the strategy, the more due diligence, time and hands on interaction required. Registration was also a factor in the timeliness of the funding process; registered products are generally more liquid, but even when they are not, the formal registration with regulators of a product reduced the due diligence and increased the speed of funding in most cases. Respondents indicated that the process generally takes anywhere from three months to two years, *presuming there is interest in a specific strategy and manager.* Firms are encouraged to take the time to understand the structural implications of this process and to ensure that their teams fully understand them. Comparing the timing of funding of a registered and liquid product, to an unregistered and illiquid product, is unrealistic. Perhaps a reasonable rule of thumb is to add two months for each year of illiquidity. A 40-act registered mutual fund that is daily liquid will take two months at a minimum to process, presuming there is immediate interest and demand. A private placement with a five-year minimum term will take ten months or longer to fully due diligence.

Keeping the Process on Track: Avoiding Detours

In discussing the research process with respondents, a few rules for the road were highlighted to help managers stay on the right track.

Avoid Resource Changes Other Than Hiring: One of the biggest risks for firms is a change in resources. Not only investment resources, which are at the top of the list, but also vendor resources, and marketing and sales resources. Consistency is critical in the institutional investment management marketing and sales process. Firms are strongly encouraged to shore up their infrastructure and confirm the commitment of their team members before they step into the market. Not only to avoid the inevitable need to explain away any changes that occur, but to avoid the perception that the firm is just getting their sea legs under them, cutting their teeth on the institutional investment management process and not fully "buttoned up" when it comes to their preparedness to take on an institutional mandate. They either "don't know what they need" in terms of resources, or have not spent the time to fully vet and incentivize their resources. Institutional researchers know that they will be tasked with explaining, and thus defending, these changes to an investment committee or directly to their client. With so many options available, why take that chance?

Changes to the investment team can cause a massive detour. Firms should do whatever they can to ensure the stability of their resources prior to engaging the institutional market. Institutional investment management research professionals are focused, from the first introduction, on who is doing what in the investment process. They want to understand where the decisions are made and what expertise the team brings to the table. When firms experience investment resource changes during the institutional sales process it raises a red flag. Often, it places the manager into a "watch list" scenario while the institution "sees" how this resource change impacts the manager's performance for a period of 12 months. Can a manager survive a junior analyst leaving? Yes. It happens. However, it will have less of an impact if the firm has clearly articulated each team member's role and responsibilities, and if the junior analyst's domain was non-core to the overall track record. It will have less of an impact if the team is sizeable. If this is the only analyst supporting a PM, the impact is perceived to be much greater.

Vendor changes are often made because a firm's first attempt at securing resources was based on budget and convenience, and not on expertise. This is a mistake and will be covered in greater detail in *Chapter 17: Resource Management.*

If there is ever a time in a firm's lifecycle when they need to engage qualified and experienced vendors, it is early on, when these resources can provide guidance and value beyond the manager's own expertise. Firms often engage small, local resources that are great partners, but lack the brand recognition and more importantly the expertise to bring the manager to institutional standards. Managers will often acknowledge this and seek to make changes well into their marketing campaigns. It is not insurmountable, but it is a reminder that the firm is "young" institutionally and might not be prepared to handle an institutional mandate of any size. Even when the change is for the better, which it typically is, it's a red flag.

Changes in marketing, and particularly in sales resources is another common challenge for firms. Institutions like consistency. They do not like getting a phone call from a new person, even if it is someone else they know, about the same manager. *"Who is on first?"* respondents asked. Reviewing *Chapter 4* in relation to the Firm's commitment, and *Chapter 17* on resources, will further the firm's knowledge regarding factors to consider in relation to marketing and sales resources.

Respect the Process—Remain Pleasant and Present: The investment management asset gathering process is a long one. Respondents, in discussing the funding process, consistently commented on managers who lacked poise and presence throughout the process. These factors eliminated them from consideration. The universe is vast, institutions have lots of choices and little time. They have their own stresses and demands. By understanding timing and the funding process, ideally managers will be better equipped to handle the frustrations inherent in waiting it out. Respondents requested four considerations from managers who are seeking to engage them:

1. ***Show Up:*** It is the manager's job, not the researcher's job nor the marketing and sales team's job, to be present through an active voice in writing and in person. Nothing replaces appropriate and timely communications from portfolio managers. These touchpoints do not need to be overly time consuming nor deep, they just need to exist.

2. ***Buck Up:*** It is a long and grueling process and institutions have lots of competing interests. Managers will not like the reception they get for one of two reasons. Either because it is non-existent in the form of a lack of response, or it is "nitpicky" in the form of what can feel like an interrogation of sorts to a manager who is passionate about their process and numbers and doesn't want to "waste time" on the little details of staff changes, process articulation or deep dive portfolio analysis. Unfortunately, this is exactly what institutions need to understand.

3. ***Respect the Process:*** Managers seek a more immediate response and believe they are being ignored for the wrong reasons. They blame the marketing and sales resources and they blame the institutional research professionals for not showing them the love fast enough. Managers and sales professionals alike may seek to circumvent the process, finding a senior institutional connection, pursuing field resources (discussed in *Chapter 5*) and going above the head of the institutional research professional. This rarely works. It is easy to underestimate the position of an investment research professional, particularly since many come across as rather youthful. While institutional research professionals could help their cause in this regard by providing more direct and timely feedback to requests from managers, they are the hiring agent and not the candidate. As the candidate, managers are encouraged to take the time to understand the prospect and their process as outlined in *Chapter 5*, and to be respectful of it.

4. ***Build a Personal Relationship:*** There is enough turnover in the institutional investment management research world that a good relationship can end up creating an asset management opportunity at an entirely different organization. Either through networking or through waiting out the institutional research professional's next move to an institution that better embraces the type of strategy the firm is offering, consider each interaction an opportunity to build a relationship that transcends the institution itself. This will pay dividends down the road.

Respondents told repeated stories of *"angry emails"* and phone calls from managers who had *"enough"*. Pleasantries had gone by the wayside and they simply couldn't understand what the problem was. Was their sales professional simply incompetent and would their direct outreach make the difference? What else could the institution need to know before funding? Why were there 445 questions in the due diligence questionnaire and even then, the funding did not come? How could this be? Part of what institutional researchers must consider is temperament.

Does the manager have the forethought and perseverance to work through the process? Are they fully committed? Do they understand what the institution is likely to need in the form of communications and portfolio analysis on a real-time basis to meet *their* client requests? The institutional marketing and sales process is not just about finding a great manager with fantastic numbers and finding a fit within an existing portfolio, it is also about finding a dependable and pleasant partner with which to work. Frustrating as the process is for managers, remaining level headed, and present is critical.

Questions Asked

Respondents were asked the following questions in bold face text specifically in relation to this chapter. The consensus answers are in italics and immediately follow the question asked.

What is the best time to market?
The middle month of the quarter, followed by the last month of the quarter.

When are the worst times to market?
The first month after quarter end; classic holiday and vacation windows.

When is your investment calendar defined and how often does that change?
It varies; change is always a possibility.

Presuming you have interest, how long does the process generally take from intro to investment?
3-24 months depending on the liquidity and registration of the investment.

What is the typical process of manager you have funded?
It varies with some common elements; see quotes. Due diligence is always an element.

Will you invest in a manager you have not met with in person?
No; liquid strategies were the only exceptions.

Will you invest in a manager you have not completed an on-site with?
Yes; we do less on-sites than we used to.

How important is team stability during the engagement process?
Critical; [it] can be overcome if not a key decision maker, however. We are also concerned about vendor resource changes and non-investment team changes.

Words to Drive By

The following quotes provide a broader sampling of the respondents' direct feedback in relation to the above questions. Firms are encouraged to drive their marketing and sales activities with these rules for the road in mind.

On Respecting the Calendar—the Best Times to Market

Mid-quarter is best; most redeem and have capital at end of quarter to place; September is [also] good.

Summertime is best—it also tells me if the manager is checked out themselves.

Those off months—Feb./March, May/June, Aug./Sept., Nov./Dec.

Products released in Q1 or Q3 get the most traction. If [you] get [the product] out Q1, [institutions] have some time to get used to it and can use [it] in tax season rebalancing; if you get out in Q3 [it] can be used for rebalancing at year-end.

Month after quarter-end we are swamped prepping updates. Second month after quarter-end we are traveling to see clients. Last month is really best for conversations.

On Respecting the Calendar—the Worst Times to Market

July because our fiscal year was June 30—perhaps asking when does your fiscal year-end? Two to three weeks before [a] board meeting we are pandemonium; middle two weeks of the month after quarter-end were reporting season. For consultants it's the end of the month after the quarter ends that should be avoided at all costs.

Don't send new things first two to three weeks after quarter-end— too much focus on attribution, commentary and client meetings; anything new will get lost in the wave. Mid-November/December [is] bad for advisors—client meetings and tax loss harvesting, and again at tax season in April.

First of the year everyone wants to meet and map out the year and see if there is a good way to get on the radar and January is [the] busiest month for year-end.

60 days after end of quarter plus or minus a week or two is when we are out talking to clients and it might be difficult because we are out meeting with our clients.

Thanksgiving on is not a good time to market; a lot of estate stuff, tax planning; quarter-end is better. The summer is interesting as lots of vacations but also very slow; July/August may be able to get in front of firms because not as many client pressures; dog days of summer are good.

On the Institutions Investment Calendar

It is a work in progress and related to demand. We are more focused in one area so more varied other places; we set up our research calendar nine months in advance in terms of onsite visits.

[It] evolves over time; we are glacial [in our pace].

Generally, set at end of year but then quarterly [we are] revisiting it; often mid-course corrections.

We meet monthly by phone and in person every six months; our priorities don't change that often.

It is an iterative process; we are constantly talking to managers and allocators and seeing what is interesting to others. [I] have a friend working at a high yield desk, always trying to figure out what the cycles are and trends. We tend to have a one to three year horizon.

On Process and Timing Presuming There Is Interest

Depends on demand; do we have an opportunity. If yes than as low as a couple of months with a number of touchpoints/analysis (meeting, data requests, rationale on past).

On average two months for liquid strategies; we are pretty thorough overall. It is not often that we are going to move on a new fund until we've gotten to know a new manager over time, this timeline is only when we know the firms quite well; with private equity we just made a commitment to a firm we talked to for three years and that is how long it took, meetings twice per year, and quarterly calls, and had access to the head of the firm. For liquid strategies we will move quicker.

If there is interest it can be 12-36 months.

Depends on structure; why it's a fit and what we expect it to do. We always meet face to face to really understand before we fund it; SMAs and illiquid LPs have a due diligence questionnaire; with interval funds [it] tends to look more like a mutual fund.

One to two years minimum; hiring a manager is time consuming and politically expensive, and not something I want to do often. I have to go through risk management, compliance, and senior management—so I really hate flipping managers. We need to feel to the best of our ability that we are hiring someone we can use for the long haul.

Definitive interest on our end for a liquid strategy is anywhere from 30-60 days for diligence but usually quicker if real interest from a client; if the interest is investment team driven but we don't know if there is adviser or client interest and need to figure where it fits—it can be highly variable. This happens often; we don't have a compelling need at the moment.

On Whether the Institution Will Invest in a Manager Without Doing an Onsite

Necessary and mandatory for both maintaining coverage and new managers.

We don't have to; it is nice if someone from [the] firm has, but [it] hasn't held us back from recommending.

It doesn't happen as much; we outsource our operational due diligence and rely on them to meet the manager; we do qualitative and quantitative and how it fits into a diversified portfolio.

We would like to visit but don't always.

We want to visit on-site to see consistency across the team in terms of answers; one quarter of the time we find inconsistencies.

On Team Stability

This is huge; depends on the set up of the firm, not an issue for Izzy Englander because they manage in pools of capital. For a single strategy organization it is a huge issue; less of an issue at a big shop, huge at a small shop.

It depends on team size and contributions and impact of analysts. For small teams it's critical (under 10 analysts), for large teams with sector overlap its ok.

Very critical; falls off the list unfortunately. Analyst exit could be ok. If it is a key member of the decision-making team we talk it through and it goes on hold if no comfort.

I identify key investment professionals—if they were to leave it would trigger a hold and a review; I've done both but can't tell the percentage. [Some firms] who lost key people had offering incentives to other key professionals to keep them on board and so we placed the manager on 'hold' and watched for 6-12 months; if any further departures we were out and that is what happened in the most recent case and often does, and so we got out.

Junior people ok, mid-level and/or non-investment senior people becomes a bit more of an issue. We just need to understand it; we frequently ask to talk to the person that left.

Summary on the Institutional Research and Funding Process

Institutions have a rhythm to their research process. Managers will increase efficiency and effectiveness by working within the institutional framework.

Understand the Institutional Process and General Timelines

Know the Calendar

Manage Expectations: Most Institutions Are Already Fully Invested

---

CHAPTER 17

Resource Management

RPM Rating on Resources

DE MINIMIS	CORE	PRIORITY	GAME CHANGER

Resources are a pivotal component of an organization's profile, and an area that firms tend to struggle with particularly early on in their development. Firms understand that they must have certain resources in place, whether internal or external, to meet institutional standards. Resource demands will ebb and flow with a firm's growth. Getting the resource equation correct is a *game changer* according to the *Resource Prioritization Matrix*. First, consider the firm's internal strengths and capabilities to help determine which activities are best completed internally v. externally. Some resources will be internal to meet institutional qualification and because they are at the heart of what a manager does, such as portfolio management. Others require external expertise, such as the firm's audit. Beyond these most obvious distinctions, there is room for both outsourcing, and building capabilities in-house. Most managers initially consider the following, generally in this order, when determining whether to build a capability in-house, or to outsource it:

Initial Manager Resource Considerations

1. Cost
2. Convenience
3. Time to Market
4. Control
5. Expertise
6. Breadth and Brand of Resource

Respondents were asked about their specific experiences with manager resources, and with internal v. external marketing resources in particular. Do institutional investment management research professionals believe they respond differently to these resources in either case? Throughout the interviews, respondents provided additional feedback on manager preparedness, which naturally related to a firm's selection of resources across functional areas from firm formation and funding, through marketing and sales. How these managers elected to build their firms' resources made a significant difference in every aspect of institutional consideration.

Re-thinking Resource Allocations

Managers have choices when it comes to resource allocation. What is assured is that several resources will be needed to provide the infrastructure required for institutional mandates. Due to the depth and scope of resources necessitated by an institutional marketing bid, managers often cobble together a mix of internal and external solutions in the following manner:

1. First, least costly and most convenient for managers is the repositioning of an internal resource;

2. Second, outsourcing to a regional vendor with limited brand strength and institutional expertise is common; and

3. Third, managers may elect to contract with nationally

recognized players, at a higher cost but with the industry expertise and breadth of resources to enhance the manager's business above and beyond the service delivery itself.

Perhaps the descriptions utilized above explain the author's perspective. However, the correct path will differ by manager, time in market, culture and function. Managers cannot always pursue nor access high-end external resources. At a minimum, firms may want to rethink their priorities when it comes to resource allocation. Here is where most managers land once they have been "around the block" regarding resource allocation and management over a series of years:

Experienced Manager Resource Considerations

1. Expertise
2. Breadth and Brand of Resource
3. Time to Market
4. Control
5. Cost
6. Convenience

Resource Considerations by Business Development Stage

There are a variety of resources needed at each stage of business development. Here are a few factors to consider at each stage:

I. *Pre-Launch*

As a component of the pre-launch process, managers are encouraged to take a step back in Part II of the book. Aspects of stepping back include ensuring the capital and resource commitment of the firm to the process, as well as full vetting of the firm and offering. Running an institutional quality investment management firm is expensive. Managers are constantly faced with the conundrum of time and money. What is worth their time, and what is worth their money? Pre-launch is the best time to fully vet resource options. It is a time when managers have less of a run rate financially, less skin in the game with previously selected resources, and more feedback from market constituents who are excited to see the firm take off, but are not yet being asked to commit capital nor their allegiance to the firm's candidacy. This time is the manager's, as discussed in Part II on stepping back, to define its resource options and priorities based on the support and feedback of organizations that are eager to see them succeed.

Resources to Tap Pre-launch Include:

Advisors: Managers are encouraged to establish an advisory board to help guide their development and to show the market that they are a known and supported entity.

Consultants: A myriad of dedicated consultants are available for managers who seek advice on various aspects of firm development. These resources can save a lot more money than they cost in good advice about what to consider, and what to skip, in building out a firm.

Network: During the pre-launch, colleagues and connections are excited to be a part of a new firm's development. They are eager to suggest resources and to provide examples of what they have seen work, and more importantly not work, on the road to asset growth. Take advantage of this network; these connections are most transparent in providing feedback and are most helpful in making suggestions *before* the manager is in the "ask" stage of business development.

Seed Capital: Managers work hard to get where they are. They have risked career and colleagues, the safety of a large corporation and their very livelihoods, all on a hunch that they could build something better on their own. That is why they established the firm in the first place. They have spent lots of time and resources getting to this point and they are reticent to share. They want the whole pie, not a part of it. This is a miss. *Seed capital can be extremely effective in helping a firm get to profitability and scale which are required elements of institutional eligibility.* Many success stories in the market have followed a common path. A manager works hard to build their firm and baseline infrastructure, and then sits at sub $100M for several years, unable to gain traction in the institutional market. They "give in" to a seed investor. Seed capital enters stage left, takes a minority ownership stake, injects the necessary capital and back office resources to immediately render the manager institutionally viable, and infuses brand and identity into the organization that was sorely needed. Institutions respond in kind with allocations. Years of footwork and preplanning have finally paid off. Yes, seed capital must be carefully vetted in terms of control rights, day-to-day operations, cultural fit, objectives and reputation of the seeder. If these hurdles can be overcome, seed capital is a highly efficient way to grow an institutional asset management firm, and in many cases, is required to do so.

Vendors: Outsourcing is the new norm in business. Firms can outsource absolutely everything, right down to portfolio management. Vendors come in many shapes, sizes, structures and experience levels. Complete the analysis of vendor options v. in-house resources via the matrix provided on page 272. Not all vendors and vendor solutions are created equal. Given the regulatory and cybersecurity environments, a complete vetting of any potential vendor is necessary before engaging. Contracts with vendors should include protective language regarding the same.

Research: Research can be generated in-house, or can be purchased. It can also be offset against trading costs in certain instances. Managers may elect to support, or even to drive their process with external research. Institutions will be most focused on two aspects of this outsourcing: (1) The use of external research positioned in the investment process and whether the positioning is consistent with the actual amount of external research employed; (2) Whether the usage of certain external research is part of a soft dollar transaction, in place as an offset to other costly services which the manager has elected to engage. Institutions will accept varying responses to these questions. They will not accept discrepancies.

II. *Launch*

In preparing to go to market, firms know they need a variety of resources in place. The buy v. build debate typically takes place on a function by function basis. Overriding the functional analysis, keep in mind that if the firm is rather new to market, at least the institutional aspect of it, it cannot afford to go to market with a vendor that is itself a babe in the woods, new and inexperienced in the institutional space. While cost and convenience might be higher, expertise and vendor brand are undeniably lesser. In the world of vendor selection and resource allocation, less can be much more. Managers will be better off outsourcing strategically to known names and experts in the field for key functions they cannot possibly perform internally, maintaining those resources that they can handle sufficiently in-house for the time being.

III. *Ongoing Maintenance*

The best case for outsourcing is made when it comes to ongoing maintenance of specific functions. Given the market's comfort with outsourcing, firms can remain agile and efficient by limiting internal staff build-outs where external resources are not only more efficient, but more focused and active in the broad market. For example, compliance requirements are constantly changing in the investment management business as new regulations are introduced, and old ones are tweaked. While firms may elect to maintain a CCO, and in many cases are required to do so under various regulatory bodies, maintaining an outsourced regulatory vendor relationship can be critical in ensuring that the firm remains abreast of all current compliance requirements. Cybersecurity and information technology are other areas where outsourcing can make tremendous sense. The market is changing rapidly; maintaining external vendor relationships with firms that specialize in these key areas will go a long way to ensuring that the firm is institutionally ready.

Impact of Culture on Resource Management

When considering what resources to hire externally, and what to maintain internally, a careful review of culture is informative. Firm culture will impact the success of both internal and external relationships. If nothing else, it should impact the terms of an agreement between the resource and the firm, as well as how the resource will be managed day-to-day. Questions the firm should ask include:

1. Are all team resources in the same location, or are they disperse? Does the singular/multiple location work culture work well for the firm?
2. How much interaction is there among team members daily? How much of the firm's activities are relegated to structured meetings where it would be simple to patch in an external resource v. how much is unstructured, impromptu back and forth between team members in the same room?
3. What external relationships are in place today and how are they working out?
4. What external relationships have succeeded and what ones have failed in the past five years? What caused this success or failure? What business functions were they performing?
5. How does the firm view the importance of marketing and sales? Does the firm view these functions as one in the same or as separate? Where does marketing and sales sit on the prioritization list for the firm? Are these functions completed 'on the side' or are they a regular and specific dialogue, and set of activities within the firm?
6. What is the firm's expectation of activity and contact between an external vendor and the in-house team? Are their defined touchpoints that will be required? How much attention will the firm require?

7. How will success be defined for an internal solution? How will it be defined for an external vendor partner? Are these expectations realistic?
8. What time frame will the team give this resource for this function? Does the firm see this as a long-term commitment or a "test case"?
9. How does the investment team anticipate working with this resource?
10. Have there been any "lessons learned" regarding in-house v. external resource allocation in the firm's history that might inform its best path moving forward?
11. Is the firm aware of the institutional market's expectations and do team members have a realistic view of the level of expertise that exists in-house currently?
12. Does the firm see the value in an external vendor relationship to further advance the firm's reputation in the market, or does it simply see an external vendor as a necessary placeholder until it can build the desired team in-house?

Impact of Capabilities on Resource Management

Culture aside, there are certain factual limitations that firms must acknowledge regarding their resource configuration. The firm's internal capabilities are a primary driver of what resources are secured, at what depth and in what order, whether internally or externally. The quickest way to establish an institutional infrastructure is to outsource its key functions. Complete an assessment of team member roles, responsibilities, backgrounds and areas of expertise as follows before determining what to outsource and what to build in-house, what resources to prioritize and what can "wait" until the firm has grown. Note that the below matrix includes "primary function" and "additional capacity" in far-right columns. Firms who have team members "wearing multiple hats" must honestly assess the capacity of its own resources, not only regarding qualifications but also regarding time. Gaps within the primary function allocation of a firm's resources represent opportunities for outsourcing and firm hiring.

FUNCTIONAL RESOURCE ASSESSMENT

Team Member	Title	Role	Education	Years of Experience	Years at Firm	Licensing	Skills	Primary Function	Currently Reports To	Additional Capacity

Note: The QR code at the front and back of the book provides complimentary access to this and many other templates for team use.

Firms, particularly in a newer stage of development, are seeking to manage resources and reduce costs. One way of doing this is to employ junior staff that can grow with the organization. This is a compelling game plan, if and only if it is supported out of the gate by industry recognized and deeply experienced vendor partners who can ensure the firm is fully up to speed on the latest in best practices. Whether the firm is considering utilizing existing staff that will be cross-trained and responsible for multiple functions, whether it considers hiring internally a resource or two, or whether it elects to outsource to a regional player or a nationally recognized brand, the firm will get what it pays for. There are of course exceptional regional vendors, individuals to hire, and junior resources that can rise fully to the occasion. Careful prioritization of highest and best use among resources will assist managers in ensuring they meet institutional qualification standards. Careful planning will save significant management time and resources in avoiding the inevitable need to micro manage insufficient and ineffective resources, or to complete a change in resources further down the road.

Avoiding the Bait and Switch in Resource Management

Firms want to get the show on the road. They are always resource constrained. To address these conflicting realities, firms will often engage the wrong resources to check the box in a cost efficient and convenient way. This includes continuing to rely on resources the firm has outgrown, or are unqualified; resources that do not have the institutional presence and expertise to be additive to the manager's value proposition. Most managers, when asked, can immediately identify which resources these are. Firms will realize, deep into the process of marketing and sales to institutions, that their resources lack the expertise and depth they require. Their only choice is to make a change.

Untimely at best, resource changes can wreak havoc on a firm's infrastructure and focus. Despite the desire to run down the road, firms are suggested to walk cautiously. Full vetting of potential resources, and clear review of their anticipated role in the process, is a required element to successful pre-launch planning. It is often the case that managers will 'outgrow' their resources and in this case changes are sometimes inevitable. However, incorporating this expectation into the game plan and mapping out resource allocations within a five-year business plan is the work of a successful firm. The five-year business plan is a common request of institutions. They want to see that the firm has thought through their resource needs now and in the future. *Establish a written five-year business plan that includes resource allocations to avoid untimely bait and switch changes when the firm can least afford the distraction.*

Don't Double Down

Firms may wish to hire multiple resources, particularly in sales, to see how much can be thrown against the proverbial wall, and what will stick. Don't double down. Respondents noted receiving *"multiple calls"* from *"different people"* on behalf of the same manager. Managers who attempt to play the field with their own resources are not perceived well by the industry. It takes time and effort to get resources integrated into the process, to manage target markets, and for the institution to respond and screen inquiries. Take the time to identify the best fit for the organization, have a shared set of goals and clear expectations for activities and outreach, and stick with the game plan for long enough to see it work. This is typically two to three years, not two or three months.

Resource Considerations: Tools by AUM

Organizations rely on a wide variety of tools to conduct business. These tools cost money. Prioritize each tool to ensure the firm is most efficiently utilizing its resources. Below is a sample set of tables for how managers might best map out their current business infrastructure, and the firm's game plan for these applications as they grow. In some instances, the cost of the tools becomes more efficient, the greater the firm's AUM. In others, the tool can become more, or less relevant as the firm's AUM grows. Completing the below analysis will assist firms in understanding their current commitments, the length and scope of them, how the team sees the tool and what factors should be under consideration regarding these resources as the firm grows.

RESOURCES AT LAUNCH

Tool	Source/ Vendor	Cost	Contractual Commitments (Length & Scope)	Vendor Experience	Firm Experience	Considerations
Investment Data/ Data Analytics						
Trading						
Account Administration/ Reporting						
Share File Sites						
Contact Management Software						
Marketing/Contact Databases						
Email Marketing / Campaign Management						
Website Hosting & Management						
Cybersecurity/ Information Technology						
Compliance						
Legal						

RESOURCES AT $100 MILLION

Tool	Source/ Vendor	Cost	Contractual Commitments (Length & Scope)	Vendor Experience	Firm Experience	Considerations
Investment Data/ Data Analytics						
Trading						
Account Administration/ Reporting						
Share File Sites						
Contact Management Software						
Marketing/Contact Databases						
Email Marketing / Campaign Management						
Website Hosting & Management						
Cybersecurity/ Information Technology						
Compliance						
Legal						

RESOURCES AT $500 MILLION

Tool	Source/ Vendor	Cost	Contractual Commitments (Length & Scope)	Vendor Experience	Firm Experience	Considerations
Investment Data/ Data Analytics						
Trading						
Account Administration/ Reporting						
Share File Sites						
Contact Management Software						
Marketing/Contact Databases						
Email Marketing / Campaign Management						
Website Hosting & Management						
Cybersecurity/ Information Technology						
Compliance						
Legal						

RESOURCES AT $1 BILLION

Tool	Source/ Vendor	Cost	Contractual Commitments (Length & Scope)	Vendor Experience	Firm Experience	Considerations
Investment Data/ Data Analytics						
Trading						
Account Administration/ Reporting						
Share File Sites						
Contact Management Software						
Marketing/Contact Databases						
Email Marketing / Campaign Management						
Website Hosting & Management						
Cybersecurity/ Information Technology						
Compliance						
Legal						

Resource Considerations by Business Function

The investment management business can be defined by a series of functions. When it comes to resource allocation, this is an effective way to think about a firm's resources and where it might elect to build internally v. engage externally. Respondents commented on their desire to understand *"Who's on first?"* at the firm for a variety of functions. In *Chapter 18: Games Managers Play,* a discussion of how managers often seek to present their resources is incorporated. As the title of this next chapter implies, managers are not always forthcoming about their scope and breadth of resources. Institutions understand that this is an expensive business, and that managers need sufficient scale in the form of AUM to offset the costs of these resources, whether they are functional tools or business personnel.

The decisions to build v. buy and hire v. outsource, are pivotal ones. Managers rarely take the time to outline these resources. Why do they have them? What are they intended to accomplish? What do they cost and what is the run rate? How experienced are they? How experienced is the firm in this area? Below is a matrix that managers can complete to better consider their resources across functional business areas. There is overlap to the above *Resource Considerations: Tools by AUM* series of matrices. This is intentional to encourage managers to think about their profile both in terms of a viable game plan as the organization grows, and in terms of in-house v. external resource prioritization. Business integration, the last column, encourages firms to consider how integrated this resource is into the day-to-day operations of the business, and how effective this has been from the perspective of the team.

INTERNAL V. EXTERNAL RESOURCES

Function	Typical Structure	Firm Profile	Cost	Run Rate & Contractual Commitment	Firm Expectations	Business Integration
Portfolio Management	In-House					
Operations	In-House					
Legal	Outsourced					
Compliance	Outsourced; In-House CCO For Oversight					
Audit	Outsourced					
Marketing	In-House					
Sales	In & Out					
Reporting	In & Out					
Information Technology	In & Out					
Administration	Outsourced					
Client Service	In-House					

Internal v. External Sales

The selection of sales support deserves special consideration. The variance in size, scope, expertise and resources applied to marketing and sales among managers is broad. In comparison, an audit is an audit. It must be done and must be done to certain specifications. Firms cannot do their own audit by design. Auditors require specific education and licensing to be qualified to complete an audit. While it can be argued that marketing and sales should be considered in a similar light, necessitating education, expertise and a certain structure, it is not required. As such firms often will jigger the most with their marketing and sales game plan, trying various resources and models on the road to AUM. Here is a basic comparison of what is typically found when comparing in-house v. outsourced sales solutions:

INTERNAL V. EXTERNAL SALES

Solution	In-House	Outsourced*
Focus	Exclusive	Non-Exclusive
Cost	Fixed Cost: Salary; Overhead; Bonus/ Commission Structure	Retainer/Draw; Commission; Potential Equity Ownership
Term	Indefinite w/ Employment Contract Benefits	One to Three Years with a Momentum Clause to Permit the Outsourced Agent(s) to Close Key Accounts Post Termination
Experience	Resumé Specific	Channel Specific; Institutional (not Individuals)
Breadth	Individual	Team
Function	Firm Defined	Third Party Defined
Integration	Present On-site	Remote
Licensing	Candidate Dependent	Broker Dealer, Affiliated with a Broker Dealer, an Investment Advisor or Municipal Advisor are Common; Outsourced Firm Manages All Compliance Oversight Of Agents

*Terms noted are typical in nature; each outsourced entity may have a unique set of criteria under which they contract with managers.

Questions Asked

Respondents were asked the following questions in bold face text specifically in relation to this chapter. The consensus answers are in italics and immediately follow the question asked.

What do you like about internal marketing professionals?
They are dedicated to the firm and tend to know the investment process fairly well. They are, on the whole, less aggressive than outsourced marketing professionals.

What do you like about outsourced/third party marketing professionals?
They can provide a variety of ideas and market feedback. It is easier to tell a third party the truth about why a manager will not be hired in most cases. They understand what we are looking for.

Do you respond differently to managers v. marketers? Do you provide more direct feedback either way?
We don't think so. We try not to, but perhaps in some cases where we know the marketer well, we do.

Words to Drive By

The following quotes provide a broader sampling of the respondents' direct feedback in relation to the above questions. Firms are encouraged to drive their marketing and sales activities with these rules for the road in mind.

On Internal Marketing

Knowledge of team and history can be really good, but that's its only advantage; also a dead end/useful life unless the role merges into a client service professional.

The person should really know what they are talking about and can answer most research questions as they are dedicated just to that manager—I have yet to find that to be true, however.

Responsiveness, deeper knowledge, particularly key with larger firms with broad investment choice.

They can speak to personalities and interaction, more soft information; there aren't that many out there, only a handful that really we can talk to in lieu of the PM.

They are in the office, face time, going to the meetings. [They] might be more in tune with what's happening.

On Outsourced/Third Party Marketing

[There is] more option to continue the dialogue as there is always something else to talk about. [We] met a music royalty fund through a third party marketing firm. An outsourced firm can manage the client better and can be told the truth "bring good Josh and not arrogant Josh." Even if they are not representing a manager they can introduce us to interesting ideas.

When times aren't great you can still get out there, more diversification; external marketer has a better grasp on what is going on in communities to whom they are marketing—they have seen more teams and consultants.

They can be thoughtful about what will work and what won't work for us; they have a broader view because they are talking to more people about more things.

I like it when they tell us there is a manager but it's not a good fit for us; it shows an understanding of what we do and like.

Individuals I speak to are those that I've built a stronger relationship with, lots of firms are providing valuable content but it doesn't have anything directly to do with their sales pitch.

Helpful information but no product pitch raises your opinion of the firm—they have given us something of value; I feel I do owe them something and will take a call because they are trying to build a relationship.

Bigger firms are trying to develop the relationship by providing useful content which goes beyond the sales pitch.

[They] can bring different ideas and I only have to deal with one person v. five or six other people; [they] know what is going on.

On the Benefits of Using External Resources

[They are] good at hard information/hard facts, but less soft nuances.

Experience and a brand we are comfortable with.

It can be an ongoing dialogue on what we need.

The benefit is casting a wide net, generating buzz and activity; network in place and a knowledgeable partner.

It can take a lot of the load off of the portfolio management team. Allow [external resources] to be the road warrior and the relationship management piece; there are different types of portfolio managers, some love marketing and being external and some hate it.

[Manager] was a terrible marketer but a great portfolio manager; [their] writing is a bit verbose and doesn't lend itself to bullet points.

Bringing in a third party marketing firm helped [the manager] be a better marketer, more succinct about pitches.

Three to five bullets is way better than eight. [Manager] needs someone to reign them in.

On Feedback Provided to Managers v. Marketers/Sales Agents

[How much feedback we give and to whom] depends on how receptive the manager is; would love to explain why I am not investing but sometimes managers take it too hard. We are starting to be clearer, and managers need to be honest with themselves.

The marketer is in a great position because they can often translate the feedback—particularly for more senior investment guys who don't take it well. Marketers can understand what the hot points are, they have heard more feedback from others as well.

Probably the same [feedback].

Manager is always the most important feedback, but we give the feedback to either. A lot depends on the quality of the sales person. Some are just excellent, they really know the product, others are just middle men—they don't add much value.

More direct with sales stuff than with a portfolio manager, but the portfolio manager conversations are a lot more detailed and fun.

No difference; sometimes it is easier to tell marketers we aren't interested as they often have other things to talk about, so it's not their only thing. We do try to be honest.

[We] might give more feedback direct to a third party marketer.

Summary on Resource Management

Resource allocation and management is a critical element to institutionalization. Firms seeking to grow must complete a detailed and ongoing analysis of their resources, both internal and external.

Rethink Resource Priorities

Complete a Thorough Internal Analysis of Resource Strengths, Knowledge and Capacity

---

Create a Five-Year Business Plan, Including an AUM Driven Resource Analysis to Avoid Unnecessary and Untimely Changes Down the Road

---

Stepping Out: Overdrive

Managers reach the final leg of the race and believe they have every-thing under control. If institutions would only give these manag-ers the opportunity, they could prove their worth and simultaneously reach their AUM goals. The road is long, and firms have invested significant resources in the effort, perhaps for several years at this point. Part V is focused on "Stepping Out", gaining some final perspective on the journey.

Marketing and selling include some gamesmanship. Managers must determine the best profile to put forward in the market provided it is a true reflection of their capabilities and process. However, sometimes gamesmanship is taken too far, employing an aspirational view of the firm instead of a realistic one. Managers play games to enhance their positioning, or to avoid a discussion on an element of their firm they believe to be negative. These games will be discussed in *Chapter 18*. They are well understood by professional researchers and unfortunately result in a few steps backwards in the process at best, elimination from consideration at worst. Games limit the firm's perceived integrity and capacity to partner fully on behalf of the institution's clients. A chapter was dedicated to gamesmanship to make it clear to firms that these games are obvious to institutional investment management research professionals. ***Presenting the firm with the highest integrity and clarity is paramount to manager success.***

Part V shifts gears to the recommendations made by institutional research professionals throughout the book. These recommendations will be synthesized here according to the ten topic areas covered in the interviews, and presented as a set of "recommendations for the road" in *Chapter 19*. Key takeaways from respondents by topic provide a framework for managers to consider in devising their own game plan.

To conclude, *Chapter 20: The Road to AUM* provides a summary review of the game plan set out in the book. Managers are encouraged to put their efforts into overdrive, rather than neutral, in revisiting their strategy, commitments, and resources dedicated to growing assets under management.

CHAPTER 18

Games Managers Play

RPM Rating on Gamesmanship

DE MINIMIS	CORE	PRIORITY	GAME CHANGER

Managers are dedicated to their craft. They are eager to demonstrate the firm's capabilities and to define what makes them different. They believe their results are better than others, which fuels the team's motivation in the marketing process. Firms hope that performance will be sufficient to offset a myriad of suboptimal profile elements related to the firm's history, team, funding, offering structure, and marketing. Performance is not enough. The firm is what institutions are considering, not a past performance track record. The suboptimal profile elements can come from anywhere and present themselves at any time. No organization is perfect. The good news is that institutions do not expect perfection, but they do expect an honest depiction of the firm, beyond performance.

The list of firm elements that are under consideration are vast. It boils down to the same five Ps previously reviewed. Presenting these elements of the firm's profile clearly and succinctly is the work of the firm. Gamesmanship will play a part; this is marketing and selling after all. However, imposture should not go so far as to call into question the validity of the manager. Respondents repeatedly discussed the games managers play in terms of specific actions and communications that left them scratching their heads. For this reason, acknowledging these tricks of the trade and how aware respondents are of them is considered a *core* element according to the *Resource Prioritization Matrix*.

Clarity Matters

In all representations, firms must be clear about the main elements of their value proposition, which can be further defined as follows:

Element	The Details
People	Experience; Backgrounds; Regulatory Records; Legal History; Compliance History; Roles and Responsibilities; Ownership and Incentive Compensation Structure
Philosophy	Clearly Defined; For How Long it Has Been a Driver; How it is Applied; When Exceptions Have Been Made
Process	Organizational Structure; Investment Team Structure, Process, Roles and Responsibilities; Investment Committee; Guidelines and Exceptions
Performance	Month by Month; Quarter by Quarter; Year by Year; Rolling Periods; Performance Analytics and Exhibits
Profile	Offering Terms and Price

The above elements can be profiled sufficiently in an email introduction, and further highlighted in an overview presentation. When it comes to institutional vetting, however, the devil is in the details. Clarity and consistency are core drivers of institutional acceptance.

Gamesmanship be Damned

Respondents interviewed spoke of the games managers play when it comes to positioning. Managers and marketing professionals alike can take these games too far, misrepresenting themselves and their firms in key areas. Institutions cannot afford to be blindsided by undiscovered firm facts. Institutions are adept at reading between the lines, understanding through thousands of manager screenings what words, or lack of words, are tiny red flags. Managers speak of transparency and integrity. They want to be transparent and honest and believe they are doing the best they can. These characteristics are in conflict when a manager is attempting to hide a less than institutional aspect of their firm or process. Managers may be seeking to downplay certain aspects of their business, or to oversell others. Either way, respondents consistently commented on the challenge of screening through these diversions, and getting managers to be more articulate and honest about what occurs day-to-day within their organizations.

Games Managers Play

Respondents were asked a variety of questions to get at the heart of the matter in relation to manager transparency and integrity. They were asked about particularly "memorable" marketing experiences. Institutional investment management research professionals responded with several examples of the games managers play; here are a few of them. To assist in reinforcing their themes, each has been given a name that matches a game we are all familiar with:

Window Dress Up

Managers put forth a fantastic profile on the web and in a pitchbook, but it is largely window dressing. The firm does not have the experience, depth or results profiled.

Musical Chairs

Managers identify certain resources that are playing specific roles within the organization. Upon further review, the resources are either playing entirely different roles in practice, or are spread so thin that their capacity to contribute meaningfully is questionable at best. Managers will also serve up specific resources on the investment team or within senior management to address various questions, even though the work is being done by more junior staffers.

Battleship

Ever tried to figure out what is happening on the other side of that game board? Managers talk to transparency, but when it comes to pinning down exactly where they are and what they are doing within their portfolio, it's a game of battleship.

Process Roulette

The more complex the investment process, the more likely process roulette is to occur. Managers want to be hired. They want their process to meet institutional expectations. Take a typical five step process of identifying investment themes, screening potential holdings, evaluating these holdings against the existing portfolio, voting on the holdings and implementing them into the portfolio. Process roulette might occur when macro factors are sometimes considered and sometimes not, when an optimizer is sometimes utilized and sometimes not, when members of the investment team are meeting regularly to discuss holdings and their implementation into the portfolio—and sometimes not.

Performance Pictionary

Managers love their growth of $10,000 charts and want the charts, and their rolling period graphs, to represent performance. These are institutions, they want and need spreadsheets with the dirty details of month to month, quarter to quarter and year to year returns since inception against an appropriate benchmark. Period.

Connect Four

Managers have an investment style, for example value or growth. This style can override their personality and culture. To reinforce their perspective, managers can be dogmatic about their approach, so much so that it impacts their presentation and presence in the market. Utilizing the value v. growth manager as one example, value oriented managers tend to believe they "know value" better than others; they often maintain an air of superiority in the investment management world. They are, as a group, loathe to spend money. They are deeply committed to finding the deal—that mispriced anomaly to be taken advantage of. This perspective permeates not only their investment management, but their entire persona, firm culture and way of doing business. It can impact the market's perception of them, and their willingness to invest in the resources and activities needed to grow.

In contrast, growth managers can be overly aggressive and sales oriented; they can never get enough. Growth managers tend to have high energy, high conviction and they are willing to invest, perhaps too much, in an idea. This growth mentality permeates the firm's culture, and their presentation. Managers play connect four as a way of ensuring they are fully understood by the market. They want to draw a straight line connecting the dots between their investment acumen as a pure value, or a pure growth player, and how they seek to present themselves in the market. Even if a manager is dogmatic about value or growth in the investment management process, it is ineffective in the marketing process. ***Effective institutional marketing requires a combination of prudence and passion, a focus on value and growth.***

Capture the Mandate Flag

Managers are frustrated when the process takes too long, and they can't get an answer from the research team. Occasionally, they will circumvent those resources, or ask their marketing and sales professionals to do the same, in an attempt to play the field. They are seeking a circuitous route.

Survivor

Managers do not like to discuss succession planning. This is not unique to the investment management industry. It is hard to imagine not being around any longer, particularly on short notice. However, this can occur, and institutions cannot risk a mandate on an ill-prepared firm that has failed to establish a sufficient succession plan. Managers will argue that the institution can simply go elsewhere if they become incapacitated. Instead, they will go elsewhere right now, having avoided the risk entirely. Managers, particularly sole proprietors, will not and should not make it as the 'last survivor' in an institutional mandate bid without a succession plan of substance.

Hide and Go Seek

Managers and their marketing and sales resources are ever present when the performance is good. They play a disappearing act when it is subpar. Respondents consistently indicated that down markets, and down performance, is exactly when they find managers most interesting, and when they know they should be considering them. Don't hide; institutions will not seek you out.

Charades

The manager presents their case but the institution "doesn't get it". The firm's first attempt at communication is passionate, calm and methodical. Then the panic to get "understood" takes hold. The manager feels compelled to jump up and down, quite literally, pinging the institution with a barrage of emails and phone calls, trying to get their point across. It isn't going to work. The extra and often frantic attempts to get the institution's attention only frustrates both parties. Move on to the next institution, or attempt to mix it up with a different presentation; share new insights and unique content. Do not continue to drill home the same basic introductory content hoping that the institution will suddenly "get it".

Monopoly

Managers have limited resources and they want to appear bigger than they are. They seek to maximize their capacity as well. Finding the right relationships and acknowledging capacity and resource constraints are critical. Not everyone needs to own Park Place to be successful. Managers who are realistic about what they can manage, and the resources they have in place to manage, are least likely to run into difficulty down the road. The market has seen remarkable catastrophes from managers who got themselves over their skis. Growing organically, adding relationships methodically and managing capacity within accepted norms for the specific strategy and structure are keys to success. As is the case in the game of monopoly, sometimes owning more real estate at the lower end of the spectrum and spreading out your risk is better than trying to manage Fifth Avenue.

Pick Up Sticks

Managers want to tell their story as broadly as possible. They presume the market will be interested based on the numbers and their unique approach. They will distribute broadly without understanding the institutions they are marketing to. Respondents noted frustration over the lack of manager understanding about what the institution does and whether a product was even a potential fit for their type of organization and portfolio. Managers pump out a bunch of materials to a broad array of institutions and wait to see which ones stick. This often means that they are marketing to organizations and walking into meetings without any knowledge of the institution itself. Like picking up sticks, they are simply in a gathering mode, not focused on specific opportunities and the most likely candidates, wasting everyone's time.

Pin the Tail on the Vendor

The infrastructure of a firm, whether fully established or in the process of launching, is constantly challenged by time and resources. Managers make decisions every day that impact the outcome of their business development efforts. They may attempt to save resources in one area, in order to expand them in another. Managers also tend to move quickly through vendors, changing horses mid-race or determining that a vendor is simply not a good "fit" for what they need. Earlier in the book, the notion of "measure twice—cut once" was highlighted. This is true in vendor selection. In a time of great outsourcing, the use of vendors is widely accepted, however they are considered a representation of the firm and its decision-making. When firms make mistakes or changes unexpectedly, which will happen, managers often blame their vendors for dropping the ball. Vendors did not create the track record, the team, or the content that serves as the basis for a firm's ability to be hired or fired. Managers are encouraged to avoid the blame game, to be fully committed when they create vendor relationships, and to ensure that the vendor has the necessary skill set and expertise to take the firm to the next level. The result is pinned "on the manager" so to speak.

Institutions Play Games Too

Managers are not the only ones who play games, or so it appears. Let's think of a few games that institutions might be accused of playing. Readers can provide their own descriptions of how institutions play these games: Red light/Green Light, 20 Questions, The Amazing Race, Scrabble, Survivor, Chutes & Ladders, Sorry.

Questions Asked

Respondents were asked the following questions in bold face text specifically in relation to this chapter. The consensus answers are in italics and immediately follow the question asked.

Any particularly memorable introductions come to mind?
Yes, many. See below.

What is your view on managers marketing to field consultants or clients in order to gain research prioritization?
Mixed reviews. It can be acceptable, if it is appropriately timed and is not implemented in an attempt to circumvent the process nor the research team.

Are direct comparisons to competitive products additive? Detractors?
Not additive. Researchers do it themselves; it could be considered cherry picking.

How often do you want to be contacted about an idea/ strategy?
Quarterly in most cases.

How important is team stability during the engagement process?
Critical; be forthcoming about it when resources change.

What do managers most often do wrong in the marketing process?
A variety of things that are obvious because we have seen so much.

What is a door closer? Biggest turn off?
Aggressive marketing tactics, lack of humility, lack of transparency, and errors are all door closers.

What are your pet peeves about the marketing process?
There are many; read on.

What has been your worst marketing experience?
Most are ok, but there have been a few stand-outs. See games managers play above and quotes below.

Words to Drive By

The following quotes provide a broader sampling of the respondents' direct feedback in relation to the above questions. Firms are encouraged to drive their marketing and sales activities with these rules for the road in mind.

On Memorable Introductions

A classic, the manager represents himself as the leader of the process and it becomes very clear, very quickly they aren't involved; not picking the names, not making the decisions. [They] may be majority owner but not the decision maker in the meetings, they are good at organization but not about the work product. We need the decision maker.

We had a much more retail oriented manager who brought too basic of materials—line chart, growth of the dollar, star ratings—we don't care. We care about what they do; some of the most interesting are when managers aren't doing well.

A manager that took a call in the middle of a meeting—just starts talking in the middle of the meeting on the phone—and then no apology.

In the 'never' category, when they send you an email, and then an hour later a voicemail, and then another email, and then they are 'in town' and want to meet the next day.

One showed up and didn't even know where he was, paperclips on his cuffs and he was the CIO so you can probably guess we've never used them.

On Playing the Field

Given that central research is all understaffed and typically more junior, an increasing number of managers can and do reach out to people that are closest to the decision makers. Economics of the consultant market have driven this reality.

There is no issue in going to a client in addition to contacting the consultant because that is smart marketing. If field consultants are hands on its ok as well, as long as they also come to research.

It's frustrating; we do all in our power to keep our advisors from reaching out to managers directly. We understand some will do that but we do everything we can; we will do accommodation meetings but largely we want to source ourselves.

[I] can count on one hand in the past 12-13 years when a client or adviser referral of a fund was actually good and subsequently implemented.

On Direct Comparisons to Competitors

[I] don't like it; it is in poor taste. [I'm] not going to trust it anyways because I don't know how they picked their peer group.

If you say [the] strategy is unique then there shouldn't be anything like it? But it's ok.

Indifferent to detracting; manager coming in has their own value-added. How are you different than peers? The allocator should know who the peers are!

We have that anyway, so it really doesn't matter. Benchmarks are a common issue, about 20% of the time there is an issue. Funds are often compared to international index but with huge U.S. exposure, or compared to large cap benchmark but should have been mid cap benchmark.

We do it because it is easier, we like to know who the competitors are but the analysis we prefer to do ourselves to be sure we are comparing apples to apples.

On Frequency of Touch Points

Twice per year or once per year but indirectly open to quarterly updates, emails.

Follow up within two weeks after an initial meeting; quarterly to every 6 months thereafter. If I am interested in it I won't forget. I make a separate file.

Quarterly—just a two-line email, "hey catching up on this, crossed $100M, on XYZ platform". Maybe a phone call every 4-5 months.

Quarterly, but really depends on the opportunity set. If the manager has a really unique position in the marketplace we might want to hear more often.

There is somewhat of a rhythm to it, quarterly updates/quarterly letters are standard once I've looked at something. Important to stay in front even if initial is "no" or "no action"; email rather than a call, so many people just don't pick up their phones anymore. I can then look at my own leisure.

On Team Stability

This is huge; depends on the set up of the firm, not an issue for Izzy Englander because they manage in pools of capital. For a single strategy organization it is a huge issue; less of an issue at a big shop, huge at a small shop.

It depends on team size and contributions and impact of analysts. For small teams its critical (under 10 analysts), for large teams with sector overlap its ok.

I identify key investment professionals—if they were to leave it would trigger a hold and a review; I've done both but can't tell the percentage. [Some firms] who lost key people had offering incentives to other key professionals to keep them on board and so we placed the manager on 'hold' and watched for 6-12 months; if any further departures we were out and that is what happened in the most recent case and often does, and so we got out.

Depends on role of [the] person and how value add; basic assumption of 5-10% attrition in any given year, above that is [a] red flag.

Junior people ok, mid-level and/or non-investment senior people becomes a bit more of an issue. We just need to understand it; we frequently ask to talk to the person that left.

On Manager Error

Marketers call relentlessly, call weekly and then call the whole team that was in the meeting. That will kill you; the deal is done.

Lack of a long-range plan and no ability to provide a 'what to expect' from the firm and strategy.

Failure to provide a sound enough case for 'how this fits in'.

Wrong structure; wrong terms before they even start.

On Door Closers

I don't like [xyz] guys—they are blind to risk.

Manager contacted us way too often, wouldn't give up to the point of annoyance.

Managers will try to get the meeting by calling the head of the firm; you might get the meeting but you won't get the business.

Lack of humility, particularly with the younger managers out there.

Style drift; we need them to stay focused and when we see what they perceive to be "little adjustments" over and over it becomes a different animal. We can't have that; they need to understand the changes they have made and how significant they are and be very sure about them.

Young managers who throw a lot against the wall and see what sticks; perseverance is a big issue.

On Pet Peeves to Avoid

The person is not doing the work but has the greatest ownership.

Managers need to be honest about when it's the best time to be in the space or not be in the space.

A star rating is not positive; we tend to shut down.

Lack of consistency; managers appear when they have great performance and don't follow up when they are under performing. We know that asset classes and managers under perform, and we want to see that so that we can hopefully understand why.

People who are obsessed with the sale. This is a long sales process, managers need to be patient. A significant number [of managers] are of the mindset that if you don't jump now than they move on and you don't hear from them for three years.

On Worst Marketing Experience

Manager came in who is very politically active and involved and lead with it and lost business because he led with it and didn't think about his audience in the sense that he might be offending people.

We are always horrified by guys who come in and only talk about what's in it for the adviser; they never get to what's in it for the investor. That might have worked in the past—that is a non-starter. People are taking on more of a fiduciary role and clients expect that and thus you need more transparency, access and focus on fees to the investor.

Manager couldn't answer several of our questions.

Manager was drilling us on what was in their materials and was openly aggravated that we hadn't spent more time reviewing them in advance.

Manager attempted to use technology and it was a colossal waste of time.

Summary on Games Managers Play

While some level of gamesmanship is expected, firms are cautioned to avoid misrepresenting their organizations during the extended marketing and sales life cycle.

Maintain a High Degree of Integrity Throughout the Marketing and Sales Process
Understand That This Is a Road Well Traveled; Institutions Know the Games Managers Play
Honesty, Patience and Showing Up Are Attributes That Differentiate a Manager

CHAPTER 19

Recommendations from the Road

RPM Rating on Respondent Recommendations

DE MINIMIS	CORE	PRIORITY	GAME CHANGER

Respondents provided a treasure trove of feedback which is presented throughout the book. These professionals commented on the biggest factors impacting their decisions, right down to the smallest details of what matters in institutional marketing. Ultimately, these are the decision makers; the professionals who have the capacity to move the needle significantly on behalf of a firm. Institutional investment management research professionals see the forest through the trees daily. They understand the scope of the marketplace and the drivers leading to institutional investment management decisions. They share in the belief that the more efficient firms can be in their institutional investment management marketing and sales activities, the more effective these firms will be in institutional asset gathering over time. Near the end of the interviews respondents were asked to give their best advice and to share their most poignant experiences. These were the questions asked of respondents in an effort to capture their recommendations:

- **What would you want managers to know before they begin marketing? If you had a good friend who wanted to grow institutional market share, what advice would you give them?**

- **What has been your worst marketing experience?**

- **What has been your best marketing experience?**

- **What is value-added to receive from a manager?**

Diversity Rules

Managers come in all shapes and sizes. They present themselves in a multitude of ways. The industry benefits from their diversity. A firm's culture, often driven by its investment management philosophy and process, tends to permeate everything it does, including its positioning and marketing. Institutional investment management research professionals have seen thousands of managers, and with them thousands of different presentations of a finite number of investment management offerings. Managers are encouraged to hold onto what makes them unique, while following a series of rules for the road to increase efficiency and results in the institutional marketing and sales process.

Respondents Top 10 Recommendations

A culmination of respondents' best advice will be provided here without regard to prioritization. As managers each present in a unique way, each will benefit uniquely from these recommendations. Whether managers are just establishing their own firms, or are years into a business development plan that has either failed to fully take off or has plateaued, the highlights below are a *game changer* according to the *Resource Prioritization Matrix*. Take what is valuable, enhance what is not meeting expectations, and heed these recommendations as the firm defines its own path to asset growth.

1. ***Do Your Homework***
   Managers so often stumble before they even get on the road. They
   fail to do the necessary work to understand the landscape and
   who they are marketing to. Do your homework. Step back and
   evaluate fully the offering, and the market the firm is pursing with
   it. Resources are wasted on the wrong product, marketing effort or
   channel. Doing the hard work in advance can ensure that managers
   are in the right place, with the right offering, ideally at the right
   time. Timing cannot always be managed; the offering and target
   market can. ***Getting in position to win means that the firm has done
   everything in its power, in advance, to understand the market and
   how they fit into it.*** Given that the majority of prospect assets are
   at work rather than sitting in cash awaiting new asset allocations,
   understanding the landscape is critical. There are lots of resources
   available to managers, whether they elect to pursue the market on
   their own or whether they engage professionals to assist them. In
   either case, there is no excuse for a lack of competitive knowledge
   and understanding in today's global, technology driven world.
   Institutional investment research professionals expect firms to have
   done their homework.

   *Do your homework on us: who is the decision maker? What is the
   decision-making process? Then follow it; and then WAIT.*

   *We have to invest in what is on the platform; [on the platform] the main
   office is doing the due diligence sniff test on track record, principals, etc.
   If it's not on our platform we can't even look at it/can't invest.*

   *What type of audience are we and what type of audience does the strat-
   egy appeal to? Is it best for tax exempt? Non-exempt? What works for
   tax exempt investors doesn't work for institution's; a low vol. five to six
   is a two to three after taxes and doesn't work.*

   *People are getting away from buckets and instead looking at opportunity
   costs, such as what is this strategy v. what I can do myself, i.e. liquid*

strategies v. illiquid, and risk budget. Managers need to understand these trends.

Horrendous is when they come in and have no idea what your business is: non-traded REIT people calling me? Know your audience—bad ones don't know the audience. [Also] sending junior people that are supposed to be product specialists and they don't have a clue, that is DOA. If you have our attention, make the meeting count—make sure your rep can answer the large majority of the questions.

2. ***Maximize Opportunities***

Managers work hard to build a track record and establish a business. Yet, repeatedly, after working for many months to get a meeting, they enter the room unprepared. Managers must step back and ensure they not only have the major touchpoints of an institutional marketing and sales effort prepared, but that the team is prepped to answer questions. Respondents reinforced throughout the interviews the surprising lack of preparation, and lack of portfolio knowledge, of presenters. This is the firm's story and the firm's opportunity. Do not waste it. Be prepared so that the firm can maximize the opportunity it has been granted. Confirm this preparation in advance through diligent trial runs, internal Q&A devil's advocate sessions and full vetting of every component of the firm's positioning that carry its brand.

People don't know how to shut up, [they] don't know how to work outside of their own story. Managers need to be agile in the face of your audience; good ones are the ones who are really prepared—spent the time ahead of time 'how do you construct portfolios', 'what is your asset allocation framework', 'what funds do you already have?'

It is great when firms come in and say 'we understand you are a mean variance shop and here is how our fund works well/doesn't work well and here is why,' 'taxable vs tax exempt,' 'asset location,' then manager frames the discussion above and beyond.

[A] long/short manager comes in and says we understand you use X and Y and here is how we would fit in and how we compare—that works.

Managers don't have enough prepared, particularly ongoing. Updates to [the] firm, three to five-year goals, products in incubation, hiring/ firing, change in PM sentiment, change in what they are finding interesting. Not necessarily top ten or bottom ten but perhaps fell outside of their traditional approach—how they came across a name differently.

3. ***Manage Costs***

   It's a marathon, not a sprint. Institutional investment management research professionals understand this. Part of the strategy is often simply "waiting it out"; watching a manager for an extended period to not only see how they perform, but how they interact and the characteristics that the team displays during this period of time. Managers often overspend initially, and have no stamina for the long run. Respondents repeatedly encouraged managers to avoid overspending, particularly on gimmicky communications. Spend wisely. Be frugal where you can, and spend where it matters. Find a balance between prudence and passion. Think about where the firm is in its current stage of development. What will work within the budget and what will match the culture? Determine what channels might make the most sense and prioritize them. ***Share the game plan internally in writing, including the length of time the firm will be committed to it and what resources will be employed by channel.*** Be sure that the team is prepared to support the effort fully and consistently. Invest in the future. Settle in for the long road.

   The process is long. Managers need to be honest about when it's the best time to be in the space or not to be in the space. Be bolder, offer more thoughts and advice and recommendations related to the space they are in particularly when it's not a good time to be in.

Managers can just be too much. And it's clear that they are spending too much. It's not sustainable. The process takes time and they need to be prepared.

It doesn't have to be fancy; [I] hate the multi-color background, artsy stuff—but just needs to be right. Plain white paper with legible black lettering is perfect for me.

4. ***Focus on Fit—Not Performance***
Managers want performance to be their story. Performance is in the rear-view mirror. Even if performance were guaranteed, performance can be derived in different ways and the combination of managers in a portfolio can lead to concentrations, or other risks, that override numbers alone. Managers must understand that performance does not sell on its own. Institutions are seeking firms that they can hire, engage and partner with for several years. They often need to introduce these firms to their end clients. Additionally, an existing portfolio is in place. Institutions must understand and defend why a certain performance track record, and manager, is the best fit for the portfolio. In many cases, they must explain why another manager should be terminated to make room. Managers rely far too much on performance to justify a lack of communication and content about the underpinnings of the portfolio. This does not assist institutions in making a case for an allocation. Managers are strongly encouraged to rethink their focus on performance, extending their purview to the broader context of the firm, its philosophy and process for money management.

Don't lead with performance, I have no idea what fund you are talking about and how to benchmark that. Much more helpful to send a teaser—one pager, then follow up. "What we are doing and why we think we are better", and give people a chance to digest.

Philosophy is number one; what makes you different? What is your edge? Performance is second.

'Uncorrelated returns' is nothing. Everyone says that.

Performance gets you in the door, it does not get you hired.

5. ***Understand What Risk Means to Institutions***
Managers focus on downside capture when it comes to risk management. They want to avoid the major misses in the market. They do not perceive their size to be a risk to larger institutions who are selecting between a series of managers, but institutions certainly do. For institutions, the risk of underperforming is rarely the biggest concern. The two risks that respondents discussed repeatedly for which managers should remain focused are: (1) firm viability and the risk of the firm failing to survive its growth years; (2) opportunity costs and the risks of what other investments were missed by allocating to this strategy. Managers can best overcome these risks by having a diligent and cost-effective business plan that is well articulated throughout the process, and by effectively communicating their "fit" into an existing and diversified portfolio.

How do you differentiate your strategy from others in the market, how do you address risks up front. There is more risk for newer firms, what are the points that will offset that?

Small market niche strategies. You could always go to the large firms to get the boilerplate strategies. If [it is] something differentiated which typically meant capacity constrained. [You] can't hire 'Bob' when 'Western' does the same thing.

There is the element of career risk going with a less tested manager. There is also firm risk. [We] can't afford to underperform; better success will be had once you know the firm you are dealing with, i.e. do you want large, established, low risk; or are you the kind of firm that wants to take some risks, wants some out of favor managers.

6. *Be Consistent: Show Up and Follow Up*

The task of the manager is to show up, and to follow up. Managers press hard up front to get in the door. They get the importance of the introduction. They will make the rounds initially and present their case. Overview marketing collateral will be created. Then the wait begins. Ongoing is a whole different ball game. Dr. Charles D. Ellis, CFA, in a speech given entitled *The Characteristics of Successful Investment Firms*, said the following:

> *"There wasn't anything unusual about what the management of any really good company was doing. They had the same recipe every other management had, but they were doing it. That made all the difference."*

Managers, despite strong recommendations from marketing and sales professionals, fail to deliver on ongoing communications. Two factors play into this typical outcome: (1) resources—the firm applied all of its resources and energy to the initial effort, expecting that the introduction itself would be so stellar that it would move the needle; and (2) commitment—firms have limited interest in focusing time and energy in the direction of marketing and sales. They truly believe that "if we build it, they will come". It is easier to blame (and to change) their marketing and sales resources, than it is to deliver on a multistage, multi-year marketing and sales campaign. The result is a series of fits and starts in institutional marketing. Institutional investment management research professionals understand these realities. In many cases institutions can simply wait managers out.

Here are the questions that institutions are asking themselves over time: How long will the firm keep pinging us? Will they send something value-added beyond the norm that we can sink our teeth into, learn from and utilize in our own work? Are they consistently pleasant, present and accountable as market conditions change? Institutions are already invested. They are not starting with a blank canvas. They have managers that they themselves have selected and entrusted with firm assets. They have long-term capital commitments to specific strategies and structures. Managers who understand that the game is one of replacement searches first and foremost, are better equipped to tolerate, and survive, the long road to assets under management. Enough media coverage on the plight of underfunded pensions and endowments has educated managers on this reality. While wealth advisors, family offices and platforms will not have issues of 'under funding', they do have committed assets and lack of platform space and/or free cash to invest in new ideas, in many cases.

Things are ebbing and flowing so I don't know if I'm going to get a mandate for something specific. Tail risk protection—I didn't have a damn name of anyone doing this. Part of this is the function and size of our team. Blackrock, JP Morgan take meetings on everything but when you are a three-person team we can't do that.

It really comes down to individuals, who is managing the fund, what is their background and history. Jumping around every one to two years is not good. Has there been greater continuity and good success [here or] somewhere else?

7. ***Structure Matters***
   Structure of firm and offering are critical elements to successful institutional asset gathering. Managers often think of product structuring, however respondents repeatedly reinforced the importance of firm structuring, and specific elements of an offering that make all the difference. Regarding the firm, managers must have the right resource game plan, including having completed an internal infrastructure review and positioning exercise before defining their best foot forward. ***Resources and representations are all about reputation; institutions want to engage with the best firms they can.*** This transcends performance. Structure relates to risk management and how the firm has built its infrastructure and offerings. Firms must fully consider their structural risks including hiring and firing, background histories, brand value of their vendor relationships positive and negative, regulatory history and ownership structure. There is

a brand value of its own to hiring and retaining certain resources. There is a brand risk in hiring others. Keep in mind that litigation risk is a hot button for institutional investment management research firms. Part of the firm's review should entail ensuring that it has fully vetted employees in terms of past employment and any regulatory or legal action. In addition, be certain that the partnership and planning is legally sound. Lastly, background checks should be completed anywhere the firm cannot risk a surprise, which is pretty much everywhere.

The second element of structure is the product offering itself. Managers must expand their universe screening beyond the obvious peer group to understand how their offering stacks up. If other managers, often larger, better branded and funded, have a similar investment strategy offered in a different vehicle structure, or on notably different terms, the manager must be aware. Top priorities for offering structural considerations are to get the vehicle, pricing and benchmark correct. Respondents repeatedly reinforced the wealth of competitive information they have at their fingertips. They identified many manager marketing attempts as a *"fool's errand"* for marketers when the pricing, structure or other related terms were off the mark. The wrong structure will not be overcome by gross outperformance, as the ultimate performance for the investor is impacted directly by the structure itself.

We get an incredible amount of manager data, enough to create a staff person and a support person and a few analysts to go through it. Stuff goes in and out of vogue. Right now is low cost, market based, replicable strategies. Everyone is focused on cost. Financial markets are strong enough that it overshadows alpha gained from higher cost strategies, so a lot is thrown out on cost.

Our due diligence has gotten a lot more structured. We have a separate risk team that completes due diligence after we do. We should not find anything on a team member that the firm is not already aware of.

[A] lower expense ratio always increases the probability that a fund will outperform over time. This is a key criteria in hiring a manager particularly when performance is below the absolute top tier.

The goal is to decline less in bear markets; it's not about finding the most alpha, it's the good risk adjusted returns. We screen out managers with poor downside capture; over 100% downside capture is too much.

8. ***Integrity Matters***
   Managers believe performance is the primary factor in institutional investment allocations. At the end of the day, it is critical and will get a firm noticed. But to get hired, the manager needs to demonstrate the depth and consistency in team and track record, over a long enough period to be considered a viable candidate. Why? Because performance rarely if ever holds up without a solid infrastructure behind it. Twelve to twenty-four months is not long enough. Thirty-six months is a minimum in most cases and that presumes everything is in place: (1) the firm has a viable team (not a husband and wife or sole proprietor for example); (2) there has been ideally no—but certainly no major—turnover; and (3) the track record shows consistent application of the process and enough time to see how it invests AND how it divests—how it exits positions and performs in regards to turnover, dispositions, etc. This *"full turn"* investment view is what organizations want and deserve to see. Institutions want to see transparency, honesty and consistency along the way.
   Managers should not wait to get to market; track records and presence need time to season. It is important to get on the radar. The mistake comes in the form of manager's expectations about what this early groundwork will lead to. Firms should not realistically expect hard dollar results from these efforts institutionally inside of a premature window. Integrity matters to institutions, and it comes in the form of clarity, mutual understanding and respect for the process. It comes with time. Managers often dismiss the importance of certain aspects of institutional due diligence.

One place in particular where managers can fail at the integrity test is in regard to the depth of team; the dreaded 'succession planning' question. It is human nature to avoid the conversation, but an institutional necessity to have it. It is not unrealistic for institutional research professionals to want to see, on paper, the organizational structure and incentives in place to keep team members happy and engaged. It is also necessary for managers to understand—particularly those in one portfolio manager shops or those with married partners—that this is an area of significant risk. Yes, of course, institutions can simply 'sell' out of a firm's strategy if the portfolio manager(s) disappear overnight, or if a 'split' happens. What is more common, however, is a steady 'quieting' of communications and worsening of results delivered by the manager, and ultimately a bad ending for all when the manager finally elects to disclose a major change in ownership or portfolio management. So why would these institutions take that risk? Is it fair to expect institutions to believe that a single portfolio manager, or a PM with one junior analyst who really has no authority, is a risk managed investment process? Integrity matters to institutions. It is delivered in the form of transparency, consistency and honest representation of the firm and its resources initially, and over time. It applies not only to the performance track record, and to any offering constraints or criteria, but also to the firm itself.

[Joe] represents himself as the leader of the process and it becomes very clear very quickly he isn't involved; [He is] not picking the names, not making the decisions. [He] may be majority owner but not the decision maker in the meetings. [Owners are] good at the organization but not about the work product; we need the decision maker.

[There is] so much competition for the investor's dollar right now. The more the track record the more confident you are to give money, but hard pressed to deal with gates and lack of transparency. The mystique is over, [managers] must be more transparent now, and there will continue to be more push back on fees.

We don't like it when the person is not doing the work but has the greatest ownership.

9. ***Keep it Interesting***

   Content and conversation must follow through on the key messaging from beginning to end. For example, if managers say, "our strength is research" that is ultimately insufficient. What specifically about the research is differentiated? How can the firm demonstrate that value-added research in subsequent conversations and materials? Whatever the firm's core messaging is, whether it be about process, transparency, team, or performance expectations, it is critical to follow it through and to reiterate the firm's position through examples. Respondents noted that managers tout their "*transparency*" but cannot provide— or do not want to provide, requested data. Managers will tout "*consistency*", but a further look at the track record does not support this. Firms will talk about "*team*", and yet a deeper dive shows a relatively divided process and infrastructure, and/or turnover ensues. Defining who a manager is and what they are best at is not completed in a few words or through historical numbers alone, it is demonstrated over months and years and this demonstration is what makes a manager investable by institutions over time. It is also exactly what makes the process take so long. Find unique ways to "show" the firm's value.

   It's on them [the manager]; you've got to be compelling. Number one thing I tell managers that I talk too at a shop like 'ABC', presume clients are fully invested at all times. [It is] not always the case but managers should presume that, so you need to justify kicking someone out; what is going to cause me to take action.

   [You] need a subject that grabs my attention; very specific—Private $300M oil and gas on shore.

   We had a much more retail oriented manager who brought too basic of materials—line chart, growth of the dollar, star ratings—we don't care.

We care about what they do; some of the most interesting are when managers aren't doing well.

One or two and they consisted around something really unusual, [they] had really tried to solve a problem, explain how something fits in well; [they] really understood what the positioning was that they brought to the table and they talked about how it would fit in. 'Here is how we might fit and how we might help you', not a generic 'Here is what we do and we are great and you should hire us'.

10. ***Good Karma Counts***
Institutional investment research professionals understand that they are in the market to discover undiscovered talent, and to bring compelling and differentiated investment ideas to the fore. They are investment professionals themselves, interested in the market and passionate about high quality investing. They love managers. The institutional investment management research process has been likened to dating. It's difficult to always understand what the criteria is that ultimately moved the needle. We know the basics must be done and done well—these requirements are spelled out throughout the book and provided in the respondents' own words. What is harder to put one's finger on, but critically important, is generating good karma. Managers must come to the table, and stay at the table for long enough, and with good energy about them, to get noticed and engaged. As the process is long and tedious, and because managers rarely take the time to ensure they are pursuing the right institutions at the right time, frustration is the norm among investment managers in the growth phase. Whether they have recently launched or have been at it for years, they tend to display similar frustrations and behaviors in the process that are unbecoming and harmful to their objectives. Institutions want to work with managers who are respectful, positive and flexible. Don't we all?

The manager is on [a mobile device] the whole time.

The manager wouldn't give any detail—said it was all proprietary or we would have to have an NDA. If you are having a meeting, be prepared to talk about what you do and how you do it.

Everyone tells you what you want to hear; the good managers have a different approach, they give you their thoughts instead of just talking through a canned template.

One of my colleagues in the room didn't iron his shirt so we aren't going to use them; bad from the get go.

I can recall more of the later than the former; one gentleman who was marketing a very small strategy and he cold called a lot, and he basically forgot who he was calling and there was this long pause, stutter—seemed he had to go to his notes to look up who he was calling.

I am not receptive to a really aggressive push for a meeting or call; perhaps only follow up one other time that year, unless a very interesting letter or piece after a particularly strong quarter. Quarterly distribution max, if we just made the allocation than don't offer the meeting—back off—biggest pet peeves.

Summary on Respondent Recommendations

Top 10 tips to crush it on the road to AUM.

Do Your Homework
Maximize Opportunities
Manage Costs
Focus on Fit, Not Performance
Understand What Risk Means to Institutions
Be Consistent: Show Up and Follow Up
Structure Matters
Integrity Matters
Keep It Interesting
Good Karma Counts

CHAPTER 20

The Road to AUM

"The only way around is through." —Robert Frost

A Game Plan

The market proliferates content in the form of blogs, commentaries, videos and short e-books written about the topics covered here. If the firm is in the market, it is bombarded by marketing and sales tips daily. This content can be helpful in its brevity, and as a reminder of factors to consider in effective business management and marketing. However, it is not a game plan. *The Road to AUM* was written to provide firms with a path to asset growth from beginning to end. The opportunity for managers who have come this far is in fully defining their own path, and ensuring it meets institutional standards in the most efficient and effective ways possible.

Guiding Principles

The big idea is simple. ***Successful asset growth is in the doing—the day-to-day work from product inception through ongoing communications.*** Consider the core message in print resources like Malcolm Gladwell's *Outliers: The Story of Success* and *The Tipping Point: How Little Things Can Make a Big Difference*, Ray Dalio's *Principles*, and a myriad of others in this genre, as better proxies for what is critical in achieving growth. The core message is brought to the fore by motivational speakers like Tony Robbins and Zig Ziglar. It is not so much what the firm is marketing and selling, as it is how the offering is structured and sold. Firms require a game plan for product development, marketing and sales that can stand the test of time, and of institutions. They must be steadfast in their commitment to it as well.

There are a series of common fits and starts that accompany organization building, institutional sales and marketing. The root causes come down to a few key elements. Firms owe it to themselves to do more work up front to ensure they are prepared, supported and committed. Marketing and sales are both costly endeavors. Successful investment management firms understand the following guiding principles that lead to growth:

I.   *Commitment*
II. *Market Knowledge*
III. *Differentiation*
IV. *Consistency*
V.   *Positivity*

I. *Commitment*

In a speech by Dr. Charles D. Ellis, CFA penned in the 80's yet relevant today: "The Characteristics of Successful Investment Firms", Dr. Ellis discusses the importance of the "*soft*" decisions; "*delicate, subtle, avoidable, easily postponed decisions on basic policy and strategy.*" He notes, "*Most organizations are uncomfortable identifying what they will not do. It is not what you are willing to do, but what you will not do that most clearly defines what you really are.*" His comments focus on the good: shared basic values and a common commitment amongst the team; and the bad: poor communication and the wrong people, as the drivers of success or failure among investment firms.

Firms must define what they are committed to. Managers will indicate that they will "*do what it takes*" and that they are "*committed for the long term*". Then, just months into an extensive and pricey marketing effort, they are frustrated and disappointed, and considering pulling the plug. An institutional marketing and sales effort will be a two to three year process at a minimum for the majority of managers. This is the length of time that respondents indicated tracking, watching, meeting with and considering managers before investing, on average. Yes, there are outliers, but for most due to a combination of firm knowledge, trends in the marketplace, market cycle dynamics and asset availability to invest, the process will run several years to grow towards a meaningful AUM.

Take the time to write down on paper, and circulate internally, what the firm is committed to. Clearly articulate the resources, time, and activities that will be completed and over what period the firm is committed to them. Ensure that the firm completes its own pre-launch puzzle as reviewed in *Chapter 4*, defining the team, offering, brand and capital commitment it is making. *Create a proactive five-year game plan. Consider resource commitments by AUM growth, not simply by the clock.* Once committed, do not make unnecessary changes. In the modern era, the desire for instant gratification impacts everyone. Institutional investment management marketing and sales is not a good proxy for instant gratification. Do the hard work of planning, make the commitment, and follow through.

Business development, marketing and sales are investments in the firm's future. How much is the firm willing to invest in itself? Invest wisely in the resources needed to achieve the firm's game plan. Be strategic in hiring; commit capital where it is necessary, and reserve capital where it is not. Stay up on technology, but do not feel compelled to dive into the latest technological advancements until the market demands it or efficiency is improved significantly by it. Outsource to gain much needed efficiency and expertise. Understand the typical path to AUM as reviewed in *Chapter 4*. Don't overdo it out of the gate; build methodically and rationally. Manage down the number of products the firm wishes to present, and manage up the quantity and quality of communications regarding the "best fit" offering(s). *Avoid spreading the resources of the firm too thin. Make a commitment the firm can stick with for three to five years. See it through.*

II. *Market Knowledge*

They say that *knowledge is power.* That holds true in the complex and competitive world of institutional investment management marketing and sales. Managers must know more about the market they are selling to. A quote from a respondent reinforces the necessity for managers to understand the marketplace:

[Referring to a manager request for review] [The] classic one is the manager who left the big firm and thinks they will get the money based on the numbers.

Avoid relying on misconceptions based on historical market norms, or based on the experiences of others. Many firms are the result of spin-out teams, or of portfolio managers with the luxury of support and capital from well-funded organizations. Establishing one's own path eliminates these supports. Understand that the market, particularly the institutional market, is looking ahead to what a firm can deliver, not in the past at what a portfolio manager did elsewhere. Colleagues may encourage a portfolio manager to start out on their own, indicating there will "certainly be demand". The portfolio manager is excited to engage with past clients and new opportunities right out of the gate, too often only to find that they must climb the ladder like everyone else, first building infrastructure, a team, and track record around them before funding comes.

Understand the marketplace; seek opportunities to gain knowledge about the best channel fit for the firm's offering, where doors might be closed and others open. **Network as much as possible to build market knowledge.** Carefully vet channel opportunities and seek first to understand what the market wants. Collect enough market knowledge to determine where the firm and its offering may fit. Work within the institutional research calendar and process. Timing is important. Keep in mind that managers are asking to be hired for their future results; institutions do not simply buy products. Market wisely with a thorough understanding of the landscape.

Managers find, when they dig deeper into why they are not winning institutional mandates, that it's often not the messaging nor the messenger keeping an offering from gaining traction. It is a variety of criteria the firm has failed to vet ahead of time. Managers can make the following mistakes, and should seek knowledge on the following subjects, when it comes to understanding the market:

- **Channel** *(Is this product institutionally ready? Does it belong in retail channels? Will wealth advisers be a good prospect base? Will institutions?)*
- **Maturity** *(Does the offering have the track record, team, and firm infrastructure required?)*
- **Terms** *(Are fees, structure, minimums, etc. within range?)*
- **Timing** *(Is the manager attempting to be first to market with a new idea, and thus serving in the role of educator? Is the manager entering mid-market, thus competing for a spot? Is the manager late to the market, seeking replacement opportunities?)*
- **Demand** *(Is there demand for the asset class? Are there capacity constraints?)*
- **Investment** *(Does the strategy incorporate elements, such as leverage, concentration or high levels of turnover, which do not meet institutional guidelines?)*

Be mindful that communications are evergreen. Everything the firm sends, each call that is made, can result in a permanent record in an institution's database. Be certain the firm has the market knowledge, and has built and positioned its offering, to have full confidence in the longevity of the content it provides.

III. *Differentiation*

Managers believe they are offering something different, yet rarely have a researched basis for that belief, nor a strategy for how they will exploit it. Start with a thorough understanding of the competition, including other firms, similar strategies in different structures, the indices and the market itself. Once the firm has confirmed what makes it truly different among a broad peer group, define a game plan for how it will engage the market regarding these differences. Respondents asked repeatedly for managers to provide a frame of reference for how the product could "fit" and for managers to be "opinionated" in sharing their market views:

[We] do need managers to clearly articulate their value add and how their strategy would benefit our client portfolios, not enough managers do that and do that well.

Fit is not simply about great performance. Fit is about bringing something different to the table. Make the firm's communications differentiated; be poignant, keep it interesting. Avoid dependency on trite words that the market dismisses as unoriginal and cliché such as "integrity", "transparency", "relative value", etc. Seek to identify the firm's differentiators in its very first communications, and reinforce them over time.

IV. *Consistency*

Firms kick-start their marketing effort with great ease and enthusiasm, then quickly revert to a performance only communications campaign. Don't waste good introductions in this way. Respondents reinforced the need for consistent presence during the marathon of institutional marketing:

Be out there and in front of people and let them know what you are doing. If it's a compelling offering people will follow up. People don't get up in the morning thinking about you and your goals.

During times of great performance, firms are laser focused on marketing. When performance is underwater, they disappear. Other factors that cause managers to disappear from the radar are lack of resources to provide content in a timely basis, and frustration over the lack of responsiveness from prospects. Consistency is a key driver of success over a multi-year marketing and sales effort to institutions. The core elements that must be in place at a minimum are reviewed in *Chapter 8*, coupled with consistent commentary and additional ongoing communications as discussed in *Chapters 14* and *15*. Proactive ongoing communications are ideal during "off cycle" periods to reinforce the firm's value proposition at times when institutions have the capacity to take notice. The core content required for these communications are best laid out through the firm's oeuvre, as discussed in *Chapter 7*, expanded upon through the application and discussion of current market events. Be prepared with a series of exhibits, commentary and presentation tools before diving into the market. These tools will assist the firm in delivering consistent, timely content. Despite distractions and competing priorities, periods of outperformance and periods of underperformance, stay the course. The firm needs to give its marketing and sales resources something to talk about, and the more consistently this content is delivered, the better. ***Create proactive, differentiated communications no less than four times per year, to maintain the firm's presence and to build understanding regarding how the firm could contribute.***

V. *Positivity*

Managers are not marketing and sales professionals; their passion lies in portfolio management. Like kids in a candy store, their eyes light up over the mere thought of security selection, trading strategies and global economics. It stands to reason that managers would prefer to spend time and energy on those who share their passion for the markets. During live meetings, institutional research professionals generally meet this criteria and managers enjoy the process. They get to talk markets and opportunities. The manager's passion for their portfolio and team comes across. Outside of this forum, when the process is a slog, requiring content to be written, drafts to be vetted, calls to be made and questions to be answered, managers grow weary. Frustration rears its ugly head, in the form of a lack of responsiveness, or in less than positive attitudes with prospects. Managers can even become defiant and argumentative, pushing back on hard questions and dragging their feet on timely responses.

Throughout the book, firms are reminded of the wide variety of factors that are in play for institutional investment management mandates.

Investment management research professionals are restricted in what they can do and when they can do it. The market is crowded, and demand will ebb and flow. Avoid taking the process too personally. Seek to build relationships with institutional investment management research professionals that will survive changes in institutional priorities, and the institutions themselves. Focus on positivity in every interaction. Everyone wants to surround themselves with positive energy. Institutions look for this strength in managers; the strength of character to persevere, positively, when the results have not yet come. Managers can offset their predisposition to impatience and frustration by seeking to understand the institution's plight, the lengthy nature of the process and by planning accordingly to survive it.

Additionally, treat the firm's resources, whether internal or external, with the utmost of respect and congeniality. ***Be positive in interactions large and small to set the standard for the firm. Resources will work harder for firms that they are passionate about. Positive energy is contagious.***

A Few Closing Notions

Get Help

Managers are encouraged to seek, and to embrace help wherever they can. The process is daunting; there are experts in the market who can make it less so. ***Firms will resist help to save money and time. This resistance rarely saves either. Engaging experienced professionals and seeking connections through vendors, associations, and publications can make all the difference.***

Enjoy the Ride

The firm has established itself and believes it offers something unique to the market. Find opportunities to engage the market on what the firm is passionate about. See the process as an opportunity to build relationships, camaraderie and a following for how the manager sees the markets. Network widely and enjoy the conversation. Get on the road. Find pleasure in the tasks of firm building—of seeing the firm's resources gain expertise and achieve success, creating new offerings and repositioning old ones, and sharing the firm's philosophy and outlook with whomever will listen. One universal truth is that business rarely comes from the expected suspects. The endgame often looks much different than what was anticipated out of the gate. Prospects who were "home runs" fell off the map. Entities that initially rejected the opportunity are those that are now prime candidates. A senior industry professional who works with a wide variety of growing investment management firms repeats a common saying that is relevant to institutional investment management marketing, and to life: *Keep the Faith*. The markets move quickly. Marketing and sales is a process that must be structured, while the outcome is inevitably unknown. Enjoy the ride.

Looking Ahead

The market has changed rapidly and will continue to do so, driven by the human spirit and ingenuity. Modern communications are wrapped into a digital ecosystem that is dynamic and global. How will this change the institutional investment management business? This business has been a holdout due to regulation and the extreme risk of poor decisions. It is easy to make a quick purchase of most anything online, or to view an engaging TED Talk or video on YouTube. Yet these decisions are not typically life-changing. Selecting a portfolio management team to run a significant asset pool of a large endowment under regulatory scrutiny is a different type of decision. Still, we anticipate that this digital ecosystem will work its way into institutional marketing and sales. When will Amazon step in? Will a cryptocurrency be the new gold standard? Will institutional investment management research professionals begin to rely more on online tools to screen managers fully? What Fintech solutions are on the horizon?

What Is Next?

Ultimately, when you need a good doctor or attorney, the human element of connecting is critical. Expect that the institutional investment management business will retain a hands-on element. Yet, the opportunity is clearly here, particularly given the regulatory hurdles and risk of legal action for poor selection, for the institutional market to become significantly more automated. Perhaps envision a market in which the databases play a more significant role in providing deeper, customized and password protected manager profiles. Envision a time when email, which is already difficult to get through, is not a viable method for reaching institutional investment management research professionals at all. A time without the telephone? Are we there already? As cyber risk and marketing fatigue continue to plague the industry due to sheer volume and global technology threats, it is easy to envision moves towards platform based manager screening that eliminates the one by one outreach that is currently the norm. The millennials may also require it, preferring short bite-sized content and a passion for self-selection. Understanding the trends and expectations of millennials in marketing and selling will become more critical. To this end, *managers that can produce the most efficient and engaging content on a consistent basis should fare well in gaining market exposure in the new economy.*

A Note to Institutional Research Professionals

Institutional research professionals have a challenging job. There was a time when there was free cash flow to put to work, notable resources and the ability to manage the scope of opportunities in the market. The world has changed; investment management research professionals have a tougher job, with fewer resources in most cases. They are responsible for screening an excessive universe of potential managers across the globe, and doing so with great diligence to ensure the firms' efficacy. They have an existing portfolio and clients to manage, and they have their own form of sales, marketing and client reporting to do in many cases. They do, however, sit in the seat of power in comparison to investment managers seeking asset growth. Institutional research professionals are asked to consider the following in their day-to-day work with the investment management community:

Be Patient

Have patience with investment managers and with their marketers as they seek to understand what is important and what process is required across a wide variety of prospects. Understand that marketers are paid to market; to provide updates and to be active. Additionally, that the regulatory environment has necessitated added steps, vetting and disclosure protocol. Be patient with the process.

Honor the Climb

Managers have worked hard to get to the table. Even if they are not a fit, honor the work they have done to get this far. Running a business is hard work. Be clear about the reality of the situation to increase efficiency—whether it be a lack of assets to invest, the unlikelihood of replacing an incumbent, or something the manager needs to improve or change to be viable. Provide feedback that is meaningful and answer as many questions as possible. Enjoy the process of discussing the markets with managers; most managers do bring something interesting to the table. Share insights and feedback that will be helpful to the manager regardless of your capacity to invest.

A Note to Marketers and Sales Professionals

Marketing and sales professionals may have the most difficult role in the investment management business development process due to their lack of control. Ultimately, they are dependent on the managers and the prospects. They must seek to affect the outcome of interactions and opportunities by bringing buyers and sellers together. Memories can be quite selective among constituents in regards to expectations, roles and responsibilities. Marketing and sales professionals must walk a fine line. Understanding that one's livelihood is at stake and that hope springs eternal, keep in mind the highbrow calling of the profession:

Guide Your Clients

Be honest about the realities of the business. Rome wasn't built in a day. Marketing and sales professionals find good in most managers and they want to help. Often, they can't. Like a dealt hand, know when to hold them and know when to fold them. Suggesting the manager head back to the drawing board can be in everyone's best interest. Encourage managers to have a business plan that covers three to five years of activity. Provide clear expectations. Define the deliverables that are necessary to market effectively in the institutional space.

Take More Time

Get to know your prospects and take a lot more time educating your clients. Marketing and sales professionals are uniquely positioned to know both constituents. Utilize this knowledge to inform the process, increasing efficiency for everyone. Avoid the desire to meet a manager's unrealistic expectations for timing and demand. Doing so can burn bridges with institutional investment management research professionals that cannot be easily repaired. You are the expert at what you do. Educate your clients accordingly.

Game Planning According to the Resource Prioritization Matrix

The book was designed to provide firms with a game plan, the details of each component are outlined throughout the last 19 chapters and provided in summary form on page 326. Remember the *Resource Prioritization Matrix*, which was designed to identify each element's level of importance in the institutional marketing and sales process so that firms can best manage their resources? The matrix is meant to do just that—assist firms in prioritizing resource allocations. Every element of an institutional marketing and sales effort is important, otherwise it would not have been included. What the rating is designed to provide is a snapshot of the *relative* importance of each element, from a resource allocation perspective. If an element is considered *de minimis* for example, it is not an area that is worthy of extensive resource allocation. If an element is considered a *game changer*, the utmost attention and resources should be applied to it.

Part I on understanding the institutional lens, Part II's sections on the pre-launch puzzle and understanding prospects, as well as Part V's section on *The Road to AUM* and defining a game plan, have each been assigned a *RPM* rating for purposes of this exercise on game planning utilizing the *Resource Prioritization Matrix*. At this point, readers understand the rationale for the *RPM* rating and can utilize these ratings to consider their resource allocations and priorities.

The Road to AUM: A Game Plan

Part I: Out of the Weeds—A View of the Forest from Institutional Investors

Element	De Minimis	Core	Priority	Game Changer
Understand the Institutional Lens		●		

Part II: Stepping Back—Getting in Position to Win

Element	De Minimis	Core	Priority	Game Changer
The Pre-Launch Puzzle: Team, Offering, Brand, Capital Commitment				●
Understand Prospects		●		
Redefine the Competition				●

Part III: Stepping In—Technology Use in Live Meetings

Element	De Minimis	Core	Priority	Game Changer
The Firm's Oeuvre: Content Library		●		
Core Collateral		●		
Databases		●		
Online Marketing				●
The Introduction				●
Face Time: The Live Meeting				●
Technology in Live Meetings	●			

Part IV: Stepping Up—Staying the Course

Element	De Minimis	Core	Priority	Game Changer
Commentary			●	
Ongoing Communications				●
The Institutional Process				●
Resource Management				●

Part V: Stepping Out—Overdrive

Element	De Minimis	Core	Priority	Game Changer
Games Managers Play		●		
Recommendations from the Road				●
The Road to AUM: A Game Plan				●

Asset Growth Awaits

If you read this far, then you have the most important skills required to succeed: humility and perseverance. Managers who understand that there is work to be done, have the best chance of succeeding. Managers are never as unique in their approach and results, as they are in their willingness to do the hard work of improving and delivering in meaningful ways. *The Road to AUM* provides a framework for driving asset growth. Ultimately, it is up to the firm to do the hard work—to step back and then step in to the race fully. **With the right resources, commitment, market knowledge and differentiation, asset growth awaits.**

About the Author

SANDRA POWERS MURPHY is a globally recognized marketing and sales consultant. After more than a decade serving in a business development capacity on behalf of State Street Global Advisors and State Street Corporation, Sandra founded ARK Global LLC. Leading the ARK Global Marketing team, Sandra drives product and business development initiatives on behalf of a diverse group of clients. Sandra has helped numerous managers expand their investor base, add product structures, secure strategic partnerships, define business plans, create market presence and improve their overall profitability. Separate and distinct from ARK Global, Sandra founded Noble Ark Ventures to serve as a consultancy and educational resource for B2B organizations regarding institutional marketing and sales best practices.

Sandra is the President of the Third Party Marketers Association as well as a member of the Women Presidents' Organization and 100 Women in Finance. Sandra is a partner of Compass Securities Corporation, member FINRA, SIPC, and a Registered Representative of ARK Global LLC, member FINRA, SIPC. Sandra holds investment industry licenses with FINRA, the MSRB and NASAA including the Series 7 and 24; 50, 53 and 54; 63 and 66 respectively. In addition, she serves on the Municipal Securities Rulemaking Board Professional Qualifications Advisory Committee. Sandra is a Licensed Certified Social Worker (LCSW) in the state of Massachusetts. Sandra lives with her husband and six children near Boston, Massachusetts.

The Roadmap to AUM
Driving Asset Under Management through Effective Marketing and Sales

PART III: Stepping In—Driving Content and Context

Resources

The below referenced resources provide a starting point for organizations seeking to expand their industry knowledge and reach. It is not intended to provide an exhaustive list of all available resources. Some organizations may provide more than one service. Resources listed are provided in alphabetical order.

The below listing is subject to ongoing changes, additions and deletions. Please scan the QR code above or visit www.noblearkventures.com for the most up to date resource listings.

Books

- Allen, James. *As a Man Thinketh*. New York: Peter Pauper Press, 1960.

- Brooks, David. *The Road to Character*. New York: Random House, 2015.

- Duhigg, Charles. *The Power Of Habit: Why We Do What We Do in Life and Business*. New York: Random House, 2012.

- Gerber, Michael E. *The E-Myth Revisited: Why Most Small Businesses Don't Work and What to Do About It*. New York: HarperBusiness, 1995.

- Gladwell, Malcolm. *Outliers: The Story of Success*. New York: Little, Brown and Company, 2008.

- Gladwell, Malcolm. *The Tipping Point*. New York: Little, Brown and Company, 2000.

- Grove, Andrew S. *Only the Paranoid Survive: How to Exploit the Crisis Points That Challenge Every Company and Career*. New York: Currency Doubleday, 1996.

- Jones, Meredith. *Women of The Street*. New York: Palgrave Macmillan US, 2015.

- Keller, Gary. Papasan, Jay. *The ONE Thing: The Surprisingly Simple Truth Behind Extraordinary Results*. Texas: Bard Press, 2013.

- Kim, W. Chan. Mauborgne, Renee. *Blue Ocean Strategy: How To Create Uncontested Market Space And Make The Competition Irrelevant.* Massachusetts: Harvard Business School Press, 2005.

- Pink, Daniel H. *Drive: The Surprising Truth About What Motivates Us.* New York: Riverhead Books, 2009.

- Sandberg, Sheryl. *Lean In: Women, Work and the Will to Lead.* New York: Alfred A. Knopf, 2013.

- Stack, Jack. Burlingham, Bo. *The Great Game of Business.* New York: Doubleday, 1994.

- Sun-tzu. Griffith, Samuel B. *The Art of War.* Oxford: Clarendon Press, 1964.

- Wiseman, Liz. McKeown, Greg. *Multipliers: How the Best Leaders Make Everyone Smarter.* New York: HarperBusiness, 2010.

- Zander, Rosamund Stone. Zander, Benjamin. *The Art of Possibility.* Massachusetts: Harvard Business School Press, 2000.

Contact Management Solutions
- Act! Premium
- C2CRM
- Claritysoft CRM
- GoldMine
- Hubspot
- Maximizer CRM
- NetSuite
- Salesforce
- Sage CRM

Content Management Solutions
- Box
- Dropbox
- SecureShare
- Seismic
- ShareFile
- Synthesis Technology

Database Vendors
- DG Analytics
- IMSS
- Jackson Analytics

Federal Regulation
- CFTC (www.cftc.gov)
- FINRA (www.finra.org)
- MSRB (www.msrb.org)
- NASAA (www.nasaa.org)
- SEC (www.sec.gov)

Industry Conferences
- Family Office Club
- Family Office Exchange
- Family Office Network
- Morningstar
- Opal Group
- Schwab IMPACT
- SkyBridge Alternatives (SALT)
- Wealth investment Exchange

Marketing Databases
- Discovery Data
- FIN Searches
- Financial Media Group
- PitchBook
- Preqin
- RIA Database
- Standard and Poor's Money Market Directories

Organizations and Associations
- 3PM
- 100 Women in Finance
- AICPA
- AIMSE
- CAIA
- CFA Institute
- Family Office Club

- FCLT Global
- ICI
- IMA
- IMCA
- NAPFA
- NAAIM

Performance Databases (Product Applicability Will Vary.)

- Albourne
- Callan
- Cambridge
- CB Insights
- DeMarche
- eQuest
- Eurekahedge
- eVestment
- FIS
- Hedge Fund Research/HFR
- Investment Metrics
- LCG
- Lipper
- Mercer
- Morningstar
- Pavilion
- PSN Informa
- Wilshire

Press and Publications

- Barron's
- Bloomberg Businessweek
- Chief Investment Officer (CIO)
- Emerging Manager Monthly
- FA Magazine
- FIN Daily
- Financial Times
- Fortune
- FundFire
- Institutional Investor
- Investment Advisor
- InvestmentNews

- Investor's Business Daily
- Mauldin
- Nonprofit News
- OnWallStreet
- Pageant Media
- Pensions & Investments
- PlanAdviser
- PlanSponsor
- The Economist

Public Relations

- Gregory FCA
- Interdependence
- JConnelly, Inc.
- MacMillan

Regulatory Compliance and GIPS Verification

- ACA Compliance Group
- Alpha Performance Verifications
- Monahan & Roth, LLC
- National Regulatory Services

Web Vendors

- BaselineGroupNY
- BKJ Productions
- DQ Communications
- FMG Suite
- Twenty Over Ten

Keep Driving to Growth

Visit www.noblearkventures.com or the QR code below to find additional resources including the Noble Ark Ventures Business Development Master Class Series.

www.ingramcontent.com/pod-product-compliance
Lightning Source LLC
Chambersburg PA
CBHW071320210326
41597CB00015B/1286